PyTorch Deep Learning Hands-On

Apply modern AI techniques with CNNs, RNNs, GANs, reinforcement learning, and more

Sherin Thomas

with Sudhanshu Passi

BIRMINGHAM - MUMBAI

PyTorch Deep Learning Hands-On

Acquisition Editor: Andrew Waldron
Acquisition Editor - Peer Reviews: Suresh Jain
Project Editor: Tom Jacob
Development Editor: Joanne Lovell
Technical Editor: Gaurav Gavas
Proofreader: Safis Editing
Indexer: Rekha Nair
Graphics: Sandip Tadge, Tom Scaria
Production Coordinator: Sandip Tadge

First published: April 2019

Production reference: 1250419

Published by Packt Publishing Ltd.
Livery Place
35 Livery Street
Birmingham B3 2PB, UK.

ISBN 978-1-78883-413-1

www.packtpub.com

`mapt.io`

Mapt is an online digital library that gives you full access to over 5,000 books and videos, as well as industry leading tools to help you plan your personal development and advance your career. For more information, please visit our website.

Why subscribe?

- Spend less time learning and more time coding with practical eBooks and Videos from over 4,000 industry professionals

- Learn better with Skill Plans built especially for you

- Get a free eBook or video every month

- Mapt is fully searchable

- Copy and paste, print, and bookmark content

Packt.com

Did you know that Packt offers eBook versions of every book published, with PDF and ePub files available? You can upgrade to the eBook version at `www.Packt.com` and as a print book customer, you are entitled to a discount on the eBook copy. Get in touch with us at `customercare@packtpub.com` for more details.

At `www.Packt.com`, you can also read a collection of free technical articles, sign up for a range of free newsletters, and receive exclusive discounts and offers on Packt books and eBooks.

Contributors

About the authors

Sherin Thomas started his career as an information security expert and shifted his focus to deep learning-based security systems. He has helped several companies across the globe to set up their AI pipelines and worked recently for CoWrks, a fast-growing start-up based out of Bengaluru. Sherin is working on several open source projects including PyTorch, RedisAI, and many more, and is leading the development of TuringNetwork.ai. Currently, he is focusing on building the deep learning infrastructure for [tensor]werk, an Orobix spin-off company.

I am indebted to a multitude of professionals who have influenced me and motivated me to write this book. Among them are my colleagues from CoWrks and my friends. I can't thank enough the technical reviewers and editorial assistants. Without them, I would not have been able to meet the deadlines. Last, and most importantly, I am indebted to my wife, Merin. Writing a book along with a day job is not easy, and without her, it would have been impossible.

Sudhanshu Passi is a technologist employed at CoWrks. Among other things, he has been the driving force behind everything related to machine learning at CoWrks. His expertise in simplifying complex concepts makes his work an ideal read for beginners and experts alike. This can be verified by his many blogs and this debut book publication. In his spare time, he can be found at his local swimming pool computing gradient descent underwater.

I would like to thank Sherin for this opportunity to be a co-author on this book. I would also like to thank my parents for their continuous support throughout the years.

About the reviewers

Bharath G. S. is an independent machine learning researcher and he currently works with glib.ai as a machine learning engineer. He also collaborates with mcg. ai as a machine learning consultant. His main research areas of interest include reinforcement learning, natural language processing, and cognitive neuroscience. Currently, he's researching the issue of algorithmic fairness in decision making. He's also involved in the open source development of the privacy-preserving machine learning platform OpenMined as a core collaborator, where he works on private and secure decentralized deep learning algorithms. You can also find some of the machine learning libraries that he has co-authored on PyPI, such as parfit, NALU, and pysyft.

Liao Xingyu is pursuing his master's degree in **University of Science and Technology of China (USTC)**. He has ever worked in Megvii.inc and JD AI lab as an intern. He has published a Chinese PyTorch book named *Learn Deep Learning with PyTorch* in China.

I am grateful for my family's support and project editor Tom's help in producing and reviewing this book.

Table of Contents

Preface

PyTorch Deep Learning Hands-On helps readers to get into the depths of deep learning quickly. In the last couple of years, we have seen deep learning become the new electricity. It has fought its way from academia into industry, helping resolve thousands of enigmas that humans could never have imagined solving without it. The mainstream adoption of deep learning as a go-to implementation was driven mainly by a bunch of frameworks that reliably delivered complex algorithms as efficient built-in methods. This book showcases the benefits of PyTorch for prototyping a deep learning model, for building a deep learning workflow, and for taking a prototyped model to production. Overall, the book concentrates on the practical implementation of PyTorch instead of explaining the math behind it, but it also links you to places that you could fall back to if you lag behind with a few concepts.

Who this book is for

We have refrained from explaining the algorithms as much as possible and have instead focused on their implementation in PyTorch, sometimes looking at the implementation of real-world applications using those algorithms. This book is ideal for those who know how to program in Python and understand the basics of deep learning. This book is for people who are practicing traditional machine learning concepts already or who are developers and want to explore the world of deep learning practically and deploy their implementations to production.

What this book covers

Chapter 1, Deep Learning Walkthrough and PyTorch Introduction, is an introduction to the PyTorch way of doing deep learning and to the basic APIs of PyTorch. It starts by showing the history of PyTorch and why PyTorch should be the go-to framework for deep learning development. It also covers an introduction of the different deep learning approaches that we will be covering in the upcoming chapters.

Chapter 2, A Simple Neural Network, helps you build your first simple neural network and shows how we can connect bits and pieces such as neural networks, optimizers, and parameter updates to build a novice deep learning model. It also covers how PyTorch does backpropagation, the key behind all state-of-the-art deep learning algorithms.

Chapter 3, Deep Learning Workflow, goes deeper into the deep learning workflow implementation and the PyTorch ecosystem that helps build the workflow. This is probably the most crucial chapter if you are planning to set up a deep learning team or a pipeline for an upcoming project. In this chapter, we'll go through the different stages of a deep learning pipeline and see how the PyTorch community has advanced in each stage in the workflow iteratively by making appropriate tools.

Chapter 4, Computer Vision, being the most successful result of deep learning so far, talks about the key ideas behind that success and runs through the most widely used vision algorithm – the **convolutional neural network (CNN)**. We'll implement a CNN step by step to understand the working principles, and then use a predefined CNN from PyTorch's nn package. This chapter helps you make a simple CNN and an advanced CNN-based vision algorithm called semantic segmentation.

Chapter 5, Sequential Data Processing, looks at the recurrent neural network, which is currently the most successful sequential data processing algorithm. The chapter introduces you to the major RNN components, such as the **long short-term memory (LSTM)** network and **gated recurrent units (GRUs)**. Then we'll go through algorithmic changes in RNN implementation, such as bidirectional RNNs, and increasing the number of layers, before we explore recursive neural networks. To understand recursive networks, we'll use the renowned example, from the Stanford NLP group, the stack-augmented parser-interpreter neural network (SPINN), and implement that in PyTorch.

Chapter 6, Generative Networks, talks about the history of generative networks in brief and then explains the different kinds of generative networks. Among those different categories, this chapter introduces us to autoregressive models and GANs. We'll work through the implementation details of PixelCNN and WaveNet as part of autoregressive models, and then look at GANs in detail.

Chapter 7, *Reinforcement Learning*, introduces the concept of reinforcement learning, which is not really a subcategory of deep learning. We'll first take a look at defining problem statements. Then we'll explore the concept of cumulative rewards. We'll explore Markov decision processes and the Bellman equation, and then move to deep Q-learning. We'll also see an introduction to Gym, the toolkit developed by OpenAI for developing and experimenting with reinforcement learning algorithms.

Chapter 8, *PyTorch to Production*, looks at the difficulties people face, even the deep learning experts, during the deployment of a deep learning model to production. We'll explore different options for production deployment, including using a Flask wrapper around PyTorch as well as using RedisAI, which is a highly optimized runtime for deploying models in multicluster environments and can handle millions of requests per second.

To get the most out of this book

- The code is written in Python and hosted on GitHub. Though the compressed code repository is available for download, the online GitHub repository will receive bug fixes and updates. Having a basic understanding of GitHub is therefore required, as is having good Python knowledge.
- Although not mandatory, the use of CUDA drivers would help to speed up the training process if you are not using any pretrained models.
- The code examples were developed on an Ubuntu 18.10 machine but will work on all the popular platforms. But if you find any difficulties, feel free to raise an issue in the GitHub repository.
- Some of the examples in the book require you to use other services or packages, such as redis-server and the Flask framework. All those external dependencies and "how-to" guides are documented in the chapters they appear.

Download the example code files

You can download the example code files for this book from your account at `http://www.packt.com`. If you purchased this book elsewhere, you can visit `http://www.packt.com/support` and register to have the files emailed directly to you.

You can download the code files by following these steps:

1. Log in or register at `http://www.packt.com`.
2. Select the **SUPPORT** tab.
3. Click on **Code Downloads & Errata**.
4. Enter the name of the book in the **Search** box and follow the on-screen instructions.

Once the file is downloaded, please make sure that you unzip or extract the folder using the latest version of:

- WinRAR / 7-Zip for Windows
- Zipeg / iZip / UnRarX for macOS
- 7-Zip / PeaZip for Linux

The code bundle for the book is also hosted on GitHub at https://github.com/hhsecond/HandsOnDeepLearningWithPytorch. We also have other code bundles from our rich catalog of books and videos available at https://github.com/PacktPublishing/. Check them out!

Download the color images

We also provide a PDF file that has color images of the screenshots/diagrams used in this book. You can download it here: http://www.packtpub.com/sites/default/files/downloads/9781788834131_ColorImages.pdf.

Conventions used

There are a number of text conventions used throughout this book.

CodeInText: Indicates code words in text, database table names, folder names, filenames, file extensions, pathnames, dummy URLs, user input, and Twitter handles. For example; "Mount the downloaded WebStorm-10*.dmg disk image file as another disk in your system."

A block of code is set as follows:

```
def forward(self, batch):
    hidden = self.hidden(batch)
    activated = torch.sigmoid(hidden)
    out = self.out(activated)
    return out
```

When we wish to draw your attention to a particular part of a code block, the relevant lines or items are set in bold:

```
def binary_encoder(input_size):
    def wrapper(num):
        ret = [int(i) for i in '{0:b}'.format(num)]
        return [0] * (input_size - len(ret)) + ret
    return wrapper
```

Any command-line input or output is written as follows:

```
python -m torch.utils.bottleneck /path/to/source/script.py [args]
```

Bold: Indicates a new term, an important word, or words that you see on the screen, for example, in menus or dialog boxes, also appear in the text like this. For example: "Select **System info** from the **Administration** panel."

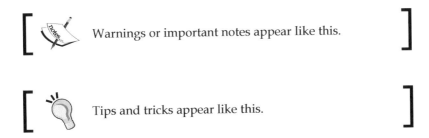

[Warnings or important notes appear like this.]

[Tips and tricks appear like this.]

Get in touch

Feedback from our readers is always welcome.

General feedback: If you have questions about any aspect of this book, mention the book title in the subject of your message and email us at customercare@packtpub.com.

Errata: Although we have taken every care to ensure the accuracy of our content, mistakes do happen. If you have found a mistake in this book we would be grateful if you would report this to us. Please visit, http://www.packt.com/submit-errata, selecting your book, clicking on the Errata Submission Form link, and entering the details.

Piracy: If you come across any illegal copies of our works in any form on the Internet, we would be grateful if you would provide us with the location address or website name. Please contact us at copyright@packt.com with a link to the material.

If you are interested in becoming an author: If there is a topic that you have expertise in and you are interested in either writing or contributing to a book, please visit http://authors.packtpub.com.

Reviews

Please leave a review. Once you have read and used this book, why not leave a review on the site that you purchased it from? Potential readers can then see and use your unbiased opinion to make purchase decisions, we at Packt can understand what you think about our products, and our authors can see your feedback on their book. Thank you!

For more information about Packt, please visit `packt.com`.

1
Deep Learning Walkthrough and PyTorch Introduction

At this point in time, there are dozens of deep learning frameworks out there that are capable of solving any sort of deep learning problem on GPU, so why do we need one more? This book is the answer to that million-dollar question. PyTorch came to the deep learning family with the promise of being NumPy on GPU. Ever since its entry, the community has been trying hard to keep that promise. As the official documentation says, PyTorch is an optimized tensor library for deep learning using GPUs and CPUs. While all the prominent frameworks offer the same thing, PyTorch has certain advantages over almost all of them.

The chapters in this book provide a step-by-step guide for developers who want to benefit from the power of PyTorch to process and interpret data. You'll learn how to implement a simple neural network, before exploring the different stages of a deep learning workflow. We'll dive into basic convolutional networks and generative adversarial networks, followed by a hands-on tutorial on how to train a model with OpenAI's Gym library. By the final chapter, you'll be ready to productionize PyTorch models.

In this first chapter, we will go through the theory behind PyTorch and explain why PyTorch gained the upper hand over other frameworks for certain use cases. Before that, we will take a glimpse into the history of PyTorch and learn why PyTorch is a need rather than an option. We'll also cover the NumPy-PyTorch bridge and PyTorch internals in the last section, which will give us a head start for the upcoming code-intensive chapters.

Understanding PyTorch's history

As more and more people started migrating to the fascinating world of machine learning, different universities and organizations began building their own frameworks to support their daily research, and Torch was one of the early members of that family. Ronan Collobert, Koray Kavukcuoglu, and Clement Farabet released Torch in 2002 and, later, it was picked up by Facebook AI Research and many other people from several universities and research groups. Lots of start-ups and researchers accepted Torch, and companies started productizing their Torch models to serve millions of users. Twitter, Facebook, DeepMind, and more are part of that list. As per the official Torch7 paper [1] published by the core team, Torch was designed with three key features in mind:

1. It should ease the development of numerical algorithms.
2. It should be easily extended.
3. It should be fast.

Although Torch gives flexibility to the bone, and the Lua + C combo satisfied all the preceding requirements, the major drawback the community faced was the learning curve to the new language, Lua. Although Lua wasn't difficult to grasp and had been used in the industry for a while for highly efficient product development, it did not have widespread acceptance like several other popular languages.

The widespread acceptance of Python in the deep learning community made some researchers and developers rethink the decision made by core authors to choose Lua over Python. It wasn't just the language: the absence of an imperative-styled framework with easy debugging capability also triggered the ideation of PyTorch.

The frontend developers of deep learning find the idea of the symbolic graph difficult. Unfortunately, almost all the deep learning frameworks were built on this foundation. In fact, a few developer groups tried to change this approach with dynamic graphs. Autograd from the Harvard Intelligent Probabilistic Systems Group was the first popular framework that did so. Then the Torch community on Twitter took the idea and implemented torch-autograd.

Next, a research group from **Carnegie Mellon University** (CMU) came up with DyNet, and then Chainer came up with the capability of dynamic graphs and an interpretable development environment.

All these events were a great inspiration for starting the amazing framework PyTorch, and, in fact, PyTorch started as a fork of Chainer. It began as an internship project by Adam Paszke, who was working under Soumith Chintala, a core developer of Torch. PyTorch then got two more core developers on board and around 100 alpha testers from different companies and universities.

The whole team pulled the chain together in six months and released the beta to the public in January 2017. A big chunk of the research community accepted PyTorch, although the product developers did not initially. Several universities started running courses on PyTorch, including **New York University (NYU)**, Oxford University, and some other European universities.

What is PyTorch?

As mentioned earlier, PyTorch is a tensor computation library that can be powered by GPUs. PyTorch is built with certain goals, which makes it different from all the other deep learning frameworks. During this book, you'll be revisiting these goals through different applications and by the end of the book, you should be able to get started with PyTorch for any sort of use case you have in mind, regardless of whether you are planning to prototype an idea or build a super-scalable model to production.

Being a **Python-first framework**, PyTorch took a big leap over other frameworks that implemented a Python wrapper on a monolithic C++ or C engine. In PyTorch, you can inherit PyTorch classes and customize as you desire. The imperative style of coding, which was built into the core of PyTorch, was possible only because of the Python-first approach. Even though some symbolic graph frameworks, like TensorFlow, MXNet, and CNTK, came up with an imperative approach, PyTorch has managed to stay on top because of community support and its flexibility.

The **tape-based autograd** system enables PyTorch to have **dynamic graph** capability. This is one of the major differences between PyTorch and other popular symbolic graph frameworks. Tape-based autograd powered the backpropagation algorithm of Chainer, autograd, and torch-autograd as well. With dynamic graph capability, your graph gets created as the Python interpreter reaches the corresponding line. This is called *define by run*, unlike TensorFlow's *define and run* approach.

Tape-based autograd uses reverse-mode automatic differentiation, where the graph saves each operation to the tape while you forward pass and then move backward through the tape for backpropagation. Dynamic graphs and a Python-first approach allow **easy debugging**, where you can use the usual Python debuggers like Pdb or editor-based debuggers.

The PyTorch core community did not just make a Python wrapper over Torch's C binary: it optimized the core and made improvements to the core. PyTorch intelligently chooses which algorithm to run for each operation you define, based on the input data.

Installing PyTorch

If you have CUDA and cuDNN installed, PyTorch installation is dead simple (for GPU support, but in case you are trying out PyTorch and don't have GPUs with you, that's fine too). PyTorch's home page [2] shows an interactive screen to select the OS and package manager of your choice. Choose the options and execute the command to install it.

Though initially the support was just for Linux and Mac operating systems, from PyTorch 0.4 Windows is also in the supported operating system list. PyTorch has been packaged and shipped to PyPI and Conda. PyPI is the official Python repository for packages and the package manager, pip, can find PyTorch under the name Torch.

However, if you want to be adventurous and get the latest code, you can install PyTorch from the source by following the instructions on the GitHub README page. PyTorch has a nightly build that is being pushed to PyPI and Conda as well. A nightly build is useful if you want to get the latest code without going through the pain of installing from the source.

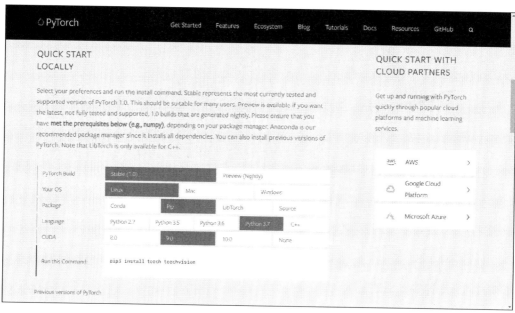

Figure 1.1: The installation process in the interactive UI from the PyTorch website

What makes PyTorch popular?

Among the multitude of reliable deep learning frameworks, static graphs or the symbolic graph-based approach were being used by almost everyone because of the speed and efficiency. The inherent problems with the dynamic network, such as performance issues, prevented developers from spending a lot of time implementing one. However, the restrictions of static graphs prevented researchers from thinking of a multitude of different ways to attack a problem because the thought process had to be confined inside the box of static computational graphs.

As mentioned earlier, Harvard's Autograd package started as a solution for this problem, and then the Torch community adopted this idea from Python and implemented torch-autograd. Chainer and CMU's DyNet are probably the next two dynamic-graph-based frameworks that got huge community support. Although all these frameworks could solve the problems that static graphs had created with the help of the imperative approach, they didn't have the momentum that other popular static graph frameworks had. PyTorch was the absolute answer for this. The PyTorch team took the backend of the well-tested, renowned Torch framework and merged that with the front of Chainer to get the best mix. The team optimized the core, added more Pythonic APIs, and set up the abstraction correctly, such that PyTorch doesn't need an abstract library like Keras for beginners to get started.

PyTorch achieved wide acceptance in the research community because a majority of people were using Torch already and probably were frustrated by the way frameworks like TensorFlow evolved without giving much flexibility. The dynamic nature of PyTorch was a bonus for lots of people and helped them to accept PyTorch in its early stages.

PyTorch lets users define whatever operations Python allows them to in the forward pass. The backward pass automatically finds the way through the graph until the root node, and calculates the gradient while traversing back. Although it was a revolutionary idea, the product development community had not accepted PyTorch, just like they couldn't accept other frameworks that followed similar implementation. However, as the days passed, more and more people started migrating to PyTorch. Kaggle witnessed competitions where all the top rankers used PyTorch, and as mentioned earlier, universities started doing courses in PyTorch. This helped students to avoid learning a new graph language like they had to when using a symbolic graph-based framework.

After the announcement of Caffe2, even product developers started experimenting with PyTorch, since the community announced the migration strategy of PyTorch models to Caffe2. Caffe2 is a static graph framework that can run your model even in mobile phones, so using PyTorch for prototyping is a win-win approach. You get the flexibility of PyTorch while building the network, and you get to transfer it to Caffe2 and use it in any production environment. However, with the 1.0 release note, the PyTorch team made a huge jump from letting people learn two frameworks (one for production and one for research), to learning a single framework that has dynamic graph capability in the prototyping phase and can suddenly convert to a static-like optimized graph when it requires speed and efficiency. The PyTorch team merged the backend of Caffe2 with PyTorch's Aten backend, which let the user decide whether they wanted to run a less-optimized but highly flexible graph, or an optimized but less-flexible graph without rewriting the code base.

ONNX and DLPack were the next two "big things" that the AI community saw. Microsoft and Facebook together announced the **Open Neural Network Exchange** (**ONNX**) protocol, which aims to help developers to migrate any model from any framework to any other. ONNX is compatible with PyTorch, Caffe2, TensorFlow, MXNet, and CNTK and the community is building/improving the support for almost all the popular frameworks.

ONNX is built into the core of PyTorch and hence migrating a model to ONNX form doesn't require users to install any other package or tool. Meanwhile, DLPack is taking interoperability to the next level by defining a standard data structure that different frameworks should follow, so that the migration of a tensor from one framework to another, in the same program, doesn't require the user to serialize data or follow any other workarounds. For instance, if you have a program that can use a well-trained TensorFlow model for computer vision and a highly efficient PyTorch model for recurrent data, you could use a single program that could handle each of the three-dimensional frames from a video with the TensorFlow model and pass the output of the TensorFlow model directly to the PyTorch model to predict actions from the video. If you take a step back and look at the deep learning community, you can see that the whole world converges toward a single point where everything is interoperable with everything else and trying to approach problems with similar methods. That's a world we all want to live in.

Using computational graphs

Through evolution, humans have found that graphing the neural network gives us the power of reducing complexity to the bare minimum. A computational graph describes the data flow in the network through operations.

A graph, which is made by a group of nodes and edges connecting them, is a decades-old data structure that is still heavily used in several different implementations and is a data structure that will be valid probably until humans cease to exist. In computational graphs, nodes represent the tensors and edges represent the relationship between them.

Computational graphs help us to solve the mathematics and make the big networks intuitive. Neural networks, no matter how complex or big they are, are a group of mathematical operations. The obvious approach to solving an equation is to divide the equation into smaller units and pass the output of one to another and so on. The idea behind the graph approach is the same. You consider the operations inside the network as nodes and map them to a graph with relations between nodes representing the transition from one operation to another.

Computational graphs are at the core of all current advances in artificial intelligence. They made the foundation of deep learning frameworks. All the deep learning frameworks existing now do computations using the graph approach. This helps the frameworks to find the independent nodes and do their computation as a separate thread or process. Computational graphs help with doing the backpropagation as easily as moving from the child node to previous nodes, and carrying the gradients along while traversing back. This operation is called automatic differentiation, which is a 40-year-old idea. Automatic differentiation is considered one of the 10 great numerical algorithms in the last century. Specifically, reverse-mode automatic differentiation is the core idea used behind computational graphs for doing backpropagation. PyTorch is built based on reverse-mode auto differentiation, so all the nodes keep the operation information with them until the control reaches the leaf node. Then the backpropagation starts from the leaf node and traverses backward. While moving back, the flow takes the gradient along with it and finds the partial derivatives corresponding to each node. In 1970, Seppo Linnainmaa, a Finnish mathematician and computer scientist, found that automatic differentiation can be used for algorithm verification. A lot of the other parallel efforts were recorded on the same concepts almost at the same time.

In deep learning, neural networks are for solving a mathematical equation. Regardless of how complex the task is, everything comes down to a giant mathematical equation, which you'll solve by optimizing the parameters of the neural network. The obvious way to solve it is "by hand." Consider solving the mathematical equation for ResNet with around 150 layers of a neural network; it is sort of impossible for a human being to iterate over such graphs thousands of times, doing the same operations manually each time to optimize the parameters. Computational graphs solve this problem by mapping all operations to a graph, level by level, and solving each node at a time. *Figure 1.2* shows a simple computational graph with three operators.

The matrix multiplication operator on both sides gives two matrices as output, and they go through an addition operator, which in turn goes through another sigmoid operator. The whole graph is, in fact, trying to solve this equation:

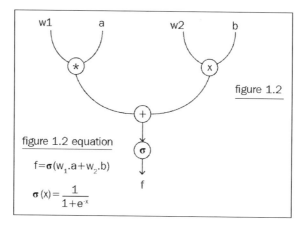

figure 1.2

figure 1.2 equation

$$f = \sigma(w_1.a + w_2.b)$$

$$\sigma(x) = \frac{1}{1+e^{-x}}$$

Figure 1.2: Graph representation of the equation

However, the moment you map it to a graph, everything becomes crystal clear. You can visualize and understand what is happening and easily code it up because the flow is right in front of you.

All deep learning frameworks are built on the foundation of automatic differentiation and computational graphs, but there are two inherently different approaches for the implementation–static and dynamic graphs.

Using static graphs

The traditional way of approaching neural network architecture is with static graphs. Before doing anything with the data you give, the program builds the forward and backward pass of the graph. Different development groups have tried different approaches. Some build the forward pass first and then use the same graph instance for the forward and backward pass. Another approach is to build the forward static graph first, and then create and append the backward graph to the end of the forward graph, so that the whole forward-backward pass can be executed as a single graph execution by taking the nodes in chronological order.

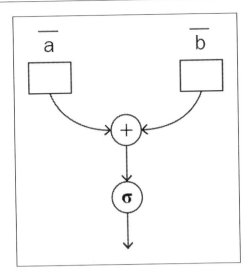

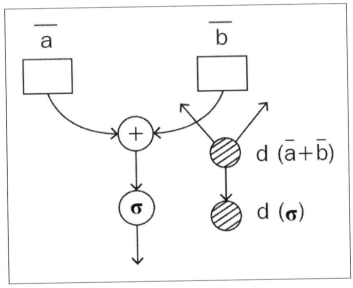

Figure 1.3 and 1.4: The same static graph used for the forward and backward pass

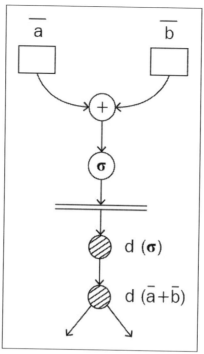

Figure 1.5: Static graph: a different graph for the forward and backward pass

Static graphs come with certain inherent advantages over other approaches. Since you are restricting the program from dynamic changes, your program can make assumptions related to memory optimization and parallel execution while executing the graph. Memory optimization is the key aspect that framework developers worry about through most of their development time, and the reason is the humungous scope of optimizing memory and the subtleties that come along with those optimizations. Apache MXNet developers have written an amazing blog [3] talking about this in detail.

The neural network for predicting the XOR output in TensorFlow's static graph API is given as follows. This is a typical example of how static graphs execute. Initially, we declare all the input placeholders and then build the graph. If you look carefully, nowhere in the graph definition are we passing the data into it. Input variables are actually placeholders expecting data sometime in the future. Though the graph definition looks like we are doing mathematical operations on the data, we are actually defining the process, and that's when TensorFlow builds the optimized graph implementation using the internal engine:

```
x = tf.placeholder(tf.float32, shape=[None, 2], name='x-input')
y = tf.placeholder(tf.float32, shape=[None, 2], name='y-input')
w1 = tf.Variable(tf.random_uniform([2, 5], -1, 1), name="w1")
```

```
w2 = tf.Variable(tf.random_uniform([5, 2], -1, 1), name="w2")
b1 = tf.Variable(tf.zeros([5]), name="b1")
b2 = tf.Variable(tf.zeros([2]), name="b2")
a2 = tf.sigmoid(tf.matmul(x, w1) + b1)
hyp = tf.matmul(a2, w2) + b2
cost = tf.reduce_mean(tf.losses.mean_squared_error(y, hyp))
train_step = tf.train.GradientDescentOptimizer(lr).minimize(cost)
prediction = tf.argmax(tf.nn.softmax(hyp), 1)
```

Once the interpreter finishes reading the graph definition, we start looping it through the data:

```
with tf.Session() as sess:
    sess.run(init)
    for i in range(epoch):
        sess.run(train_step, feed_dict={x_: XOR_X, y_: XOR_Y})
```

We start a TensorFlow session next. That's the only way you can interact with the graph you built beforehand. Inside the session, you loop through your data and pass the data to your graph using the `session.run` method. So, your input should be of the same size as you defined in the graph.

If you have forgotten what XOR is, the following table should give you enough information to recollect it from memory:

INPUT	OUTPUT	
A	B	A XOR B
0	0	0
0	1	1
1	0	1
1	1	0

Using dynamic graphs

The imperative style of programming has always had a larger user base, as the program flow is intuitive to any developer. Dynamic capability is a good side effect of imperative-style graph building. Unlike static graphs, dynamic graph architecture doesn't build the graph before the data pass. The program will wait for the data to come and build the graph as it iterates through the data. As a result, each iteration through the data builds a new graph instance and destroys it once the backward pass is done. Since the graph is being built for each iteration, it doesn't depend on the data size or length or structure. Natural language processing is one of the fields that needs this kind of approach.

For example, if you are trying to do sentiment analysis on thousands of sentences, with a static graph you need to hack and make workarounds. In a vanilla **recurrent neural network (RNN)** model, each word goes through one RNN unit, which generates output and the hidden state. This hidden state will be given to the next RNN, which processes the next word in the sentence. Since you made a fixed length slot while building your static graph, you need to augment your short sentences and cut down long sentences.

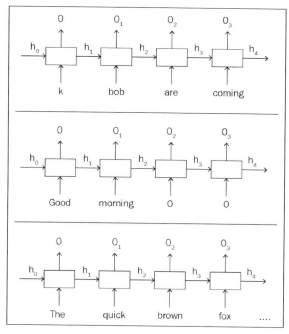

Figure 1.6: Static graph for an RNN unit with short, proper, and long sentences

The static graph given in the example shows how the data needs to be formatted for each iteration such that it won't break the prebuilt graph. However, in the dynamic graph, the network is flexible such that it gets created each time you pass the data, as shown in the preceding diagram.

The dynamic capability comes with a cost. Your graph cannot be preoptimized based on assumptions and you have to pay for the overhead of graph creation at each iteration. However, PyTorch is built to reduce the cost as much as possible. Since preoptimization is not something that a dynamic graph is capable of doing, PyTorch developers managed to bring down the cost of instant graph creation to a negligible amount. With all the optimization going into the core of PyTorch, it has proved to be faster than several other frameworks for specific use cases, even while offering the dynamic capability.

Following is a code snippet written in PyTorch for the same XOR operation we developed earlier in TensorFlow:

```
x = torch.FloatTensor(XOR_X)
y = torch.FloatTensor(XOR_Y)
w1 = torch.randn(2, 5, requires_grad=True)
w2 = torch.randn(5, 2, requires_grad=True)
b1 = torch.zeros(5, requires_grad=True)
b2 = torch.zeros(2, requires_grad=True)

for epoch in range(epochs):
    a1 = x @ w1 + b1
    h1 = a2.sigmoid()
    a2 = h2 @ w2 + b1
    hyp = a3.sigmoid()
    cost = (hyp - y).pow(2).sum()
    cost.backward()
```

In the PyTorch code, the input variable definition is not creating placeholders; instead, it is wrapping the variable object onto your input. The graph definition is not executing once; instead, it is inside your loop and the graph is being built for each iteration. The only information you share between each graph instance is your weight matrix, which is what you want to optimize.

In this approach, if your data size or shape is changing while you're looping through it, it's absolutely fine to run that new-shaped data through your graph because the newly created graph can accept the new shape. The possibilities do not end there. If you want to change the graph's behavior dynamically, you can do that too. The example given in the recursive neural network session in *Chapter 5*, *Sequential Data Processing*, is built on this idea.

Exploring deep learning

Since man invented computers, we have called them intelligent systems, and yet we are always trying to augment their intelligence. In the old days, anything a computer could do that a human couldn't was considered artificial intelligence. Remembering huge amounts of data, doing mathematical operations on millions or billions of numbers, and so on was considered artificial intelligence. We called Deep Blue, the machine that beat chess grandmaster Garry Kasparov at chess, an artificially intelligent machine.

Eventually, things that humans can't do and a computer can do became just computer programs. We realized that some things humans can do easily are impossible for a programmer to code up. This evolution changed everything. The number of possibilities or rules we could write down and make a computer work like us with was insanely large. Machine learning came to the rescue. People found a way to let the computers to learn the rules from examples, instead of having to code it up explicitly; that's called machine learning. An example is given in *Figure 1.9*, which shows how we could make a prediction of whether a customer will buy a product or not from his/her past shopping history.

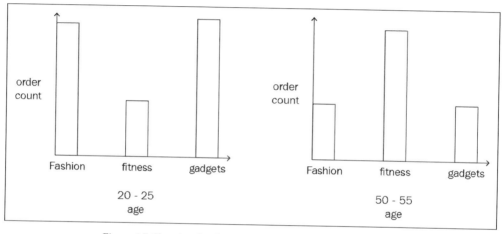

Figure 1.7: Showing the dataset for a customer buying a product

We could predict most of the results, if not all of them. However, what if the number of data points that we could make a prediction from is a lot and we cannot process them with a mortal brain? A computer could look through the data and probably spit out the answer based on previous data. This data-driven approach can help us a lot, since the only thing we have to do is assume the relevant features and give them to the black box, which consists of different algorithms, to learn the rules or pattern from the feature set.

There are problems. Even though we know what to look for, cleaning up the data and extracting the features is not an interesting task. The foremost trouble isn't this, however; we can't predict the features for high-dimensional data and the data of other media types efficiently. For example, in face recognition, we initially found the length of particulars in our face using the rule-based program and gave that to the neural network as input, because we thought that's the feature set that humans use to recognize faces.

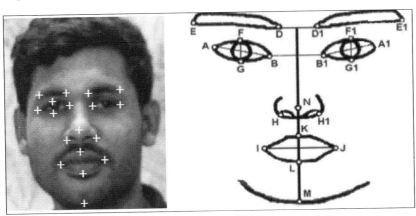

Figure 1.8: Human-selected facial features

It turned out that the features that are so obvious for humans are not so obvious for computers and vice versa. The realization of the feature selection problem led us to the era of deep learning. This is a subset of machine learning where we use the same data-driven approach, but instead of selecting the features explicitly, we let the computer decide what the features should be.

Let's consider our face recognition example again. FaceNet, a 2014 paper from Google, tackled it with the help of deep learning. FaceNet implemented the whole application using two deep networks. The first network was to identify the feature set from faces and the second network was to use this feature set and recognize the face (technically speaking, classifying the face into different buckets). Essentially, the first network was doing what we did before and the second network was a simple and traditional machine learning algorithm.

Deep networks are capable of identifying features from datasets, provided we have large labeled datasets. FaceNet's first network was trained with a huge dataset of faces with corresponding labels. The first network was trained to predict 128 features (generally speaking, there are 128 measurements from our faces, like the distance between the left eye and the right eye) from every face and the second network just used these 128 features to recognize a person.

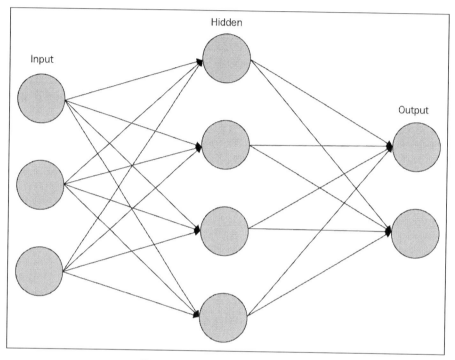

Figure 1.9: A simple neural network

A simple neural network has a single hidden layer, an input layer, and an output layer. Theoretically, a single hidden layer should be able to approximate any complex mathematical equation, and we should be fine with a single layer. However, it turns out that the single hidden layer theory is not so practical. In deep networks, each layer is responsible for finding some features. Initial layers find more detailed features, and final layers abstract these detailed features and find high-level features.

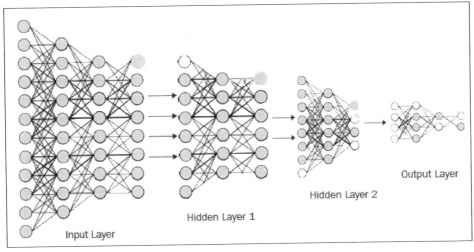

Figure 1.10: A deep neural network

Getting to know different architectures

Deep learning has been around for decades, and different structures and architectures evolved for different use cases. Some of them were based on ideas we had about our brain and some others were based on the actual working of the brain. All the upcoming chapters are based on the state-of-the-art architectures that the industry is using now. We'll cover one or more applications under each architecture, with each chapter covering the concepts, specifications, and technical details behind all of them, obviously with PyTorch code.

Fully connected networks

Fully connected, or dense or linear, networks are the most basic, yet powerful, architecture. This is a direct extension of what is commonly called machine learning, where you use neural networks with a single hidden layer. Fully connected layers act as the endpoint of all the architectures to find the probability distribution of the scores we find using the below deep network. A fully connected network, as the name suggests, has all the neurons connected to each other in the previous and next layers. The network might eventually decide to switch off some neurons by setting the weight, but in an ideal situation, initially, all of them take part in the communication.

Encoders and decoders

Encoders and decoders are probably the next most basic architecture under the deep learning umbrella. All the networks have one or more encoder-decoder layers. You can consider hidden layers in fully connected layers as the encoded form coming from an encoder, and the output layer as a decoder that decodes the hidden layer into output. Commonly, encoders encode the input into an intermediate state, where the input is represented as vectors and then the decoder network decodes this into an output form that we want.

A canonical example of an encoder-decoder network is the **sequence-to-sequence (seq2seq)** network, which can be used for machine translation. A sentence, say in English, will be encoded to an intermediate vector representation, where the whole sentence will be chunked in the form of some floating-point numbers and the decoder decodes the output sentence in another language from the intermediate vector.

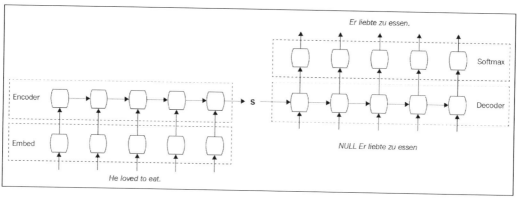

Figure 1.11: Seq2seq network

An autoencoder is a special type of encoder-decoder network and comes under the category of unsupervised learning. Autoencoders try to learn from unlabeled data, setting the target values to be equal to the input values. For example, if your input is an image of size 100 x 100, you'll have an input vector of dimension 10,000. So, the output size will also be 10,000, but the hidden layer size could be 500. In a nutshell, you are trying to convert your input to a hidden state representation of a smaller size, re-generating the same input from the hidden state.

If you were able to train a neural network that could do that, then voilà, you would have found a good compression algorithm where you could transfer high-dimensional input to a lower-dimensional vector with an order of magnitude's gain.

Autoencoders are being used in different situations and industries nowadays. You'll see a similar architecture in *Chapter 4, Computer Vision*, when we discuss semantic segmentation.

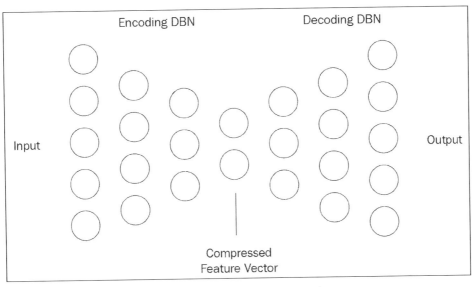

Figure 1.12: Structure of an autoencoder

Recurrent neural networks

RNNs are one of the most common deep learning algorithms, and they took the whole world by storm. Almost all the state-of-the-art performance we have now in natural language processing or understanding is because of a variant of RNNs. In recurrent networks, you try to identify the smallest unit in your data and make your data a group of those units. In the example of natural language, the most common approach is to make one word a unit and consider the sentence as a group of words while processing it. You unfold your RNN for the whole sentence and process your sentence one word at a time. RNNs have variants that work for different datasets and sometimes, efficiency can be taken into account while choosing the variant. Long **short-term memory (LSTM)** and **gated recurrent units (GRUs)** cells are the most common RNN units.

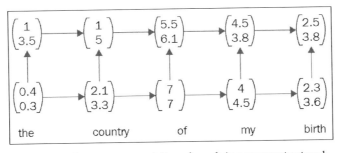

Figure 1.13: A vector representation of words in a recurrent network

Recursive neural networks

As the name indicates, recursive neural networks are tree-like networks for understanding the hierarchical structure of sequence data. Recursive networks have been used a lot in **natural language processing** applications, especially by Richard Socher, a chief scientist at Salesforce, and his team.

Word vectors, which we will see soon in *Chapter 5, Sequential Data Processing,* are capable of mapping the meaning of a word efficiently into a vector space, but when it comes to the meaning of the overall sentence, there is no go-to solution like word2vec for words. Recursive neural networks are one of the most used algorithms for such applications. Recursive networks can make a parse tree and compositional vectors, and map other hierarchical relations, which, in turn, help us to find the rules that combine words and make sentences. The **Stanford Natural Language Inference** group has found a renowned and well-used algorithm called **SNLI**, which is a good example of recursive network use.

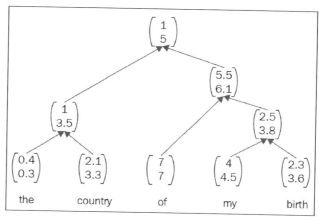

Figure 1.14: Vector representation of words in a recursive network

Convolutional neural networks

Convolutional neural networks (CNNs) enabled us to get super-human performance in computer vision. We hit human accuracy in the early 2010s, and we are still gaining more accuracy year by year.

Convolutional networks are the most understood networks, as we have visualizers that show what each layer is doing. Yann LeCun, the **Facebook AI Research (FAIR)** head, invented CNNs back in the 1990s. We couldn't use them then, since we did not have enough dataset and computational power. CNNs basically scan through your input like a sliding window and make an intermediate representation, then abstract it layer by layer before it reaches the fully connected layer at the end. CNNs are used in non-image datasets successfully as well.

The Facebook research team found a state-of-the-art natural language processing system with convolutional networks that outperforms the RNN, which is supposed to be the go-to architecture for any sequence dataset. Although several neuroscientists and a few AI researchers are not fond of CNNs, since they believe that the brain doesn't do what CNNs do, networks based on CNNs are beating all the existing implementations.

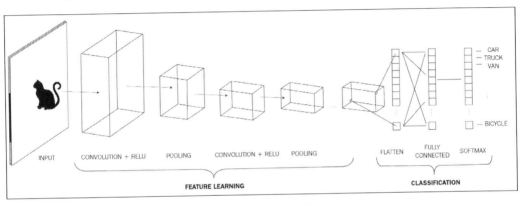

Figure 1.15: A typical CNN

Generative adversarial networks

Generative adversarial networks (GANs) were invented by Ian Goodfellow in 2014 and since then, they have turned the whole AI community upside down. They were one of the simplest and most obvious implementations, yet had the power to fascinate the world with their capabilities. In GANs, two networks compete with each other and reach an equilibrium where the generator network can generate the data, which the discriminator network has a hard time discriminating from the actual image. A real-world example would be the fight between police and counterfeiters.

A counterfeiter tries to make fake currency and the police try to detect it. Initially, the counterfeiters are not knowledgeable enough to make fake currency that look original. As time passes, counterfeiters get better at making currency that looks more like original currency. Then the police start failing to identify fake currency, but eventually they'll get better at it again. This generation-discrimination process eventually leads to an equilibrium. The advantages of GANs are humungous and we'll discuss them in depth later.

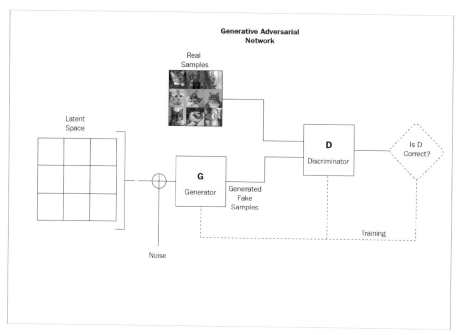

Figure 1.16: GAN setup

Reinforcement learning

Learning through interaction is the foundation of human intelligence. Reinforcement learning is the methodology leading us in that direction. Reinforcement learning used to be a completely different field built on top of the idea that humans learn by trial and error. However, with the advancement of deep learning, another field popped up called deep reinforcement learning, which combines the power of deep learning and reinforcement learning.

Modern reinforcement learning uses deep networks to learn, unlike the old approach where we coded those rules explicitly. We'll look into Q-learning and deep Q-learning, showing you the difference between reinforcement learning with and without deep learning.

Reinforcement learning is considered as one of the pathways toward general intelligence, where computers or agents learn through interaction with the real world and objects or experiments, or from feedback. Teaching a reinforcement learning agent is comparable to training dogs through negative and positive rewards. When you give a piece of biscuit for picking up the ball or when you shout at your dog for not picking up the ball, you are reinforcing knowledge into your dog's brain through negative and positive rewards. We do the same with AI agents, but the positive reward will be a positive number, and the negative reward will be a negative number. Even though we can't consider reinforcement learning as another architecture similar to CNN/RNN and so on, I have included this here as another way of using deep neural networks to solve real-world problems:

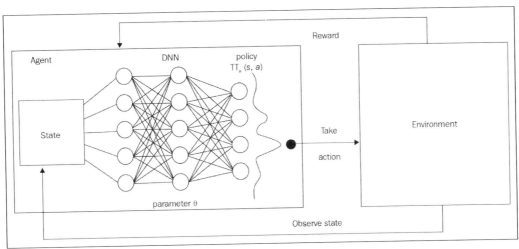

Figure 1.17: Pictorial representation of a reinforcement learning setup

Getting started with the code

Let's get our hands dirty with some code. If you have used NumPy before, you are at home here. Don't worry if you haven't; PyTorch is made for making the beginner's life easy.

Being a deep learning framework, PyTorch can be used for numerical computing as well. Here we discuss the basic operations in PyTorch. The basic PyTorch operations in this chapter will make your life easier in the next chapter, where we will try to build an actual neural network for a simple use case. We'll be using Python 3.7 and PyTorch 1.0 for all the programs in the book. The GitHub repository is also built with the same configuration: PyTorch from PyPI instead of Conda, although it is the recommended package manager by the PyTorch team.

Learning the basic operations

Let's start coding by importing `torch` into the namespace:

```
import torch
```

The fundamental data abstraction in PyTorch is a `Tensor` object, which is the alternative of `ndarray` in NumPy. You can create tensors in several ways in PyTorch. We'll discuss some of the basic approaches here and you will see all of them in the upcoming chapters while building the applications:

```
uninitialized = torch.Tensor(3,2)
rand_initialized = torch.rand(3,2)
matrix_with_ones = torch.ones(3,2)
matrix_with_zeros = torch.zeros(3,2)
```

The `rand` method gives you a random matrix of a given size, while the `Tensor` function returns an uninitialized tensor. To create a tensor object from a Python list, you call `torch.FloatTensor(python_list)`, which is analogous to `np.array(python_list)`. `FloatTensor` is one among the several types that PyTorch supports. A list of the available types is given in the following table:

Data type	CPU tensor	GPU tensor
32-bit floating point	`torch.FloatTensor`	`torch.cuda.FloatTensor`
64-bit floating point	`torch.DoubleTensor`	`torch.cuda.DoubleTensor`
16-bit floating point	`torch.HalfTensor`	`torch.cuda.HalfTensor`
8-bit integer (unsigned)	`torch.ByteTensor`	`torch.cuda.ByteTensor`
8-bit integer (signed)	`torch.CharTensor`	`torch.cuda.CharTensor`
16-bit integer (signed)	`torch.ShortTensor`	`torch.cuda.ShortTensor`
32-bit integer (signed)	`torch.IntTensor`	`torch.cuda.IntTensor`
64-bit integer (signed)	`torch.LongTensor`	`torch.cuda.LongTensor`

Table 1.1: DataTypes supported by PyTorch. Source: http://pytorch.org/docs/master/tensors.html

With each release, PyTorch makes several changes to the API, such that all the possible APIs are similar to NumPy APIs. Shape was one of those changes introduced in the 0.2 release. Calling the `shape` attribute gives you the shape (size in PyTorch terminology) of the tensor, which can be accessible through the `size` function as well:

```
>>> size = rand_initialized.size()
>>> shape = rand_initialized.shape
>>> print(size == shape)
True
```

The `shape` object is inherited from Python tuples and hence all the possible operations on a tuple are possible on a `shape` object as well. As a nice side effect, the `shape` object is immutable.

```
>>> print(shape[0])
3
>>> print(shape[1])
2
```

Now, since you know what a tensor is and how one can be created, we'll start with the most basic math operations. Once you get acquainted with operations such as multiplication addition and matrix operations, everything else is just Lego blocks on top of that.

PyTorch tensor objects have overridden the numerical operations of Python and you are fine with the normal operators. Tensor-scalar operations are probably the simplest:

```
>>> x = torch.ones(3,2)
>>> x
tensor([[1., 1.],
        [1., 1.],
        [1., 1.]])
>>>
>>> y = torch.ones(3,2) + 2
>>> y
tensor([[3., 3.],
        [3., 3.],
        [3., 3.]])
>>>
>>> z = torch.ones(2,1)
>>> z
tensor([[1.],
        [1.]])
>>>
>>> x * y @ z
tensor([[6.],
        [6.],
        [6.]])
```

Variables x and y being 3 x 2 tensors, the Python multiplication operator does element-wise multiplication and gives a tensor of the same shape. This tensor and the z tensor of shape 2 x 1 is going through Python's matrix multiplication operator and spits out a 3 x 1 matrix.

You have several options for tensor-tensor operations, such as normal Python operators, as you have seen in the preceding example, in-place PyTorch functions, and out-place PyTorch functions.

```
>>> z = x.add(y)
>>> print(z)
tensor([[1.4059, 1.0023, 1.0358],
        [0.9809, 0.3433, 1.7492]])
>>> z = x.add_(y)   #in place addition.
>>> print(z)
tensor([[1.4059, 1.0023, 1.0358],
        [0.9809, 0.3433, 1.7492]])
>>> print(x)
tensor([[1.4059, 1.0023, 1.0358],
        [0.9809, 0.3433, 1.7492]])
>>> print(x == z)
tensor([[1, 1, 1],
        [1, 1, 1]], dtype=torch.uint8)
>>>
>>>
>>>
>>> x = torch.rand(2,3)
>>> y = torch.rand(3,4)
>>> x.matmul(y)
tensor([[0.5594, 0.8875, 0.9234, 1.1294],
        [0.7671, 1.7276, 1.5178, 1.7478]])
```

Two tensors of the same size can be added together by using the + operator or the add function to get an output tensor of the same shape. PyTorch follows the convention of having a trailing underscore for the same operation, but this happens in place. For example, a.add(b) gives you a new tensor with summation ran over a and b. This operation would not make any changes to the existing a and b tensors. But a.add_(b) updates tensor a with the summed value and returns the updated a. The same is applicable to all the operators in PyTorch.

In-place operators follow the convention of the trailing underscore, like add_ and sub_.

Matrix multiplication can be done using the function matmul, while there are other functions like mm and Python's @ for the same purpose. Slicing, indexing, and joining are the next most important tasks you'll end up doing while coding up your network. PyTorch enables you to do all of them with basic Pythonic or NumPy syntax.

Indexing a tensor is like indexing a normal Python list. Indexing multiple dimensions can be done by recursively indexing each dimension. Indexing chooses the index from the first available dimension. Each dimension can be separated while indexing by using a comma. You can use this method when doing slicing. Start and end indices can be separated using a full colon. The transpose of a matrix can be accessed using the attribute t; every PyTorch tensor object has the attribute t.

Concatenation is another important operation that you need in your toolbox. PyTorch made the function cat for the same purpose. Two tensors of the same size on all the dimensions except one, if required, can be concatenated using cat. For example, a tensor of size 3 x 2 x 4 can be concatenated with another tensor of size 3 x 5 x 4 on the first dimension to get a tensor of size 3 x 7 x 4. The stack operation looks very similar to concatenation but it is an entirely different operation. If you want to add a new dimension to your tensor, stack is the way to go. Similar to cat, you can pass the axis where you want to add the new dimension. However, make sure all the dimensions of the two tensors are the same other than the attaching dimension.

split and chunk are similar operations for splitting your tensor. split accepts the size you want each output tensor to be. For example, if you are splitting a tensor of size 3 x 2 with size 1 in the 0th dimension, you'll get three tensors each of size 1 x 2. However, if you give 2 as the size on the zeroth dimension, you'll get a tensor of size 2 x 2 and another of size 1 x 2.

The squeeze function sometimes saves you hours of time. There are situations where you'll have tensors with one or more dimension size as 1. Sometimes, you don't need those extra dimensions in your tensor. That is where squeeze is going to help you. squeeze removes the dimension with value 1. For example, if you are dealing with sentences and you have a batch of 10 sentences with five words each, when you map that to a tensor object, you'll get a tensor of 10 x 5. Then you realize that you have to convert that to one-hot vectors for your neural network to process.

You add another dimension to your tensor with a one-hot encoded vector of size 100 (because you have 100 words in your vocabulary). Now you have a tensor object of size 10 x 5 x 100 and you are passing one word at a time from each batch and each sentence.

Now you have to split and slice your sentence and most probably, you will end up having tensors of size 10 x 1 x 100 (one word from each batch of 10 with a 100-dimension vector). You can process it with a 10 x 100-dimension tensor, which makes your life much easier. Go ahead with `squeeze` to get a 10 x 100 tensor from a 10 x 1 x 100 tensor.

PyTorch has the anti-squeeze operation, called `unsqueeze`, which adds another fake dimension to your tensor object. Don't confuse `unsqueeze` with `stack`, which also adds another dimension. `unsqueeze` adds a fake dimension and it doesn't require another tensor to do so, but `stack` is adding another tensor of the same shape to another dimension of your reference tensor.

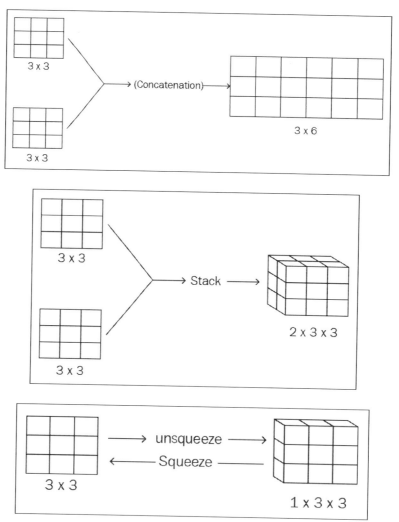

Figure 1.18: Pictorial representation of concatenation, stack, squeeze, and unsqueeze

If you are comfortable with all these basic operations, you can proceed to the second chapter and start the coding session right now. PyTorch comes with tons of other important operations, which you will definitely find useful as you start building the network. We will see most of them in the upcoming chapters, but if you want to learn that first, head to the PyTorch website and check out its tensor tutorial page, which describes all the operations that a tensor object can do.

The internals of PyTorch

One of the core philosophies of PyTorch, which came about with the evolution of PyTorch itself, is interoperability. The development team invested a lot of time into enabling interoperability between different frameworks, such as ONNX, DLPack, and so on. Examples of these will be shown in later chapters, but here we will discuss how the internals of PyTorch are designed to accommodate this requirement without compromising on speed.

A normal Python data structure is a single-layered memory object that can save data and metadata. But PyTorch data structures are designed in layers, which makes the framework not only interoperable but also memory-efficient. The computationally intensive portion of the PyTorch core has been migrated to the C/C++ backend through the ATen and Caffe2 libraries, instead of keeping this in Python itself, in favor of speed improvement.

Even though PyTorch has been created as a research framework, it has been converted to a research-oriented but production-ready framework. The trade-offs that came along with multi-use case requirements have been handled by introducing two execution types. We'll see more about this in *Chapter 8, PyTorch to Production*, where we discuss how to move PyTorch to production.

The custom data structure designed in the C/C++ backend has been divided into different layers. For simplicity, we'll be omitting CUDA data structures and focusing on simple CPU data structures. The main user-facing data structure in PyTorch is a THTensor object, which holds the information about dimension, offset, stride, and so on. However, another main piece of information THTensor stores is the pointer towards the THStorage object, which is an internal layer of the tensor object kept for storage.

```
x = torch.rand(2,3,4)
x_with_2n3_dimension = x[1, :, :]
scalar_x = x[1,1,1]       # first value from each dimension

# numpy like slicing
x = torch.rand(2,3)
print(x[:, 1:])           # skipping first column
```

```
print(x[:-1, :])              # skipping last row


# transpose
x = torch.rand(2,3)
print(x.t())                  # size 3x2


# concatenation and stacking
x = torch.rand(2,3)
concat = torch.cat((x,x))
print(concat)                 # Concatenates 2 tensors on zeroth dimension


x = torch.rand(2,3)
concat = torch.cat((x,x), dim=1)
print(concat)                 # Concatenates 2 tensors on first dimension


x = torch.rand(2,3)
stacked = torch.stack((x,x), dim=0)
print(stacked)                # returns 2x2x3 tensor


# split: you can use chunk as well
x = torch.rand(2,3)
splitted = x.split(split_size=2, dim=0)
print(splitted)               # 2 tensors of 2x2 and 1x2 size


#sqeeze and unsqueeze
x = torch.rand(3,2,1) # a tensor of size 3x2x1
squeezed = x.squeeze()
print(squeezed)               # remove the 1 sized dimension


x = torch.rand(3)
with_fake_dimension = x.unsqueeze(0)
print(with_fake_dimension)            # added a fake zeroth dimension
```

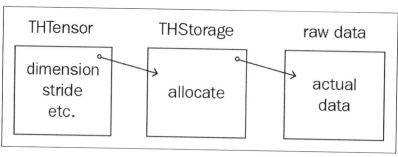

Figure 1.19: THTensor to THStorage to raw data

As you may have assumed, the **THStorage** layer is not a smart data structure and it doesn't really know the metadata of our tensor. The **THStorage** layer is responsible for keeping the pointer towards the raw data and the allocator. The allocator is another topic entirely, and there are different allocators for CPU, GPU, shared memory, and so on. The pointer from **THStorage** that points to the **raw data** is the key to interoperability. The **raw data** is where the actual data is stored but without any structure. This three-layered representation of each tensor object makes the implementation of PyTorch memory-efficient. Following are some examples.

Variable x is created as a tensor of size 2 x 2 filled with 1s. Then we create another variable, xv, which is another view of the same tensor, x. We flatten the 2 x 2 tensor to a single dimension tensor of size 4. We also make a NumPy array by calling the .NumPy() method and storing that in the variable xn:

```
>>> import torch
>>> import numpy as np >>> x = torch.ones(2,2)
>>> xv = x.view(-1)
>>> xn = x.numpy()
>>> x
tensor([[1., 1.],
        [1., 1.]])
>>> xv
tensor([1., 1., 1., 1.])
>>> xn
array([[1. 1.],
       [1. 1.]], dtype=float32)
```

PyTorch provides several APIs to check internal information and storage() is one among them. The storage() method returns the storage object (THStorage), which is the second layer in the PyTorch data structure depicted previously. The storage object of both x and xv is shown as follows. Even though the view (dimension) of both tensors is different, the storage shows the same dimension, which proves that THTensor stores the information about dimensions but the storage layer is a dump layer that just points the user to the raw data object. To confirm this, we use another API available in the THStorage object, which is data_ptr. This points us to the raw data object. Equating data_ptr of both x and xv proves that both are the same:

```
>>> x.storage()
 1.0
 1.0
 1.0
 1.0
[torch.FloatStorage of size 4]
```

```
>>> xv.storage()
1.0
1.0
1.0
1.0
[torch.FloatStorage of size 4]
>>> x.storage().data_ptr() == xv.storage().data_ptr()
True
```

Next, we change the first value in the tensor, which is at the indices 0, 0 to 20. Variables x and xv have a different THTensor layer, since the dimension has been changed but the actual raw data is the same for both of them, which makes it really easy and memory-efficient to create *n* number of views of the same tensor for different purposes.

Even the NumPy array, xn, shares the same raw data object with other variables, and hence the change of value in one tensor reflects a change of the same value in all other tensors that point to the same raw data object. DLPack is an extension of this idea, which makes communication between different frameworks easy in the same program.

```
>>> x[0,0]=20
>>> x
tensor([[20.,  1.],
        [ 1.,  1.]])
>>> xv
tensor([20.,  1.,  1.,  1.])
>>> xn
array([[20.,  1.],
       [ 1.,  1.]], dtype=float32)
```

Summary

In this chapter, we learned about the history of PyTorch, and the pros and cons of a dynamic graph library over a static one. We also glanced over the different architectures and models that people have come up with to solve complicated problems in all kinds of areas. We covered the internals of the most important thing in PyTorch: the Torch tensor. The concept of a tensor is fundamental to deep learning and will be common to all deep learning frameworks you use.

In the next chapter, we'll take a more hands-on approach and will be implementing a simple neural network in PyTorch.

References

1. Ronan Collobert, Koray Kavukcuoglu, and Clement Farabet, *Torch7: A Matlab-like Environment for Machine Learning* (`https://pdfs.semanticscholar.org/3449/b65008b27f6e60a73d80c1fd990f0481126b.pdf?_ga=2.194076141.1591086632.1553663514-2047335409.1553576371`)

2. PyTorch's home page: `https://pytorch.org/`

3. *Optimizing Memory Consumption in Deep Learning* (`https://mxnet.incubator.apache.org/versions/master/architecture/note_memory.html`)

2
A Simple Neural Network

Learning the PyTorch way of building a neural network is really important. It is the most efficient and clean way of writing PyTorch code, and it also helps you to find tutorials and sample snippets easy to follow, since they have the same structure. More importantly, you'll end up with the efficient form of your code, which is also highly readable.

Don't worry, PyTorch is not trying to add another spike into your learning curve by implementing a brand-new methodology. If you know how to code in Python, you'll feel at home right away. However, we won't learn those building blocks as we did in the first chapter; in this chapter, we will build a simple network. Instead of choosing a typical entry-level neural network use case, we'll be teaching our network to do mathematics in the NumPy way. Then we'll convert that to a PyTorch network. By the end of this chapter, you will have the skills to become a PyTorch developer.

Introduction to the neural network

In this section, we'll go through the problem statement at hand and the dataset we are using. Then, we'll go and build a basic neural network, before building it up to a proper PyTorch network.

The problem

Have you ever played the game **Fizz buzz**? Don't worry if you haven't. The following is a simple explanation of what the game is about.

As per Wikipedia, Fizz buzz [1] is a group word game for children that teaches them about division. Players take turns to count incrementally. Any number divisible [2] by three is replaced by the word fizz and any number divisible by five is replaced by the word buzz. Numbers divisible by both become fizz buzz.

Fizz buzz has been used in a fun example by Joel Grus, one of the research engineers at the **Allen Institute of Artificial Intelligence (AI2)**, while writing a blog post [3] on TensorFlow. Although this particular example doesn't solve any practical problems, the blog post got quite a lot of traction and it is fun to see how a neural network learns to find a mathematical pattern from a number stream.

Dataset

Building a data pipeline is as important as the architecture of your network, especially when you train your network in real time. The data that you get from the wild is never going to be clean, and you'll have to process it before throwing it at your network. For example, if we were to collect data for predicting whether a person buys a product or not, we would end up having outliers. Outliers could be of any kind and unpredictable. Somebody could have made an order accidently, for example, or they could have given access to their friends who then made the order, and so on.

Theoretically, deep neural networks are ideal for finding patterns and solutions from your dataset because they are supposed to mimic the human brain. However, in practice, this is often not quite the case. Your network will be able to solve problems easily by finding the pattern if your data is clean and properly formatted. PyTorch gives data preprocessing wrappers out of the box, which we will discuss in *Chapter 3, Deep Learning Workflow*. Along with that, we'll discuss how to format or clean a dataset.

For simplicity, we are going to use some simple functions for generating our data. Let's start by building the simple dataset for the *FizBuz* model. When our model gets a number, it should predict the next output, as if it is a person playing the game. For example, if the input is three, the model should predict the next number is four. If the input is eight, the model should say "fizz," since nine is divisible by three.

We would not want our model to suffer from complicated output. So, to make it easy for our model, we will formulate the problem as a simple classification problem where the model classifies the output to four different categories: **fizz**, **buzz**, **fizzbuzz**, and **continue_without_change**. For any input model, we will try to make a probability distribution over these four classes, and with training, we can try to make the probability distribution concentrated over the correct class.

We will also convert the input number to binary-encoded form, which is easier for the network to process than whole numbers.

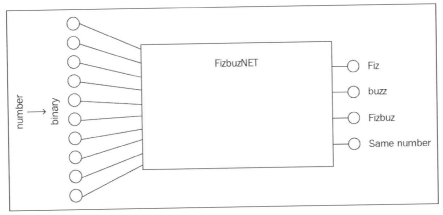

Figure 2.1: Input-to-output mapping

The following code generates the input in binary form and the output as a vector of size four:

```
def binary_encoder(input_size):
    def wrapper(num):
        ret = [int(i) for i in '{0:b}'.format(num)]
        return [0] * (input_size - len(ret)) + ret
    return wrapper


def get_numpy_data(input_size=10, limit=1000):
    x = []
    y = []
    encoder = binary_encoder(input_size)
    for i in range(limit):
        x.append(encoder(i))
        if i % 15 == 0:
            y.append([1, 0, 0, 0])
        elif i % 5 == 0:
            y.append([0, 1, 0, 0])
        elif i % 3 == 0:
            y.append([0, 0, 1, 0])
        else:
            y.append([0, 0, 0, 1])
    return training_test_gen(np.array(x), np.array(y))
```

The encoder function encodes the input to binary numbers, which makes it easy for the neural network to learn. Passing numerical values directly to the neural network places more constraints on the network. Don't worry about the `training_test_gen` function in the last line; we'll talk about it more in *Chapter 3, Deep Learning Workflow*. For now, just remember it's going to split the dataset into a training and testing set, and return them as NumPy arrays.

With the information we possess so far about our dataset, we can architect the network as follows:

- We have converted the input to a binary of 10 digits, so our first input layer needs 10 neurons to accept these 10 digits.

- Since our output is always going to be a vector of size four, we need to have four output neurons.

- It looks like we have a fairly simple problem to solve: comparing the fictional impulses deep learning is making in the current world. We could have a single hidden layer of size 100 to start with.

- As it's always better to batch data before processing, to get good results, we'll have our input batched with 64 data points. Check out the *Finding error* section close to the end of this chapter to understand why batching is better.

Let's define the hyperparameters and call the function we defined previously to get training and testing data. There are five typical hyperparameters we'll be defining for all sorts of neural network models:

```
epochs = 500
batches = 64
lr = 0.01
input_size = 10
output_size = 4
hidden_size = 100
```

We need to define the input and output sizes on top of the program, which will help us to use the input and output sizes in different places, such as the network designing function. Hidden size is the number of neurons in the hidden layer. If you were to design the neural network manually, the size of the weight matrix is `input_size` x `hidden_size`, which converts your input of size `input_size` to size `hidden_size`. `epoch` is the counter value for iterating over the network. The concept of `epoch` ultimately depends on how a programmer defines the iteration process. Normally, for each epoch, you run over the whole dataset and then repeat that for each epoch.

```
for i in epoch:
    network_execution_over_whole_dataset()
```

The learning rate decides how fast we want our network to take feedback from the error on each iteration. It decides what to learn from the current iteration by forgetting what the network learned from all the previous iterations. Keeping the learning rate as one makes the network take the complete error into consideration and adjust the weight with the complete error. A learning rate of zero means zero information passing to the network. The learning rate will be the selection factor in the equation of the gradient update in a neural network. For each neuron, we run the following equation to update the weight of the neuron:

*weight -= lr * loss*

A small learning rate helps the network to take small steps climbing down the mountain, while a large learning rate helps the network to take big steps. However, that comes at a cost. Once the loss gets close to the minima, a high learning rate might let the network jump over the minima and cause the network to never find the minima. More technically, at each iteration, the network makes a linear approximation over the approximation, and the learning rate controls this approximation.

If the loss function is highly curved, taking long steps with a high learning rate might result in a bad model. So, an ideal learning rate is always subject to the problem statement and the model architecture at hand. The fourth chapter of *Deep Learning Book* [4] is a good source for understanding the importance of learning. A good pictorial representation from the famous Andrew Ng course on Coursera gives a succinct view of how the learning rate affects the network learning.

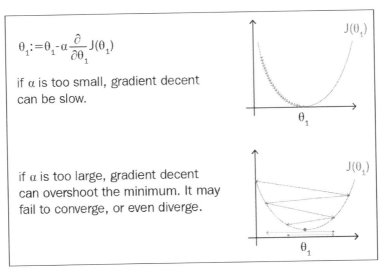

$$\theta_1 := \theta_1 - \alpha \frac{\partial}{\partial \theta_1} J(\theta_1)$$

if α is too small, gradient decent can be slow.

if α is too large, gradient decent can overshoot the minimum. It may fail to converge, or even diverge.

Figure 2.2: A small learning rate and a large learning rate

Novice model

Now we are going to build a novice, NumPy-like model, not using any PyTorch-specific approach. Then, in the next session, we'll convert the same model to PyTorch's method. If you come from a NumPy background, you'll feel at home, but if you are an advanced deep learning practitioner who has used other frameworks, please take the liberty of skipping this session.

Autograd

So, now that we know which type our tensors should be, we can create PyTorch tensors from the NumPy array we got from `get_numpy_data()`.

```
x = torch.from_numpy(trX).type(dtype)
y = torch.from_numpy(trY).type(dtype)
w1 = torch.randn(input_size, hidden_size,
                 requires_grad=True).type(dtype)
w2 = torch.randn(hidden_size, output_size,
                 requires_grad=True).type(dtype)
b1 = torch.zeros(1, hidden_size, requires_grad=True).type(dtype)
b2 = torch.zeros(1, output_size, requires_grad=True).type(dtype)
```

That might look intimidating to a beginner, but once you learn the basic building blocks, it's just six lines of code. We are starting with the most important module in PyTorch, which is autograd, the backbone of the PyTorch framework. It helps the user to do automatic differentiation, which led us through all breakthroughs in the deep learning field.

Note: Automatic differentiation, sometimes known as algorithmic differentiation, is the technique of exploiting the execution order of functions by computer programs. Two major approaches to automatic differentiation are forward mode and reverse mode. In forward-mode automatic differentiation, we find the derivative of the outer function first and go inside recursively until we explore all the child nodes. Reverse-mode automatic differentiation is the exact opposite and is being used by the deep learning community and frameworks. It was first published by Seppo Linnainmaa in his master's thesis in 1970. The major building block of reverse mode differentiation is the memory that stores intermediate variables and the functionality that made those variables calculate the derivative, while moving back from a child node to a parent node.

As the PyTorch home page says, central to all neural networks in PyTorch is the autograd package. PyTorch acquired dynamic capability with the help of the autograd package. When the program executes, autograd writes each operation to the tape-like data structure and stores it in memory.

This is one of the key features of reverse-mode automatic differentiation. This helps PyTorch to be dynamic, since whatever the user writes as an operation in the forward pass can be written to the tape, and when backpropagation starts, autograd can move backward through the tape and take the gradient along with it until it reaches the outermost parent.

The tape or memory write is a comparatively negligible task and PyTorch exploits that behavior in each forward pass by writing the operations onto the tape and destroying the tape after the backward pass. Although I will try to avoid as much mathematics as possible in this book, a mathematical example of how autograd works should definitely help you. In the following two diagrams, the backpropagation algorithm and autograd's approach of using the chain rule are explained. We have a small network in the following diagram, which has one multiplication node and one addition node. The multiplication node gets the input tensor and the weight tensor, which is passed to the addition node for adding with bias.

$$Out = X * W + B$$

Since we divide the equation into several steps, we can find the slope for each stage based on the next stage, which is then chained together by using the chain rule to get the error on weights based on the final output. The second diagram shows how autograd chains each of those derivative terms to get the final error.

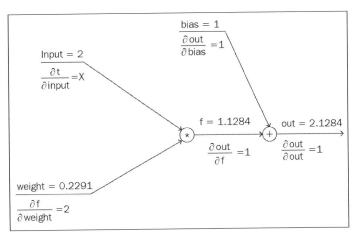

Figure 2.3: How autograd works

$$\text{weight gradient} = \frac{\partial t}{\partial \text{weight}} = \boxed{\frac{\partial t}{\partial \text{weight}} * \boxed{\frac{\partial \text{out}}{\partial t} \times \boxed{\frac{\partial \text{out}}{\partial \text{out}}}}}$$

Figure 2.4: The chain rule used by autograd

The preceding diagram can be converted to a PyTorch graph with the following code:

```
>>> import torch
>>> inputs = torch.FloatTensor([2])
>>> weights = torch.rand(1, requires_grad=True)
>>> bias = torch.rand(1, requires_grad=True)
>>> t = inputs @ weights
>>> out = t + bias
>>> out.backward()
>>> weights.grad
tensor([2.])
>>>bias.grad
tensor([1.])
```

Normally, users can access autograd using two major APIs, which take care of almost all the operations you will encounter when building a neural network.

Autograd attributes of a tensor

Tensors, when becoming part of a graph, need to store information that is needed for autograd for automatic differentiation. The tensor acts as a node in the computational graph and connects to other nodes through functional module instances. Tensor instances mainly have three attributes for supporting autograd: .grad, .data, and grad_fn() (watch out for letter cases: **Function** represents the PyTorch Function module, while **function** represents Python functions).

The .grad attribute stores the gradient at any point in time and all the backward calls accumulate the current gradient to the .grad attribute. The .data attribute gives access to the bare tensor object that has the data in it.

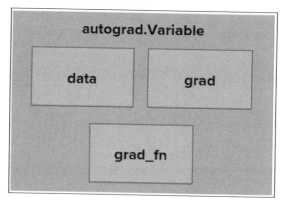

Figure 2.5: data, grad, and grad_fn

In case you are wondering, the `required_grad` parameter in the preceding code snippet informs the tensor or autograd-engine that it needs the gradient while doing backpropagation. When we create the tensor, we can specify whether we need that tensor to carry the gradient or not. In our example, we are not updating the input tensor with the gradient (the input never changes): we just need to change the weights. Since we are not changing the input in iterations, we don't need the input tensor to have the gradient computed. So, while wrapping the input tensor, we pass `False` as the `required_grad` parameter and for weights, we pass `True`. Check the `grad` and `data` attributes of the tensor instance we created before.

Tensor and `Function` instances are interconnected when they are in a graph, and together, they make the acyclic computational graph. Each tensor other than the tensor explicitly made by the user is connected to a function. (If the user did not create a tensor explicitly, it must be created by a function. For example, *c* in the expression *c = a + b* is created by the addition function.) You can access the creator function by calling `grade_fn` on the tensor. Printing the values of `grad`, `.data`, and `.grade_fn()` gives us the following result:

```
print(x.grad, x.grad_fn, x)
# None None tensor([[...]])
print(w1.grad, w1.grad_fn, w1)
# None None tensor([[...]])
```

Our input, x, and first-layer weight matrix, w1, don't have `grad` or `grad_fn` right now. We'll see soon how and when those attributes get updated. The `.data` attribute of x is 900 x 10 shaped since we pass 900 data points, each of size 10 (a binary encoded number). Now you are ready to move to data iteration.

We have our input, weights, and biases ready and waiting for data to come in. As we have already seen before, PyTorch is a dynamic graph-based network that builds the computational graph on each iteration. So, when we iterate through the data, we are essentially building the graph on the fly and calling backpropagation on it when we reach the last or root node. Here is a code snippet showing this:

```
for epoch in range(epochs):
    for batch in range(no_of_batches):
        start = batch * batches
        end = start + batches
        x_ = x[start:end]
        y_ = y[start:end]

        # building graph
        a2 = x_.matmul(w1)
        a2 = a2.add(b1)
        print(a2.grad, a2.grad_fn, a2)
```

```
# None <AddBackward0 object at 0x7f5f3b9253c8>
        tensor([[...]])
h2 = a2.sigmoid()
a3 = h2.matmul(w2)
a3 = a3.add(b2)
hyp = a3.sigmoid()
error = hyp - y_
output = error.pow(2).sum() / 2.0

# backpropagation
w1.grad.zero_()
w2.grad.zero_()
b1.grad.zero_()
b2.grad.zero_()
output.backward()

print(x.grad, x.grad_fn, x)
# None None tensor([[...]])
print(w1.grad, w1.grad_fn, w1)
# tensor([[...]], None, tensor([[...]]
print(a2.grad, a2.grad_fn, a2)
# None <AddBackward0 object at 0x7f5f3d42c780>
        tensor([[...]])

# parameter update
with torch.no_grad():
    w1 -= lr * w1.grad
    w2 -= lr * w2.grad
    b1 -= lr * b1.grad
    b2 -= lr * b2.grad
```

The preceding code snippet is the same as you have seen in *Chapter 1, Deep Learning Walkthrough and PyTorch Introduction,* which explained static and dynamic computational graphs, but here we look at the code from another perspective: the model explanation. It starts with looping through batches for each epoch and processing each batch with the model we are building now. Unlike the static computational graph-based framework, we haven't built the graph yet; we have just defined the hyperparameters and made tensors from our data.

Building the graph

We are building the graph as shown in the following diagram:

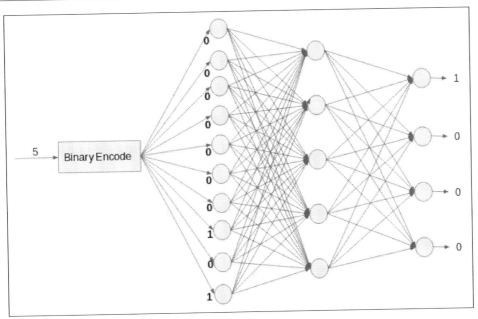

Figure 2.6: Network architecture

The first layer consists of a matrix multiplication and addition between the batched input matrix, weights, and biases. At this point, the a2 tensor should have one grad_ fn, which should be the backward operation of the matrix addition. However, since we haven't done the backward pass yet, .grad should return None and .data, as always, will return the tensor with the result from the matrix multiplication and bias addition. The neuronal activity is defined by the sigmoid activation function, which gives us the output in **h2** (which stands for hidden units in layer two). The second layer follows the same structure: matrix multiplication, bias addition, and sigmoid. We get hyp at the end, which has the predicted result:

```
print(a2.grad, a2.grad_fn, a2)
# None <AddBackward0 object at 0x7f5f3b9253c8> tensor([[...]])
```

> **Softmax**: It's unusual to have a sigmoid layer spitting out the prediction for a classification problem, but we kept it as such since that makes our model fairly simple to understand, because it's repeating the first layer. Normally, classification problems are handled by the softmax layer and cross-entropy loss, which increases the probability of one class over another. Since the probability of all the classes should add up to one, increasing the probability of one class reduces the probability of other classes, which is a nice feature to have. There will be more on that in future chapters.

Finding error

It's time to find out how well our model predicted in Fizz buzz. We are using the most basic regression loss called the **mean squared error** (**MSE**). Initially, we find the difference between the prediction and output of each element in the batch (remember the vector of size four we created for each input data point?). Then we square all the differences and sum all of them together to get a single value. Don't worry about the division by 2.0 if you are not familiar with loss functions. That is just there for making the mathematics neat while doing backpropagation.

Backpropagation

People coming from a NumPy background, be ready to be blown away. People who started a deep learning career in advanced frameworks like TensorFlow or PyTorch, don't take it for granted. The powerful feature of the modern-day framework, automatic differentiation, made backpropagation a one-liner. The last node in our graph was the loss result we just found. Now we have a single value that states how badly (or well) our model predicted the result and we need to update the parameters based on that value. Backpropagation is here to help. We need to take this loss and move back to each neuron to find the contribution of each neuron.

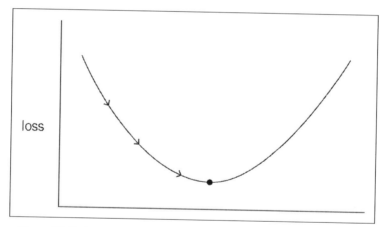

Figure 2.7: Backpropagation and loss reduction with the mountain example

Consider the graph of the loss function where the Y axis is the error (how bad our model was). Initially, the model's prediction would be random and really bad for the dataset as a whole, that is, the error in the Y axis is really high. We need to move it down like climbing down a mountain: we want to climb down the mountain and find the lowest point in the valley that gives a close-to-accurate result.

Backpropagation achieves this by finding the direction each parameter should move in, so that the overall movement of the loss value climbs down the mountain. We seek help from calculus for doing this. The derivative of any function with respect to the final error can tell us what the slope is of the function in the preceding graph. So, backpropagation helps us by taking the derivative of each neuron (each neuron is a non-linear function, usually) with respect to the final loss and telling us the direction we have to move in.

It wasn't an easy process before we had frameworks. Finding derivatives of each parameter and updating was, in fact, a tedious and error-prone task. In PyTorch, all you have to do is call `backward` on the last node, which will backpropagate and update the. `grad` attribute with gradients.

PyTorch's `backward` function does the backpropagation and finds the error for each neuron. However, we need to update the weight of the neuron based on this error factor. The process of updating the error found is called optimization, generally, and there are different strategies for optimization. PyTorch has given us another module called `optim` for different optimization algorithm implementations. We used the basic and most popular optimization algorithm in the previous implementation called **stochastic gradient descent (SGD)**. We'll see different optimization algorithms in later chapters when we work with complex neural networks.

PyTorch also gives us more flexibility by separating backpropagation and optimization as different steps. Remember, backpropagation accumulates the gradients in the `.grad` attribute. This is helpful, especially if our project is more research-oriented or if we want to go deep into the weight-gradient relation, or if we want to see how the gradients are being changed. Sometimes, we wish to update all the parameters other than a particular neuron's, or sometimes we might think updating a particular layer is unnecessary. During those instances where you need more control of parameter updates, having an explicit parameter update step is a great benefit.

Before moving forward, we check all the tensors we checked before to see what has changed after the backward pass.

```
print(x.grad, x.grad_fn, x)
# None None tensor([[...]])
print(w1.grad, w1.grad_fn, w1)
# tensor([[...]], None, tensor([[...]])
print(a2.grad, a2.grad_fn, a2)
# None <AddBackward0 object at 0x7f5f3d42c780> tensor([[...]])
```

Things have changed! Since we created the input tensor with `required_grad` as `False`, we first print to check the attributes of the input haven't shown any difference. `w1` has changed. Before the backward pass, the `.grad` attribute was `None`, and now it has got some gradients. That's refreshing!

Weights are the parameters we need to change based on the gradient, and we got the gradient for them. We don't have a gradient function, since it's created by the user, so `grad_fn` is still `None`, and `.data` is still the same. If we try to print the value of the data, it will still be the same, as the backward pass will not update the tensors implicitly. In summary, among `x`, `w1`, and `a2`, only `w1` got the gradient. This is because the intermediate nodes created by the internal functions like `a2` will not save the gradients, since they are parameter-less nodes. The only parameters that affect the output of the neural network are the weights we have defined for the layers.

Parameter update

The parameter update or optimization step takes the gradient generated by backpropagation and updates the weights using some strategies to reduce the contribution factor from the parameter by a small step. This step is then repeated until we find a good set of parameters.

All user-created tensors require that gradient has value in the `gradient` attribute, and we need to update the parameter. All the parameter tensors have the `.data` attribute and `.grad` attribute, which have tensor values and gradients, respectively. Obviously, what we need to do is take the gradient and subtract that from the data. However, it turns out that reducing the whole gradient from the parameter is not a good idea. The idea behind that is that the amount of parameter updates decides how much the network learns from each example (each iteration), and we don't want our network to learn false information if a particular example we gave was an outlier.

We want our network to be generalized, learning a bit from all the examples and eventually becoming good at generalizing any new examples. So, instead of reducing the whole gradient from the data, we use the learning rate to decide how much the gradient should be used in a particular update. Finding the optimal learning rate is always an important decision because that affects the overall performance of the model. The basic rule of thumb is to find a learning rate that is small enough that the model will eventually learn and high enough that it won't take forever to converge.

The preceding described training strategy is called gradient descent. The more sophisticated training strategies like Adam will be discussed in a later chapter. Gradient descent itself has evolved from two other variants. The most primitive version of gradient descent is SGD, mentioned earlier. With SGD, each network execution runs on a single sample and updates the model with the gradient gained from one sample, then moves on to the next sample.

The major disadvantage of SGD is inefficiency. For instance, consider our *FizBuz* dataset with 1,000 samples each of size 10. Executing one sample at a time requires us to pass the tensor of size 1 x 10 as the input to the hidden layer, with a weight tensor of 10 x 100, which converts the 1 x 10 input to a 1 x 100 hidden state. For processing the whole of our dataset, we have to run 1,000 iterations. Normally, we'd be running our model on GPUs with thousands of cores, but with one sample at a time, we'll not be using the full power of our GPU. Now think about passing the whole dataset at in a single stretch. The first layer gets the input of size 1,000 x 10, which gets transferred to a hidden state of size 1,000 x 100. Now that is efficient, since tensor multiplication will be executed on the multi-core GPU parallelly.

The variant of gradient descent that uses the full dataset is called batched gradient descent. It is not quite better than SGD; while batched gradient descent increases efficiency practically, it reduces the generalization capability of the network. SGD has to move through noises one by one, so it will have a high rate of jerking, which causes the network to move out of local minima, while batched gradient descent avoids the chances of getting stuck at the local minima.

Another major drawback of batched gradient descent is its memory consumption. Since the whole batch is being processed together, the huge dataset should be loaded to RAM or GPU memory, which is not practical in most cases where we try to train with millions of samples. The next variant is a mixture of both the preceding approaches called mini-batch gradient descent (although it is mini-batch gradient descent by definition, SGD is what people use typically to refer to it).

Everything else remains the same other than the new hyperparameters, learning rate, and batch size that we introduced just now. We update the .data attribute with the learning rate times the .grad attribute, and we do this for each iteration. Choosing the batch size is almost always dependent on memory availability. We try to make the mini-batch as big as possible, so that it can be placed in the GPU memory. Dividing the whole batch into mini-batches makes sure that each gradient update creates enough jerking to throw the model out of the local minima, while using the full power provided by the GPU.

We have reached the last part of our model-building journey. Everything so far was intuitive and easy, but the last part is a bit confusing. What does zero_grad do? Remember the first print statement on weight w1.grad? It was empty and now it has the gradient from the current backward pass. So, we need to empty the gradient before the next backward pass because the gradient gets accumulated, not rewritten. We call zero_grad() on each tensor on each iteration after the parameter update and move on to the next iteration.

.grad_fn holds the graph together by connecting the functions and tensors. Each possible operation on a tensor is defined in the Function module. .grad_fn of all the tensors always points toward a function object unless a user creates it. PyTorch lets you traverse through your graph backward by using grad_fn. From any node in your graph, you can reach any of the parent nodes by calling next_functions on the return value of grad_fn.

```
# traversing the graph using .grad_fn
print(output.grad_fn)
# <DivBackward0 object at 0x7eff00ae3ef0>
print(output.grad_fn.next_functions[0][0])
# <SumBackward0 object at 0x7eff017b4128>
print(output.grad_fn.next_functions[0][0].next_functions[0][0])
# <PowBackward0 object at 0x7eff017b4128>
```

Printing grad_fn on the output tensor just after the training reveals its creator, and in the case of output, it is the division operator that does the last division-by-two operation. Then the next_functions call on any gradient functions (or backward functions) will show us the way back to the input node. In the example, the division operator follows the sum function, which adds up the squared errors of all the data points in a batch. The next operator is the power operator, which was used for squaring the individual errors. The following diagram shows the idea of chaining tensors using functions:

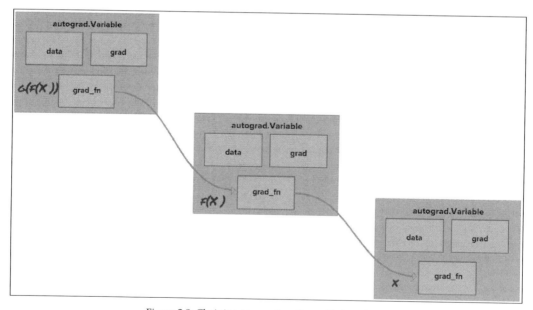

Figure 2.8: Chaining tensors together with functions

The PyTorch way

So far, we have developed a simple two-layer neural network in a hybrid NumPy-PyTorch style. We have coded each operation line by line, like how we do it in NumPy, and we have adopted automatic differentiation from PyTorch so that we don't have to code the backward pass.

On the way, we have learned how to wrap matrices (or tensors) in PyTorch, and that helps us with backpropagation. The PyTorch way of doing the same thing is a bit more convenient and that is what we are going to discuss in this section. PyTorch gives access to almost all the functionality required for a deep learning project inbuilt. Since PyTorch supports all the mathematical functions available in Python, it's not a tough task to build one function if it's not available in the core. You can not only build any functionality you need, but PyTorch defines the derivative function of the functionality you build implicitly.

PyTorch is helpful for people who need to know the low-level operations, but at the same time, PyTorch comes with high-level APIs through the `torch.nn` module. So, if the user doesn't want to know what is happening inside the black box, but just needs to build the model, PyTorch allows them to do so. Similarly, if the user doesn't like some uplifting happening under the hood and needs to know what exactly is going on, PyTorch offers that flexibility as well. Building this combination onto a single framework was a gamechanger and made PyTorch one of the favorite frameworks for the whole deep learning community.

High-level APIs

High-level APIs allow beginners to start building a network right from scratch, and at the same time, they allow an advanced user to spend time on other critical parts and leave the invented modules to PyTorch. All the modules in PyTorch that are required to build a neural network are Python class instances that have the forward and backward functions. When you start executing your neural network, under the hood, you are executing the forward function, which in turn adds the operations onto the tape. Since PyTorch knows the derivative function of all the operations, it's easy for PyTorch to move back through the tape. Now we are going to modularize our code to small units to make the same *FizBuz* net.

Modularized code has the same structure, since we get the data and create the tensor from the NumPy data input. The rest of the "complicated" code can be replaced with the model class we have created.

```
net = FizBuzNet(input_size, hidden_size, output_size)
```

We made the class flexible to accept any input size and output size, which makes it easier for us if we are changing our mind to pass one-hot encoding instead of binary encoding the input. So, where is this `FizBuzNet` coming from?

```
class FizBuzNet(nn.Module):
    """
    2 layer network for predicting fiz or buz
    param: input_size -> int
    param: output_size -> int
    """

    def __init__(self, input_size, hidden_size, output_size):
        super(FizBuzNet, self).__init__()
        self.hidden = nn.Linear(input_size, hidden_size)
        self.out = nn.Linear(hidden_size, output_size)

    def forward(self, batch):
        hidden = self.hidden(batch)
        activated = torch.sigmoid(hidden)
        out = self.out(activated)
        return out
```

We have defined the structure of `FizBuzNet` and wrapped it inside a Python class inherited from `torch.nn.Module`. The nn module in PyTorch is the high-level API for accessing all the popular layers in the deep learning world. Let's take it step by step.

nn.Module

The high-level API that allows users to write other high-level APIs is `nn.Module`. You can define each separable part of your network as a separate Python class and inherit from `nn.Module`. For example, let's say you want to make a deep learning model to trade cryptocurrencies. You've collected trading data from some exchange for each coin and parsed that data to some form that you can pass to your network. Now you are in a dilemma: how do you rank each coin? A simple approach would be to one-hot encode the coins and pass that to a neuron, but you are not happy with that. Another, fairly simple, approach is to make another small model to rank the coin, and you can pass the rank from this small model to your main model as one input. Aha! That seems simple and smart, but again, how do you do that? Let's take a look at the following diagram:

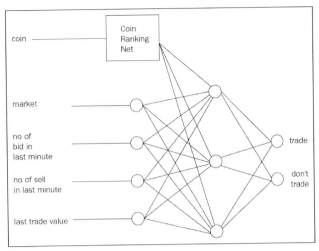

Figure 2.9: A simple network for coin ranking and passing the output to the major network

nn.Module makes it easier for you to have such nice abstractions. When you initialize the class object, __init__() will be called, which in turn initializes the layers and returns the object. nn.Module implements two major functions, __call__ and backward(), and the user needs to override forward and __init__().

Once the layer-initialized object is returned, input data can be passed to the model by calling the model object itself. Usually, Python objects are not callable. To call object methods, the user has to call them explicitly. However, nn.Module implements the magic function __call__(), which in turn calls the forward function the user has defined. The user has the privilege of defining whatever they want in the forward call.

As far as PyTorch knows how to backpropagate what's in forward, you are safe. However, if you have custom functions or layers in forward, PyTorch allows you to override the backward function, and that will be executed while moving back through the tape.

The user has the option to build the layers in the __init__() definition, which takes care of the weight and bias creation we have done in the novice model by hand. In our following FizBuzNet, lines in __init__() create the linear layers. The linear layer is also called the fully connected or dense layer, which does the matrix multiplication between the weights and the input, and bias addition, internally:

```
self.hidden = nn.Linear(input_size, hidden_size)
self.out = nn.Linear(hidden_size, output_size)
```

Let's look at the source code of `nn.Linear` from PyTorch, which should give us enough understanding about how `nn.Module` works and also how can we extend `nn.Module` to create another custom module:

```
class Linear(Module):
    def __init__(self, in_features, out_features, bias):
        super(Linear, self).__init__()
        self.in_features = in_features
        self.out_features = out_features
        self.weight = Parameter(torch.Tensor(out_features,
                                        in_features))
        self.bias = Parameter(torch.Tensor(out_features))

    def forward(self, input):
        return input.matmul(self.weight.t()) + self.bias
```

The code snippet is a modified version of the Linear layer from the PyTorch source code. Wrapping the tensor with `Parameter` must look like a strange thing to you, but don't worry about it. The `Parameter` class adds the weights and biases to the list of module parameters and will be available when you call `model.parameters()`. The initializer saves all the arguments as object attributes. The `forward` function does exactly what we did in our custom Linear layer in the previous example.

```
a2 = x.matmul(w1)
a2 = a2.add(b1)
```

There are more important functionalities of `nn.module` that we will be using in future chapters.

apply()

This is a function that helps us with applying a custom function to all the parameters of the model. It is often used to make custom weight initialization, but generally, `model_name.apply(custom_function)` executes `custom_function` on each model parameter.

cuda() and cpu()

These functions have the same purpose as we discussed before. However, `model.cpu()` converts all the parameters to CPU tensors, which is handy when you have more than a few parameters in your model and converting each of them separately is cumbersome.

```
net = FizBuzNet(input_size, hidden_size, output_size)
net.cpu()      # convert all parameters to CPU tensors
net.cuda()     # convert all parameters to GPU tensors
```

This decision should be uniform across the entire program. If we decide to keep our net on GPU and if we pass a CPU tensor (the storage of the tensor is on CPU memory), it won't be able to process it. While creating the tensor itself, PyTorch allows you to do this by passing the tensor type as an argument to the factory function. The ideal way to make this decision is to test whether CUDA is available or not with PyTorch's inbuilt `cuda.is_available()` function and create tensors accordingly:

```
if torch.cuda.is_available():
    xtype = torch.cuda.FloatTensor
    ytype = torch.cuda.LongTensor
else:
    xtype = torch.FloatTensor
    ytype = torch.LongTensor
x = torch.from_numpy(trX).type(xtype)
y = torch.from_numpy(trY).type(ytype)
```

We don't stop here. If you have started your operation on GPU and you have a CPU-optimized operation in between your script, you can convert your GPU tensors to CPU tensors just by calling the CPU method and vice versa. We will see such examples in future chapters.

train() and eval()

As the names indicate, these functions tell PyTorch that the model is running in training mode or evaluation mode. This has some effect only if you want to turn off or on the modules, such as `Dropout` or `BatchNorm`. We will use them quite often in future chapters.

parameters()

A call on `parameters()` returns all the model parameters, which are useful in the case of optimizers or if you want to do experiments with parameters. In the novice model we developed, it had four parameters, w1, w2, b1, and b2, and we updated the parameters with gradients line by line. However, in `FizBuzNet`, since we have a model class and we haven't created the weights and biases of our model, the `.parameter()` call is the way to go.

```
net = FizBuzNet(input_size, hidden_size, output_size)

#building graph
# backpropagation
# zeroing the gradients

with torch.no_grad():
    for p in net.parameters():
        p -= p.grad * lr
```

Instead of a user writing down each parameter update line by line, we can generalize to a `for` loop since `.parameters()` returns all the parameters that are special tensors and have `.grad` and `.data` attributes. We have better approaches to update the weights, but this is one of the most common and intuitive ways that people update the weights if they don't need any fancy update strategies like Adam, and so on.

zero_grad()

This is a convenience function to make the gradients zero. But unlike the way we did this in the novice model, it's an easier and straightforward function call. With models powered with `zero_grad`, we don't have to find each parameter and call `zero_grad` on it separately, but a single call on the model object will zero the gradient of all the parameters.

Other layers

The *nn* module is rich with the different layers you would need to build almost everything with current deep learning techniques.

An important layer that comes with `nn.Module` is the sequential container, which provides an easy API to make a model object without having the user write the class structure if the structure of the model is sequential and straightforward. `FizBuzNet` with the structure **Linear | Sigmoid | Linear | Sigmoid** can be implemented with Sequential with a single line of code, and this will act exactly like the `FizBuzNet` network we have built before:

```
import torch.nn as nn

net = nn.Sequential(
    nn.Linear(i, h),
    nn.Sigmoid(),
    nn.Linear(h, o),
    nn.Sigmoid())
```

The functional module

The `nn.functional` module comes with operations we require to connect the network nodes together. In our models, we use the sigmoid from the `functional` module as the non-linear activation. The `functional` module has a lot more functionalities, such as all the mathematical functions you are doing that are pointed to the `functional` module. In the following example, the multiplication operator calls the `mul` operator from the `functional` module:

```
>>> a = torch.randn(1,2)
>>> b = torch.randn(2,1,requires_grad=True)
>>> a.requires_grad
```

```
False
>>> b.requires_grad
True
>>> c = a @ b
>>> c.grad_fn
<MmBackward at 0x7f1cd5222c88>
```

The `functional` module has layers as well, but it is less abstractive than what nn offers and more abstractive than the way we built the novice model:

```
>>> import torch
>>> import torch.nn.functional as F
>>> a = torch.Tensor([[1,1]])
>>> w1 = torch.Tensor([[2,2]])
>>> F.linear(a,w1) == a.matmul(w1.t())
tensor([[1]], dtype=torch.uint8)
```

As given in the preceding example, `F.linear` allows us to pass the weights and inputs and returns the same value as if it were a normal `matmul` we used in the novice model. Other layer functions in `functional` also work in the same way.

> **Sigmoid activation**: Activation functions create the non-linearity between the layers of the neural network. This is essential because without non-linearity, the layers are just multiplying the input values with weights. In that case, a single layer of a neural network can do the exact functionality of 100 layers; it's just a matter of increasing or decreasing the value of the weights. Sigmoid activation is probably the most traditional activation function. It squashes the input to the range of [0,1].

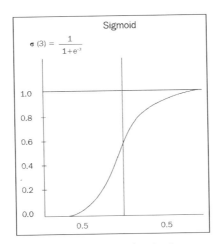

Figure 2.10: Sigmoid activation

Though sigmoid acts non-linearly on the input, it doesn't produce output that is centered on zero. Vanishing gradients and computationally expensive exponentiation are other disadvantages of sigmoid and because of these reasons, almost all deep learning practitioners don't use sigmoid for any use cases these days. Finding suitable non-linearity is a major field of research and people have come up with much better solutions like ReLU, Leaky ReLU, and ELU. We will see most of them in the future chapters.

Inside the `forward` function of our `FizBuzNet`, we have two linear layers and two non-linear activation layers. Usually, the output returns from the `forward` function are the logits that represent the probability distribution, where the correct class gets high value, but in our model, we are returning the output from sigmoid.

The loss function

Now we have the prediction returned by `FizBuzNet`, we need to find out how well our model predicted and then backpropagate that error. We call the loss function to find the error. There are different loss functions prevalent in the community. PyTorch comes with all the popular loss functions inbuilt in the nn module. Loss functions accept the logits and the actual value, and apply the loss functionality on them to find the loss score. This process gives the error rate, which represents how good or bad the model's prediction is. In the novice model, we used the basic MSE loss, which has been defined as `MSELoss()` in the nn module.

```
loss = nn.MSELoss()
output = loss(hyp, y_)
output.backward()
```

The nn module has more sophisticated losses than those we'll see in future chapters, but for our current use case, we'll go with `MSELoss`. The loss node we created with `nn.MSELoss()` is equivalent to the loss we defined in the first example:

```
error = hyp - y_
output = error.pow(2).sum() / 2.0
```

The node returned by `loss(hyp, y_)` will then be the leaf node on which we can call backward to find the gradients.

Optimizers

In the novice model, after we called `backward()`, we updated the weight by subtracting a small factor of the gradient. We did that by calling weight parameters explicitly.

```
# updating weight
```

```
with torch.no_grad():
    w1 -= lr * w1.grad
    w2 -= lr * w2.grad
    b1 -= lr * b1.grad
    b2 -= lr * b2.grad
```

However, we cannot do that for big models with lots of parameters. A better alternative is looping over `net.parameters()` as we have seen before, but doing so has the major disadvantage of looping over the parameters from Python, which is a boilerplate. Moreover, there are different strategies for weight updates. The one we used is the most basic gradient descent method. The complex methods handle learning rate decay, momentum, and more. These help the network to reach the global minima faster than normal SGD.

The `optim` package is the alternative that PyTorch provides to handle the weight updates efficiently. Additional to that, the user can call `zero_grad` on the optimizer object once it is initialized with model parameters. So, there are no more `zero_grad` calls on each weight-bias parameter explicitly as we did previously.

```
w1.grad.zero_()
w2.grad.zero_()
b1.grad.zero_()
b2.grad.zero_()
```

The `optim` package has all the popular optimizers inbuilt. Here we use the exact same simple optimizer – SGD:

```
optimizer = optim.SGD(net.parameters(), lr=lr)
```

The `optimizer` object now has the model parameters. The `optim` package provides a convenient function called `step()`, which does the parameter update based on the strategy defined by the optimizer:

```
for epoch in range(epochs):
    for batch in range(no_of_batches):
        start = batch * batches
        end = start + batches
        x_ = x[start:end]
        y_ = y[start:end]
        hyp = net(x_)
        loss = loss_fn(hyp, y_)
        optimizer.zero_grad()
        loss.backward()
        optimizer.step()
```

Here is the code that loops over the batches and calls the `net` with the input batch. The `hyp` returned by the `net(x_)` is then passed to the loss function along with the actual value, `y_`. The error returned by the loss function is used as the leaf node to call `backward()`. Then we call the `step()` function of `optimizer`, which updates the parameters. After the update, the user is responsible for zeroing the gradients, which is now possible with `optimizer.zero_grad()`.

Summary

In this chapter, we have learned how to build a simple neural network in the most basic way and convert that to a PyTorch's way. The basic building block of deep learning starts here. Once we know how and why the methodology we follow exists, we'll be able to take the big steps. Any deep learning model, regardless of the size, usage, or algorithm, can be built with the concepts we have learned in this chapter. Because of that, understanding this chapter thoroughly is critical for going through future chapters. In the next chapter, we will dive into the deep learning workflow.

References

1. Fizz buzz Wikipedia page, `https://en.wikipedia.org/wiki/Fizz_buzz`
2. Division (mathematics) Wikipedia page, `https://en.wikipedia.org/wiki/Division_(mathematics)`
3. Joel Grus, *Fizz Buzz in Tensorflow*, `http://joelgrus.com/2016/05/23/fizz-buzz-in-tensorflow/`
4. Ian Goodfellow, Yoshua Bengio and Aaron Courville, *Deep Learning Book*, `http://www.deeplearningbook.org/`

3
Deep Learning Workflow

Although deep learning is making a big shift from just being in academia to being in industry and powering millions of users' requests every day, the new players in the field still struggle to set up a workflow for the deep learning pipeline. This chapter is designed to cover the portion of workflow that PyTorch can help with.

PyTorch was started as a research framework by a Facebook intern and it has grown to the stage where the backend is backed by a super-optimized Caffe2 core. So, in a nutshell, PyTorch can be used as a research or prototype framework and at the same time, it can be used to write an efficient model with serving modules, and it also can be deployable to single-board computers and mobile devices.

A typical deep learning workflow starts with ideation and research around a problem statement, which is where the architectural design and model decisions come into play. The theoretical model is then experimented with using prototypes. This includes trying out different models or techniques like skip connection, or making decisions on what not to try out. Also, choosing the right dataset for the prototyping and adding the seamless integration of the dataset to the pipeline is crucial for this stage. Once the model is implemented and verified with training and validation sets, the model can then be optimized for production serving. A five-stage deep learning workflow is depicted in the following diagram:

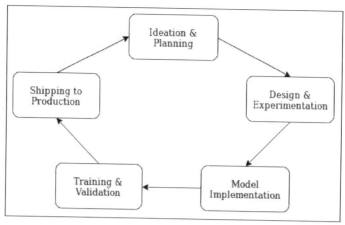

Figure 3.1: Deep learning workflow

The preceding deep learning workflow is fairly equivalent to the workflow implemented by almost everyone in the industry, even for highly sophisticated implementations, with slight variations. This chapter explains the first and last stages briefly, and goes into the core of the intermediate three stages, which are design and experimentation, model implementation, and training and validation.

The last stage in the workflow is usually where people struggle a lot, especially if the scale of the application is quite large. I mentioned earlier that although PyTorch was built as a research-oriented framework, the community managed to integrate Caffe2 to the backend of PyTorch, which is powering thousands of models used by Facebook. Hence shipping the model to production is discussed thoroughly in *Chapter 8*, *PyTorch to Production*, with examples using ONNX, PyTorch JIT, and so on, to showcase how to ship PyTorch models to serve millions of requests, as well as the migration of models to single-board computers and mobile devices.

Ideation and planning

Usually, in an organization the product team shows up with a problem statement for the engineering team, wanting to know whether they can solve it or not. This is the start of the ideation phase. In academia, this could be the decision phase, where candidates have to find a problem for their thesis. In the ideation phase, the engineers brainstorm and find the theoretical implementations that could potentially solve the problem. Along with converting the problem statement to a theoretical solution, the ideation phase is where we decide what the data types are and what dataset we should use to build the **proof of concept** (POC) of the **minimum viable product** (MVP). This is the stage where the team decides which framework to go with by analyzing the behavior of the problem statement, existing available implementations, available pretrained models, and so on.

This stage is very common in the industry and I have thousands of examples where a well-planned ideation phase helped the team to roll out a reliable product on time, while a non-planned ideation phase destroyed the whole product creation.

Design and experimentation

After the theoretical foundation of the problem statement is built, we move to the design and/or experimentation phase where we build the POC by trying out several model implementations. The crucial part of design and experimentation lies in the dataset and the preprocessing of the dataset. For any data science project, the major time share is spent on data cleaning and preprocessing. Deep learning is no different from this.

Data preprocessing is one of the vital parts of building a deep learning pipeline. Real-world datasets are not cleaned or formatted, usually, for a neural network to process. Conversion to floats or integers, normalization and so on, is required before further processing. Building a data processing pipeline is also a non-trivial task, which consists of writing a lot of boilerplate code. To make it much easier, dataset builders and `DataLoader` pipeline packages are built into the core of PyTorch.

The dataset and DataLoader classes

Different types of deep learning problems require different types of datasets and each of them might require different types of preprocessing depending on the neural network architecture we use. This is one of the core problems in deep learning pipeline building.

Although the community has made the datasets for different tasks available for free, writing a preprocessing script is almost always painful. PyTorch solves this problem by giving abstract classes to write custom datasets and data loaders. The example given here is a simple `dataset` class to load the `fizbuz` dataset we used in *Chapter 2, A Simple Neural Network*, but extending this to handle any type of dataset is fairly straightforward. PyTorch's official documentation uses a similar approach to preprocess an image dataset before passing that to a complex **convolutional neural network (CNN)** architecture.

A `dataset` class in PyTorch is a high-level abstraction that handles almost everything required by the data loaders. The custom `dataset` class defined by the user needs to override the `__len__` function and `__getitem__` function of the parent class, where `__len__` is being used by the data loaders to determine the length of the dataset and `__getitem__` is being used by the data loaders to get the item. The `__getitem__` function expects the user to pass the index as an argument and get the item that resides on that index:

```
from dataclasses import dataclass
from torch.utils.data import Dataset, DataLoader

@dataclass(eq=False)
class FizBuzDataset(Dataset):
    input_size: int
    start: int = 0
    end: int = 1000

    def encoder(self,num):
        ret = [int(i) for i in '{0:b}'.format(num)]
        return[0] * (self.input_size - len(ret)) + ret

    def __getitem__(self, idx):
        x = self.encoder(idx)
        if idx % 15 == 0:
            y = [1,0,0,0]
        elif idx % 5 ==0:
            y = [0,1,0,0]
        elif idx % 3 == 0:
            y = [0,0,1,0]
        else:
            y = [0,0,0,1]
        return x,y

    def __len__(self):
        return self.end - self.start
```

The implementation of a custom dataset uses brand new `dataclasses` from Python 3.7. `dataclasses` help to eliminate boilerplate code for Python magic functions, such as `__init__`, by using dynamic code generation. This needs the code to be type-hinted and that's what the first three lines inside the class are for. You can read more about `dataclasses` in the official documentation [1] of Python.

The `__len__` function returns the difference between the end and start value passed to the class. In the `fizbuz` dataset, the data is being generated by the program. The implementation of data generation is inside the `__getitem__` function, where the class instance generates the data based on the index passed by `DataLoader`. PyTorch made the class abstraction as generic as possible such that the user could define what the data loader should return for each ID. In this particular case, the class instance returns an input and output for each index where the input, x, is the binary-encoder version of the index itself and output is one-hot encoded output with four states. The four states represent where the next number is a multiple of three (fizz), or a multiple of five (buzz), or a multiple of three and five (fizzbuzz), or not a multiple of three or five.

For Python newbies, the way the dataset works can be understood by looking first at the loop that loops over the integers, starting from zero to the length of the dataset (the length is being returned by the __len__ function when len(object) is called). The following snippet shows the simple loop.

```
dataset = FizBuzDataset()
for i in range(len(dataset)):
    x, y = dataset[i]

dataloader = DataLoader(dataset, batch_size=10, shuffle=True,
                        num_workers=4)
for batch in dataloader:
    print(batch)
```

The DataLoader class accepts a dataset class that is inherited from torch.utils.data.Dataset. DataLoader accepts dataset and does non-trivial operations such as mini-batching, multithreading, shuffling, and more, to fetch the data from the dataset. It accepts a dataset instance from the user and uses the sampler strategy to sample data as mini-batches.

The num_worker argument decides how many parallel threads should be operating to fetch the data. This helps to avoid CPU bottleneck so that the CPU can catch up with the GPU's parallel operations. Data loaders allow users to specify whether to use pinned CUDA memory or not, which copies the data tensors to CUDA's pinned memory before returning it to the user. Using pinned memory is the key to fast data transfers between devices, since the data is loaded into the pinned memory by the data loader itself, which is done by multiple cores of the CPU anyway.

Most often, especially while prototyping, custom datasets might not be available for developers, and in such cases, they have to rely on existing open datasets. The good thing about working on open datasets is that most of them are free from licensing burdens and thousands of people have already tried preprocessing them, so the community will help out. PyTorch came up with utility packages for all three types of datasets with pretrained models, preprocessed datasets, and utility functions to work with these datasets.

Utility packages

The community made three different utility packages for vision (torchvision), text (torchtext), and audio (torchaudio). All of them address the same problem for different data domains and stop the user worrying about the data processing and cleaning up in almost all the use cases that a user might have. In fact, all the utility packages are easily pluggable to any sort of programs that may or may not understand PyTorch's data structures.

torchvision

```
pip install torchvision
```

torchvision is the most mature and most used utility package from PyTorch, and consists of datasets, pretrained models, and transformation scripts prebuilt. torchvision has powerful APIs that enable the user to do the preprocessing of data easily, and it is especially helpful in the prototyping stage where the dataset might not even be available.

The functionality of torchvision has been divided into three: preloaded, downloadable datasets for almost all sorts of computer vision problems; pretrained models for popular computer vision architectures; and common transformation functions used in computer vision problems. An additional perk is that the simplicity of the functional APIs of the torchvision package lets the user write custom datasets or transformation functions. Following is a table of all the current datasets available in the torchvision package with their description:

Dataset	Description
MNIST	Dataset of 70,000 28 x 28 handwritten digits.
KMNIST	Hiragana characters arranged like normal MNIST.
Fashion-MNIST	An MNIST-like dataset of 70,000 28 x 28 labeled fashion images.
EMNIST	This dataset is a set of 28 x 28 handwritten character digits.
COCO	Large-scale object detection, segmentation, and captioning dataset.
LSUN	Large-scale Scene Understanding Challenge dataset similar to COCO.
Imagenet-12	A dataset of 14 million images for the Large-Scale Visual Recognition Challenge 2012.
CIFAR	A dataset of 60,000 32 x 32 color images labeled in 10/100 classes.
STL10	Another image dataset inspired by CIFAR.
SVHN	A dataset of Street View House Numbers, similar to MNIST.
PhotoTour	A dataset of tourist places provided by the University of Washington.

One example with the MNIST dataset is given in the following snippet of code. All the datasets in the preceding table need one positional argument to be passed, which is the path where the dataset to be downloaded is or the path where the dataset is stored if it has been downloaded already. The return value from the datasets prints the basic information about the status of the datasets. Later, we'll be using the same dataset to enable transformations and see how descriptive the output from the datasets is.

```
>>> mnist = v.datasets.MNIST('.', download=True)
Downloading …
```

```
Processing...
Done!
```

```
>>> mnist
Dataset MNIST
    Number of datapoints: 60000
    Split: train
    Root Location: .
    Transforms (if any): None
    Target Transforms (if any): None
```

`torchvision` uses Pillow (`PIL`) as the default backend for loading the image. But with the convenient function `torchvision.set_image_backend(backend)`, it can be changed to any compatible backend. All the data provided by `torchvision` is inherited from the `torch.utils.data.Dataset` class and hence `__len__` and `__getitem__` have been implemented for each of those. Both of those magic functions enable all these datasets to be compatible with `DataLoader`, just like how we implemented the simple dataset and loaded it with `DataLoader`.

```
>>> mnist[1]
(<PIL.Image.Image image mode=L size=28x28 at 0x7F61AE0EA518>, tensor(0))
>>> len(mnist)
60000
```

What if the user has image data already that needs to be read from a location on the disk? The traditional way of doing this is by writing a preprocessing script that loops through the images and loads them using any package like, `PIL` or `skimage`, and passes that to PyTorch (or any other framework), possibly through NumPy.

`torchvision` has a solution for that also. Once the image dataset is stored in the disk with the proper directory hierarchy, `torchvision.ImageFolder` can assume the needed information from the directory structure itself, just like how we do it with our custom script, and make loading much easier for the user. The given code snippet and folder structure shows the simple steps needed for it to work. Once the images are stored in the last folder in the hierarchy as the class name (the name of the image doesn't really matter here), then `ImageFolder` reads the data and accumulates the required information smartly:

```
>>> images = torchvision.datasets.ImageFolder('/path/to/image/folder')
>>> images[0]
(<PIL.Image.Image image mode=RGB size=1198x424 at 0x7F61715D6438>, 0)
```

```
/path/to/image/folder/class_a/img1.jpg
/path/to/image/folder/class_a/img2.jpg
/path/to/image/folder/class_a/img3.jpg
/path/to/image/folder/class_a/img4.jpg


/path/to/image/folder/class_b/img1.jpg
/path/to/image/folder/class_b/img2.jpg
/path/to/image/folder/class_b/img3.jpg
```

torchvision's `models` module is packed with several popular models that can be used out of the box. Since most of the high-level models nowadays use transfer learning to get the benefit of weights learned by other architectures (for example, the semantic segmentation model in the third chapter uses a trained resnet18 network), this is one of the most used `torchvision` functionalities. The following code snippet shows how to download the resnet18 model from `torchvision.models`. The flag `pretrained` tells `torchvision` to use just the model or get the pretrained model downloaded from the PyTorch servers.

```
>>> resnet18 = torchvision.models.resnet18(pretrained=False)
>>> resnet18 = torchvision.models.resnet18(pretrained=True)
>>> for param in resnet18.layer1.parameters():
        param.requires_grad = False
```

PyTorch's Python APIs allow freezing parts of the model that the user decides to make non-trainable. An example of this is given in the preceding code. The loop that iterates over the parameter of layer 1 of `resnet18` gives access to the `requires_grad` attribute of each parameter, which is what autograd looks for while backpropagating to make gradient updates. Setting `requires_grad` to `False` masks that particular parameter from `autograd` and keeps the weights frozen.

torchvision's `transforms` module is another major player, which has utility modules for data preprocessing and data augmentation. The `transforms` module gives out-of-the-box implementation for commonly used preprocessing functionalities, such as padding, cropping, grayscaling, affine transformation, conversion of an image to PyTorch tensors, and more, and a few implementations for data augmentation, such as flip, random cropping and, color jittering. The `Compose` utility groups several transformations together to make a single pipeline object.

```
transform = transforms.Compose(
    [
        transforms.ToTensor(),
        transforms.Normalize(mean, std),
    ]
)
```

The preceding example shows how `transforms.Compose` groups `ToTensor` and `Normalize` together to make a single pipeline. `ToTensor` converts the three-channeled input RGB image to a three-dimensional tensor with size *channel × width × height*. This is the dimension order expected by vision networks in PyTorch.

`ToTensor` also converts the pixel values from a range of 0 to 255 for each channel to a range of 0.0 to 1.0. `Transforms.Normalize` is the simple normalization with mean and standard deviation. So, `Compose` loops through all the transformations and calls the transformation with the result from the previous transformation. Following is the `__call__` function of `torchvision`'s transformation compose copied from the source code:

```
def __call__(self, img):
    for t in self.transforms:
        img = t(img)
    return img
```

Transformation comes up with a lot of utilities and all of them are useful in different instances. It's always good to look at the ever-improving documentation of `torchvision` to understand more functionalities in detail.

torchtext

```
pip install torchtext
```

Unlike the other two utility packages, `torchtext` keeps its own API structure, which is entirely different from `torchvision` and `torchaudio`. `torchtext` is a very powerful library that can do the required preprocessing tasks for a **natural language processing (NLP)** dataset. It comes with a set of datasets for common NLP tasks, but unlike `torchvision`, it doesn't have pretrained networks available for download.

`torchtext` can be plugged to any Python packages on the input or output side. Normally, spaCy or NLTK are good options for helping `torchtext` do the preprocessing and vocabulary loading. `torchtext` gives Python data structures as output and hence can be connected to any kind of output framework, not just PyTorch. Since `torchtext`'s API is not similar to `torchvision` or `torchaudio`, and it's not as straightforward as others, the next section runs through an example that shows the major role `torchtext` has in NLP.

`torchtext` by itself is a wrapper utility rather than supporting linguistic operations, and that's why I used spaCy in the example that follows. For the example, we use the **Text REtrieval Conference (TREC)** dataset, which is a question classifier.

Text	Label
How do you measure earthquakes?	DESC
Who is Duke Ellington?	HUM

A normal data preprocessing pipeline for NLP tasks on this type of dataset includes:

- Dividing the dataset into train, test, and validation sets.
- Converting the dataset to a form that a neural network could understand. Numericalizing, one-hot encoding, and word embedding, are common methods.
- Batching.
- Padding to the length of the longest sequence.

Without a helper class like `torchtext`, these mundane tasks are depressing and not rewarding. We'll use `torchtext`'s powerful APIs to simplify all these tasks.

`torchtext` has two main modules: the `Data` module and the `Datasets` module. As the official documentation states, the `Data` module hosts several data loaders, abstractions, and iterators of text (including vocabulary and word vectors), while the `Datasets` module has prebuilt datasets for common NLP tasks.

We will use the `Data` module in this example to load tab-separated data and preprocess it with spaCy's tokenization, before converting the text to vectors.

```
spacy_en = spacy.load('en')

def tokenizer(text):
    return [tok.text for tok in spacy_en.tokenizer(text)]

TEXT = data.Field(sequential=True, tokenize=tokenizer, lower=True)
LABEL = data.Field(sequential=False, use_vocab=True)

train, val, test = data.TabularDataset.splits(
    path='./data/', train='TRECtrain.tsv',
    validation='TRECval.tsv', test='TRECtest.tsv', format='tsv',
    fields=[('Text', TEXT), ('Label', LABEL)])
```

The first portion of the preceding snippet loads the English language in spaCy and defines the tokenizer function. The next part is where the input and output fields are defined using `torchtext.data.Field`. The `Field` class is used for defining the preprocessing steps before loading the data into `DataLoader`.

The `Field` variable TEXT is being shared between all the input sentences and the `Field` variable LABEL is being shared between all the output labels. TEXT in the example is set to be sequential, which tells the `Field` instance that the data is sequentially dependent and tokenization would be a better option to chunk it into smaller pieces. If `sequential` is set to `False`, then no tokenization would be applied on the data.

Since `sequential` is `True` for TEXT, the tokenization function we developed is set as `tokenizer`. This option defaults to `str.split` of Python, but we needed more intelligent tokenization and that's where spaCy's tokenization could help us.

Another important modification that the normal NLP pipeline does is converting all the data to the same case. Setting `lower` to `True` makes that happen but it is by default `False`. The `Field` class accepts numerous other parameters apart from the three given in the example, which includes `fix_length` to fix the length of the sequences; `pad_token`, which defaults to `<pad>` and is used to pad the sequence to match `fixed_length` or the length of the longest sequence in the batch; and `unk_token`, which defaults to `<unk>`, and is used to replace tokens that don't have a vocabulary vector.

The official documentation of `Field` covers all the parameters in detail. The LABEL field's `sequential` is set to `False` since we have only one word as a label. This is so handy for different instances, especially cases like language translation where both input and output are sequences.

Another important argument to `Field` is `use_vocab`, which is set to `True` by default. This argument tells the `Field` instance whether to use the vocabulary builder for the data or not. In the example dataset, we use both input and output as words, and it makes sense to convert even the output to word vectors, but in almost all cases, the output will be a one-hot encoded vector or will be numericalized. Setting `use_vocab` to `False` helps in those cases where `torchtext` won't try to convert it to indices of a word-embedding dictionary.

Once the preprocessing mechanisms are set using `Field`, we can pass them to `DataLoader` a long with the data location. Now it's `DataLoader`'s responsibility to load the data from the disk and pass it through the pre-processing pipeline.

The `Data` module comes with several `DataLoader` instances out of the box. The one we are using here is `TabularDataset`, since our data is in TSV format. `torchtext`'s official documentation shows other examples, such as JSON loaders. `TabularDataset` accepts the path to the location of the data in the disk and the name of the training, testing, and validation data. This comes in super handy for loading different datasets because loading a dataset to memory is done in less than five lines of code. As I stated earlier, we pass the `Field` objects we made before to `DataLoader` and it knows how to preprocess now. `DataLoader` returns the `torchtext` object for the training, test, and validation data.

We still have to build the vocabulary from some pretrained word-embedding dictionary and convert our dataset to indices in the dictionary. The `Field` object allows this by giving away the API called `build_vocab`. But here it gets a little bizarre and becomes something like a circular dependency, but don't worry; we'll get used to it.

Field's build_vocab requires us to pass the data object returned by the DataSet. split method in the previous step. This is how the Field knows the words present in the dataset, the length of the total vocabulary, and so on. The build_vocab method also can download the pretrained vocabulary vector for you if you don't have one already. The available word embeddings through torchtext are:

- Character n-gram
- FastText
- GloVe vectors

```
TEXT.build_vocab(train, vectors="glove.6B.50d")
LABEL.build_vocab(train, vectors="glove.6B.50d")
train_iter, val_iter, test_iter = data.Iterator.splits(
    (train, val, test), sort_key=lambda x: len(x.Text),
    batch_sizes=(32, 99, 99), device=-1)

print(next(iter(test_iter)))

# [torchtext.data.batch.Batch of size 99]
# [.Text]:[torch.LongTensor of size 16x99]
# [.Label]:[torch.LongTensor of size 99]
```

Once the vocabulary is built, we can ask torchtext to give us the iterator, which can be looped over to execute the neural network. The preceding snippet shows how build_vocab accepts parameters and then how we can call the Iterator package's splits function to create three different iterators for our training, validation, and test data.

The device argument is set to -1 for it to use the CPU. If it's 0, Iterator loads the data to the default GPU or we can specify the device number. Batch size expects the batch sizes for each dataset we pass. In this case, we have three datasets for training, validation, and test, and hence we pass a tuple with three batch sizes.

sort_key sorts the dataset with the lambda function we pass. Sorting of the dataset in some cases helps, while in most cases, randomness helps the network to learn general cases. Iterator is smart enough to batch the input dataset with the batch size passed through the argument, but it's not stopping there; it can dynamically pad all the sequences to the length of the longest sequence in each batch. The output from Iterator (as shown by the print statement) gives the TEXT data with the size 16x99, where 99 is the batch size we passed for the test dataset and 16 is the length of the longest sequence in that particular batch.

What if the `Iterator` class needs to handle things more cleverly? What if the dataset is for language modeling and we need a dataset for **backpropagation through time** (**BPTT**). `torchtext` has abstracted modules for those as well, which are inherited from the `Iterator` class we just used. The `BucketIterator` module does smarter grouping of sequences together so that sequences with the same length will be in single group, and this reduces the length of unnecessary padding that introduces noise into the dataset. `BucketIterator` also shuffles the batches in each epoch and keeps enough randomness in the dataset, making the network not learn from the order of the dataset, which is essentially not teaching any real-world information.

`BPTTIterator` is another module inherited from the `Iterator` class helping in the language modeling dataset and it needs to get a label from *t+1* for each input from *t*, where *t* is time. `BPTTIterator` takes a continuous stream of input data and a continuous stream of output data (the input stream and output stream could be different in the case of translation networks or they could be the same in the case of language-modeling networks) to convert it to an iterator that follows the time series rule described previously.

`torchtext` also has saved datasets for out-of-the-box use cases. What follows is an example of how easy it is to get access to a usable version of a dataset:

```
>>> import torchtext
>>> from torchtext import data
>>> TextData = data.Field()
>>> LabelData = data.Field()
>>> dataset = torchtext.datasets.SST('torchtextdata', TextData,
LabelData)
>>> dataset.splits(TextData, LabelData)
(<torchtext.datasets.sst.SST object at 0x7f6a542dcc18>, <torchtext.
datasets.sst.SST object at 0x7f69ff45fcf8>, <torchtext.datasets.sst.SST
object at 0x7f69ff45fc88>)
>>> train, val, text = dataset.splits(TextData, LabelData)
>>> train[0]
<torchtext.data.example.Example object at 0x7f69fef9fcf8>
```

Here we download the SST sentiment analysis dataset and used the same `dataset.splits` method to get `data` objects that have `__len__` and `__getitem__` defined as similar to the `torch.utils.data.datasets` instances we have seen before.

The following table shows currently available datasets in `torchtext` and the tasks they are specific to:

Dataset	Task
BaBi	Question answering
SST	Sentiment analysis
IMDB	Sentiment analysis
TREC	Question classification
SNLI	Entailment
MultiNLI	Entailment
WikiText2	Language modeling
WikiText103	Language modeling
PennTreebank	Language modeling
WMT14	Machine translation
IWSLT	Machine translation
Multi30k	Machine translation
UDPOS	Sequence tagging
CoNLL2000Chunking	Sequence tagging

torchaudio

The utility for audio is probably the least mature package out of all the utility packages of PyTorch. The fact that it cannot be installed over `pip` proves this claim. However, `torchaudio` covers the basic use case for any problem statement in the audio domain. Also, PyTorch added several convenient functions like **Inverse Fast Fourier Transform** (**IFFT**) and **Sparse Fast Fourier Transform** (**SFFT**) to the core, showing the advancement in the audio domain that PyTorch is making.

`torchaudio` is dependent on **Sound eXchange** (**SoX**), the cross-platform audio format changer. Once the dependencies are installed, it can be installed from source with the Python setup file.

```
python setup.py install
```

`torchaudio` comes with two prebuilt datasets, some transformations, and a loading and saving utility for audio files. Let's dive into each of them. Loading and saving audio files is always painful and dependent on several other packages. `torchaudio` makes it much easier by giving a simple load-and-save functional API. `torchtext` can load any common audio files and convert them to PyTorch tensors. It can also normalize and denormalize the data, as well as write back to disk in any common format. The saved API accepts the file path and infers the format of the output from the file path to convert it to that format, before writing it back to disk.

```
>>> data, sample_rate = torchaudio.load('foo.mp3')
>>> print(data.size())
torch.Size([278756, 2])
>>> print(sample_rate)
44100
>>> torchaudio.save('foo.wav', data, sample_rate)
```

As with `torchvision`, `torchaudio`'s datasets are inherited directly from `torch. utils.data.Dataset`, which means they have `__getitem__` and `__len__` implemented already, and are compatible with `DataLoader`. Now, `torchaudio`'s `datasets` module is preloaded with two different audio datasets, VCTK and YESNO, both of which have similar APIs as `torchvision`'s datasets. An example of loading the YESNO dataset using the Torch `DataLoader` is given as follows:

```
yesno_data = torchaudio.datasets.YESNO('.', download=True)
data_loader = torch.utils.data.DataLoader(yesno_data)
```

The `transforms` module is also inspired by the `torchvision` API, and with `Compose`, we can wrap one or more transformations together into a single pipeline. An example taken from the official documentation is given here. It composes `Scale` transformation and `PadTrim` transformation sequentially into a single pipeline. The list of all available transformations is explained in detail in the official documentation.

```
transform = transforms.Compose(
    [
        transforms.Scale(),
        transforms.PadTrim(max_len=16000)
    ]
)
```

Model implementation

Implementing the model is, after all, the most important step in our pipeline. In a way, we have built the whole pipeline for this step. Apart from building the network architecture, there are numerous details we need to consider to optimize our implementation (in terms of effort, time, and perhaps code efficiency as well).

In this session, we will discuss profiling and bottleneck tools available in the PyTorch package itself and `ignite`, a recommended trainer utility for PyTorch. The first part covers bottleneck and profiling utility, which is essential when the model starts underperforming and you need to know what went wrong where. The second part of this session explains `ignite`, the trainer module.

A trainer network is not really an essential component, but it is a good-to-have helper utility that saves a lot of time writing boilerplate and fixing bugs. Sometimes, it can reduce the number of lines of your program by half, which also helps to improve readability.

Bottleneck and profiling

PyTorch's Python-first approach prevented the core team from building a separate profiler for the first year, but when modules started moving to C/C++ core, the need for an independent profiler over Python's cProfiler became clear, and that's where the story of `autograd.profiler` begins.

This section is going to be more tables and statistics rather than step-by-step guidance because PyTorch has already made profiling as simple as possible. For profiling, we will use the same *FizBuz* model we developed in the second chapter. Although `autograd.profiler` can profile all the operations inside the graph, in this example, only the forward pass of the main network is profiled and not the loss functions and the backward passes.

```
with torch.autograd.profiler.profile() as prof:
    hyp = net(x_)


print(prof)
print(prof.key_averages())
print(prof.table('cpu_time'))
prof.export_chrome_trace('chrometrace')
```

The first `print` statement just spit outs the t profile output in a tabular form, while the second `print` statement groups the op nodes together and averages the time taken for a particular node. This is shown in the following screenshot:

Name	CPU time	CUDA time	Calls	CPU total	CUDA total
t	15.758us	0.000us	2	31.516us	0.000us
expand	6.203us	0.000us	2	12.405us	0.000us
addmm	898.371us	0.000us	2	1796.742us	0.000us
sigmoid	14.462us	0.000us	2	28.923us	0.000us

Figure 3.2: autograd.profiler output grouped by name

The next `print` statement sorts the data based on the head passed as the argument in increasing order. This helps with finding the node that takes more time and perhaps provides some way to optimize the model.

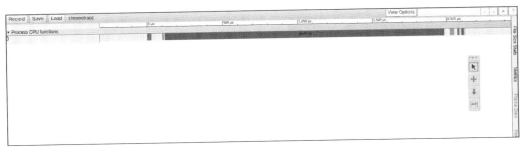

Name	CPU time	CUDA time	Calls	CPU total	CUDA total
sigmoid	2.524us	0.000us	1	2.524us	0.000us
expand	4.325us	0.000us	1	4.325us	0.000us
t	5.140us	0.000us	1	5.140us	0.000us
expand	9.168us	0.000us	1	9.168us	0.000us
addmm	16.646us	0.000us	1	16.646us	0.000us
sigmoid	29.335us	0.000us	1	29.335us	0.000us
t	30.314us	0.000us	1	30.314us	0.000us
addmm	1858.968us	0.000us	1	1858.968us	0.000us

Figure 3.3: autograd.profiler output ordered on CPU time

The last `print` statement is just another way of visualizing the execution time on the Chrome trace tool. The `export_chrome_trace` function accepts a file path and writes output to the file that is understandable by the Chrome tracer:

Figure 3.4: autograd.profiler output converted to chrometrace

But if the user needs to combine `autograd.profiler` and the cProfiler (which will turn out to give us a succinct correlation between several node operations), or if the user needs to just call another utility instead of changing the source code for fetching the profiled information, bottleneck is the way to go. Bottleneck is the Torch utilities and can be executed as a Python module from the command line:

```
python -m torch.utils.bottleneck /path/to/source/script.py [args]
```

Bottleneck finds more information about the environment, and also gives the profiled information from `autograd.profiler` and cProfiler. But for both, bottleneck executes the program twice, and hence reducing the number of epochs would be a good option to make the program stop its execution in a decent amount of time. I used bottleneck on the same program from the second chapter and here are the output screens:

```
--------------------------------------------------------------------------
  Environment Summary
--------------------------------------------------------------------------
PyTorch 2018.05.07 compiled w/ CUDA 8.0.61
Running with Python 3.6 and

`pip3 list` truncated output:
msgpack-numpy (0.4.1)
numpy (1.14.2)
torch (2018.5.7, /home/sherin/miniconda3/lib/python3.6/site-packages)
torchaudio (0.1, /home/sherin/mypro/audio)
torchtext (0.2.3)
torchvision (0.2.1)
```

Figure 3.5: Bottleneck output on the environment summary

```
--------------------------------------------------------------------------
  autograd profiler output (CPU mode)
--------------------------------------------------------------------------
        top 15 events sorted by cpu_time_total

------------------  ---------------  ---------------  ---------------  ---------------  ---------------
Name                       CPU time        CUDA time            Calls        CPU total       CUDA total
------------------  ---------------  ---------------  ---------------  ---------------  ---------------
AddmmBackward             233.993us          0.000us                1        233.993us          0.000us
t                         100.119us          0.000us                1        100.119us          0.000us
addmm                      79.638us          0.000us                1         79.638us          0.000us
_cast_float                70.043us          0.000us                1         70.043us          0.000us
mm                         61.899us          0.000us                1         61.899us          0.000us
_mm                        53.449us          0.000us                1         53.449us          0.000us
AddmmBackward              47.908us          0.000us                1         47.908us          0.000us
zeros_like                 46.894us          0.000us                1         46.894us          0.000us
ExpandBackward             46.219us          0.000us                1         46.219us          0.000us
uniform_                   44.824us          0.000us                1         44.824us          0.000us
addmm                      42.784us          0.000us                1         42.784us          0.000us
sqrt                       40.520us          0.000us                1         40.520us          0.000us
sqrt                       39.984us          0.000us                1         39.984us          0.000us
sum                        39.054us          0.000us                1         39.054us          0.000us
MseLossBackward            39.017us          0.000us                1         39.017us          0.000us
```

Figure 3.6: Bottleneck output showing autograd.profiler

```
--------------------------------------------------------------------------
  cProfile output
--------------------------------------------------------------------------
         6532 function calls (6524 primitive calls) in 0.149 seconds

   Ordered by: internal time
   List reduced from 81 to 15 due to restriction <15>

   ncalls  tottime  percall  cumtime  percall filename:lineno(function)
        1    0.071    0.071    0.071    0.071 {method 'run_backward' of 'torch._C._EngineBase' objects}
        2    0.015    0.008    0.015    0.008 {method 'sigmoid' of 'torch._C._TensorBase' objects}
        8    0.015    0.002    0.015    0.002 {method 'add_' of 'torch._C._TensorBase' objects}
        1    0.011    0.011    0.011    0.011 {built-in method ones_like}
     1000    0.008    0.000    0.008    0.000 bottleneck_support.py:16(<listcomp>)
        2    0.005    0.003    0.005    0.003 {built-in method addmm}
        2    0.004    0.002    0.004    0.002 {built-in method numpy.core.multiarray.array}
     1000    0.004    0.000    0.013    0.000 bottleneck_support.py:15(wrapper)
        1    0.003    0.003    0.003    0.003 {built-in method torch._C._nn.mse_loss}
        1    0.003    0.003    0.021    0.021 bottleneck_support.py:39(get_data)
        4    0.002    0.001    0.002    0.001 {method 'sqrt' of 'torch._C._TensorBase' objects}
     1004    0.001    0.000    0.001    0.000 {method 'format' of 'str' objects}
        2    0.001    0.000    0.001    0.000 {method 'type' of 'torch._C._TensorBase' objects}
        1    0.001    0.001    0.149    0.149 bottleneck_support.py:1(<module>)
        1    0.001    0.001    0.001    0.001 {method 'permutation' of 'mtrand.RandomState' objects}
```

Figure 3.7: Bottleneck output showing cProfile output

Training and validation

We have reached the final step in the deep learning workflow, although the workflow actually ends with the deployment of the deep model to production, which we'll cover in *Chapter 8, PyTorch to Production*. After all the preprocessing and model building, now we have to train the network, test the accuracy, and validate the reliability. Most of the existing code implementation that we see in the open source world (even in this book) uses a straightforward approach, where we explicitly write each line that is required for training, testing, and validation in favor of readability, since specific tools that can avoid the boilerplates increase the learning curve, especially for newcomers. It became clear that a tool that could avoid the boilerplate would be a lifesaver for programmers who play with neural networks on a day-to-day basis. So, the PyTorch community built not one but two tools: torchnet and ignite. This session is only about ignite, since that is found to be more useful and abstract than torchnet, but both are actively developed tools and could be potentially merged in the near future.

Ignite

Ignite [2] is a neural network training tool that abstracts away certain boilerplate code in favor of clean and elegant code. Ignite's core is the `Engine` module. This module is immensely powerful because:

- It runs the model based on default/custom trainer or evaluator.
- It can accept handlers and metrics, and act on them.
- It can make triggers and execute callbacks.

Engine

`Engine` accepts a trainer function that is essentially the typical loop used to train a neural network algorithm. It includes looping over the epoch, looping over the batches, zeroing the existing gradient value, calling the model with batch, calculating the loss, and updating the gradient. This is shown in the following example, which is taken from *Chapter 2, A Simple Neural Network*:

```
for epoch in range(epochs):
    for x_batch, y_batch in dataset:
        optimizer.zero_grad()
        hyp = net(x_batch)
        loss = loss_fn(hyp, y_batch)
        loss.backward()
        optimizer.step()
```

Engine can help you to avoid the first two loops and will do it for you if you define the function that needs to do the rest of the code. What follows is the rewritten version of the preceding code snippet that is compatible with Engine:

```
def training_loop(trainer, batch)
    x_batch, y_batch = process_batch(batch)
    optimizer.zero_grad()
    hyp = net(x_batch)
    loss = loss_fn(hyp, y_batch)
    loss.backward()
    optimizer.step()


trainer = Engine(training_loop)
```

That's smart but that's not saving a lot of a user's time and not keeping promises such as removing boilerplates. All it does is remove two for loops and add one more line of Engine object creation. That's not really the purpose of Ignite. Ignite tries to make coding fun and flexible at the same time, helping to avoid boilerplates.

Ignite has come up with some functions that are commonly used, such as supervised training or supervised evaluation, and also gives the flexibility to the user to define their own training functions for instances like training GANs, **reinforcement learning (RL)** algorithms, and so on.

```
from ignite.engine import create_supervised_trainer,
create_supervised_evaluator

epochs = 1000
train_loader, val_loader = get_data_loaders(train_batch_size,
val_batch_size)
trainer = create_supervised_trainer(model, optimizer, F.nll_loss)
evaluator = create_supervised_evaluator(model)
trainer.run(train_loader, max_epochs=epochs)
evaluator.run(val_loader)
```

The functions create_supervised_trainer and create_supervised_evaluator return an Engine object that has a function like training_loop to execute the common pattern of the code, like the one given precedingly. Apart from the given arguments, both functions accept a device (CPU or GPU) also, which returns a trainer or evaluator Engine instance that runs on the device we specified. Now things are getting better, right? We passed the defined model, the optimizer we wanted, and the loss function we are using, but what do we do after we have a trainer and an evaluator object?

The Engine object has the run method defined, which makes the loop start the execution based on the epochs and loader we pass into the run function. As usual, the run method makes the trainer loop from zero to the number of epochs. For each iteration, our trainer runs through the loader to do the gradient update.

Once the training is done, `evaluator` kicks off with `val_loader` and makes sure things are getting better by running through the same model with the evaluation dataset.

That was fun, but still there are missing pieces. What if the user needs to run `evaluator` after each epoch, or what if the user needs the trainer to print the accuracy of the model to the terminal, or plot that to a Visdom, Turing, or Network graph? Is there a way in the preceding setup to know what the validation accuracy is? You can do most of it by overriding the default logger of `Engine`, which is essentially a Python logger saved in the `trainer_logger` variable, but the actual answer is events.

Events

Ignite opens up a special way to interact with the loop by events or triggers. Each setup function will get triggered when the event occurs and does what the user defines in the function. Through that, it is flexible enough for the user to set up any sort of event, and this makes the user's life easier by avoiding writing those complex events into the loop and making the loop bigger and unreadable. The currently available events in `Engine` are:

- EPOCH_STARTED
- EPOCH_COMPLETED
- STARTED
- COMPLETED
- ITERATION_STARTED
- ITERATION_COMPLETED
- EXCEPTION_RAISED

The best and recommended way of setting function triggers on these events is by Python decorators. The `on` method of the trainer accepts one of these events as an argument and returns a decorator that sets the custom function to be triggered on the event. A couple of commonly seen events and use cases are given here:

```
@trainer.on(Events.ITERATION_COMPLETED)
def log_training_loss(engine):
    epoch = engine.state.epoch
    iteration = engine.state.iteration
    loss = engine.state.output
    print("Epoch:{epoch} Iteration:{iteration} Loss: {loss}")

@trainer.on(Events.EPOCH_COMPLETED)
def run_evaluator_on_training_data(engine):
```

```
        evaluator.run(train_loader)

    @trainer.on(Events.EPOCH_COMPLETED)
    def run_evaluator_on_validation_data(engine):
        evaluator.run(val_loader)
```

By now, I must have convinced you that Ignite is a must-have tool for your toolbox. The `@trainer.on` decorator has been set for three events in the preceding example; in fact, on two events where we set two functions on the EPOCH_COMPLETED event. With the first function, we are printing the status of the training to the terminal. But there is something we haven't seen yet. State is the `state` variable that `Engine` keeps to hold the information about the execution. In the example, we see that the state holds information about the epoch, iteration, and even the output, which is essentially the loss for the training loop. A `state` attribute holds the epoch, iteration, current data, metrics if there are any (we'll see what the metrics are soon); the max epoch we set while calling the `run` function, and the output from the `training_loop` function.

> **Note**: In the case of `create_supervised_trainer`, the `training_loop` function returns the loss, and in the case of `create_supervised_evaluator`, the `training_loop` function returns the output of the model. But if we are defining a custom `training_loop` function, whatever this function returns is what `Engine.state.output` holds.

The second and third event handlers are running `evaluator` on EPOCH_COMPLETED but with a different dataset. In the first function, `evaluator` uses the training dataset and in the second, it uses the evaluation dataset. That is great because now we can run `evaluator` whenever one epoch is completed, not like at the end of the whole execution like in the first example. But other than just running it, the handler hasn't really done anything. Normally, this is where we check the average accuracy and average loss, and we do more complex analysis like confusion metrics creation, which we'll see next. But the major takeaway for now is: it is possible to set *n* number of handlers for a single event and Ignite will just call all of them sequentially without any hesitation. What follows is the internal `_fire_event` function of the event, which gets triggered on each event from the `training_loop` function.

```
    def _fire_event(self, event_name, *event_args):
        if event_name in self._event_handlers.keys():
            self._logger.debug("firing handlers for event %s",
    event_name)
            for func, args, kwargs in
    self._event_handlers[event_name]:
                func(self, *(event_args + args), **kwargs)
```

In the next section, we will make the EPOCH_COMPLETED event handler do more sensible things with Ignite's metrics.

Metrics

Just like `Engine`, metrics is also an important part of Ignite's source code, which is continuously evolving. Metrics wraps several commonly used metrics for analyzing the performance and efficiency of a neural network into simple configurable classes that are comprehensible by `Engine`. Currently built metrics are given next. We'll use some of them to build the preceding event handler:

- `Accuracy`
- `Loss`
- `MeanAbsoluteError`
- `MeanPairwiseDistance`
- `MeanSquaredError`
- `Precision`
- `Recall`
- `RootMeanSquaredError`
- `TopKCategoricalAccuracy`
- `RunningAverageŁ`
- `IoU`
- `mIoU`

Ignite has a parent `metrics` class, which is being inherited by all the classes in the list. Setting metrics can be done by passing the dictionary object with a user-readable name as the key and an instantiated object of one of the preceding classes as the value to the `Engine` creation call. So, we are redefining the creation of `evaluator` with metrics now.

```
metrics = {'accuracy': Accuracy(), 'null': Loss(F.null_loss)}
evaluator = create_supervised_evaluator(model, metrics=metrics)
```

The initializer of `Engine` gets the metrics and calls the `Metrics.attach` function to set up the triggers for calculating the metrics on EPOCH_STARTED, ITERATION_COMPLETED, and EPOCH_COMPLETED. The `attach` function from the `Metrics` source code is as follows:

```
def attach(self, engine, name):
    engine.add_event_handler(Events.EPOCH_STARTED, self.started)
    engine.add_event_handler(Events.ITERATION_COMPLETED,
self.iteration_completed)
    engine.add_event_handler(Events.EPOCH_COMPLETED,
self.completed, name)
```

Once the event handlers are set by `Engine`, they automatically gets called when an event occurs. The `EPOCH_STARTED` event cleans up the metrics by calling a `reset()` method and makes the storage clean for the current epoch metrics collection.

The `ITERATION_COMPLETED` trigger will call the `update()` method of the corresponding metrics and do the metrics update. For example, if the metrics equals the loss, it calculates the current loss by calling the loss function we have passed as an argument to the `Loss` class while creating `Engine`. The calculated loss is then saved to object variables for future use.

The `EPOCH_COMPLETED` event will be the final event, which uses whatever is updated in `ITERATION_COMPLETED` to compute the final metric score. All of this happens as a flow without the user knowing anything, once the `metrics` dictionary is passed as an argument to `Engine` creation. The following code snippet shows how the user can fetch this information back on the `EPOCH_COMPLETED` trigger, which runs `evaluator`:

```
@trainer.on(Events.EPOCH_COMPLETED)
def run_evaluator_on_validation_data(engine):
    evaluator.run(val_loader)
    metrics = evaluator.state.metrics
    avg_accuracy = metrics['accuracy']
    avg_null = metrics['nll']
    print(f"Avg accuracy: {avg_accuracy} Avg loss: {avg_nll}")
```

The `metrics` state is saved in the `Engine` state variable as a dictionary with the same name as the user passed initially, with the output as the value. Ignite just makes the whole flow smooth and seamless for the user, such that the user doesn't have to worry about writing all the mundane code.

Saving checkpoints

Another perk of using Ignite is the checkpoint saving feature, which is not available in PyTorch. People have come up with different approaches for writing and loading checkpoints effectively. `ModelCheckpoint` is part of Ignite's handlers, which can be imported like this:

```
from ignite.handlers import ModelCheckpoint
```

Ignite's checkpoint saver has very simple APIs to work with. The user needs to define where the checkpoint should be saved, how frequently checkpoints should be saved, and what the objects are to be saved other than default parameters like iteration count, epoch number for resuming the operation, and more. In the example, we are checkpointing for each hundredth iteration. The defined values then can be passed as arguments to the `ModelCheckpoint` module to get the checkpoint event handler object.

The returned handler has all the features of a normal event handler and can be set for any events that Ignite has triggered. In the following example, we set it for an `ITERATION_COMPLETED` event:

```
dirname = 'path/to/checkpoint/directory'
objects_to_checkpoint = {"model": model, "optimizer": optimizer}
engine_checkpoint = ModelCheckpoint(
    dirname=dirname,
    to_save=objects_to_checkpoint,
    save_interval=100)
trainer.add_event_handler(Events.ITERATION_COMPLETED, engine_
checkpoint)
```

The trigger calls the handler on each `ITERATION_COMPLETED` event, but we needed it to save only for every hundredth iteration, and Ignite doesn't have a methodology for customizing events. Ignite solves this problem by giving the user flexibility to do this check inside the handlers. In the case of the checkpoint handler, Ignite checks internally whether the currently completed iteration is the hundredth or not and saves it only if the check passes, as given in the following code snippet:

```
if engine.state.iteration % self.save_interval !=0:
    save_checkpoint()
```

Saved checkpoints can be loaded with `torch.load('checkpoint_path')`. This will have you the dictionary `objects_to_checkpoint` back that has the model and optimizer.

Summary

This chapter was all about how to build a basic pipeline for deep learning development. The system we have defined in this chapter is a very common/general approach followed by different sorts of companies, with slight changes. The benefit of starting with a generic workflow like this is that you can build a really complex workflow as your team/project grows on top of it.

Also, having a workflow in the early stage of development itself will make your sprints stable and predictable. Finally, the division between steps in the workflow helps with defining roles for the team members, setting deadlines for each step, trying to accommodate each of them in sprints efficiently, and executing the steps in parallel.

The PyTorch community is making different tools and utility packages to incorporate into the workflow. `ignite`, `torchvision`, `torchtext`, `torchaudio`, and so on are such examples. As the industry grows, we could see a lot of such tools emerging, which could be fitted into different parts of this workflow to help us with iterating through it easily. But the most important part of it is: start with one.

In the next chapter, we will explore computer vision and CNNs.

References

1. Python official documentation for `dataclasses`, `https://docs.python.org/3/library/dataclasses.html`

2. Examples used in *Ignite* section are inspired by Ignite's official examples, `https://github.com/pytorch/ignite/blob/master/examples/mnist/mnist.py`

4
Computer Vision

Computer vision is the stream of engineering that gives eyes to a computer. It powers all sorts of image processing, such as face recognition in an iPhone, Google Lens, and so on. Computer vision has been around for decades and is probably best explored with the help of artificial intelligence, which will be demonstrated in this chapter.

We reached human accuracy in computer vision years ago in the ImageNet challenge. Computer vision has gone through an enormous amount of change in the last decade, from being an academically oriented object detection problem to a segmentation problem used by self-driving cars on real roads. Although people had come up with many different network architectures to solve computer vision, **convolutional neural networks (CNNs)** beat all of them.

In this chapter, we will discuss basic CNNs built on PyTorch and variants of them that have been successfully used in some state-of-the-art models powering several applications by big companies.

Introduction to CNNs

CNNs are a decades-old machine learning algorithms that never proved their power until Geoffrey Hinton and his lab came up with AlexNet. Since then, CNNs have been through several iterations. Now we have a few different architectures built on top of CNNs, which power all the computer vision implementations around the world.

A CNN is a network architecture that fundamentally consists of small networks, almost like the simple feedforward network introduced in *Chapter 2, A Simple Neural Network*, but for solving problems with images as input. CNNs consist of neurons that have non-linearity, weight parameters, biases, and spit out one loss value based on which the whole network is rearranged using backpropagation.

If this sounds similar to simple fully connected networks, what makes CNNs special for processing images? CNNs let the developer make certain assumptions that are applicable to images, such as the spatial relation of pixel values.

Simple fully connected layers have more weights because they store the information to process everything in weights. Another feature of a fully connected layer makes it incapable of doing image processing: it cannot take spatial information into account, since it removes the order/arrangement structure of the pixel values while processing.

CNNs consist of several three-dimensional kernels moving through the input tensor like a sliding window until they cover the whole tensor. A kernel is a three-dimensional tensor where its depth and the depth of the input tensor (in the first layer it is three; the depth of an image is in RGB channels) is the same. The height and width of the kernel could be lower than or equal to the height and width of the input tensor. If the height and width of the kernel are the same as those of the input tensor, then the setup is quite similar to that of a normal neural network.

Each time a kernel makes a move through the input tensor, it could spit out a single value output, which goes through a non-linearity. Each slot that the kernel covers from the input image, while moving as a sliding window, will have this output value. The sliding window movement creates an output feature map (essentially a tensor). So, we can increase the number of kernels to get more feature maps and, theoretically, each feature map is capable of holding one particular type of information.

Figure 4.1: Different layers showing different information
Source: *Visualizing and Understanding Convolutional Networks*, Matthew D. Zeiler and Rob Fergus

Since the same kernel is being used to cover the whole image, we are reusing the kernel parameters, which in turn reduces the number of parameters.

A CNN essentially downgrades the dimensionality of the image in the x and y axes (height and width), and increases the depth (z axis). Each slice in the z axis is one feature map as described previously, created by each of those multidimensional kernels.

Dimensionality downgrading in CNN helps the CNN to be positionally invariant. Positional invariance helps it to identify objects in a different part of the image. For example, if you have two images of a cat, where the cat is on the left side in one image and the right side in the other, you would want your network to identify the cat from both, right?

CNNs achieve positional invariance by two mechanisms: striding and pooling. The stride value decides how aggressive the sliding window movement is. Pooling is an inherent part of CNNs. We have three main type of pooling: max-pooling, min-pooling, and average-pooling. Pooling takes the highest value from a sub-block of the input tensor in the case of max-pooling, or the smallest value for min-pooling, and an average of all the values in the case of average-pooling. The input and output of the pooling layer and convolutional kernels are essentially the same. Both move as a sliding window over the input tensor and output a single value.

What follows is a depiction of how CNNs work. To understand CNNs more in depth, check out CS231N from Stanford University. Or if you need a quick introduction to CNNs through an animated video, Udacity [1] has an excellent resource.

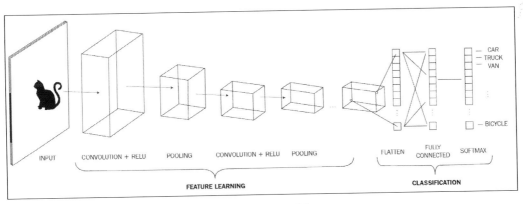

Figure 4.2: A CNN

There are four main types of operation for building the complete CNN network:

- Convolutional layer
- Non-linearity layer
- Pooling layer
- Fully connected layer

Computer vision with PyTorch

PyTorch provides several convenient functions for computer vision, which includes convolutional layers and pooling layers. PyTorch provides `Conv1d`, `Conv2d`, and `Conv3d` under the `torch.nn` package. As it sounds, `Conv1d` handles one-dimensional convolution, while `Conv2d` works with two-dimensional convolution with inputs like images, and `Conv3d` operates a three-dimensional convolution on inputs like videos. Obviously, this is confusing since the dimension specified never considered the depth of the input. For instance, `Conv2d` handles four-dimensional input among which the first dimension would be batch size, the second dimension would be the depth of the image (in RGB channels), and the last two dimensions would be the height and width of the image.

Apart from the higher-layer functions for computer vision, `torchvision` has some handy utility functions for setting up the network. We'll explore some of those in this chapter.

This chapter explains PyTorch using two neural network applications:

- **Simple CNN**: A simple neural network architecture for classifying CIFAR10 images
- **Semantic segmentation**: An advanced example using the concept from the simple CNN for semantic segmentation

Simple CNN

We are developing a CNN to do a simple classification task. The idea of using a simple CNN is to get an understanding of how a CNN works. Once we clear the basics, we'll move to an advanced network design where we use the high-level PyTorch functions that do the same thing as this application but more efficiently.

We will use CIFAR10 as the input dataset, which consists of 60,000 32x32 color images in 10 classes, with 6,000 images per class. `torchvision` has higher-level functions that download and process the dataset. As in the examples we have seen in *Chapter 3, Deep Learning Workflow*, we download the dataset and then convert it using transformations, and wrap it under the `get_data()` function.

```
def get_data():
    transform = transforms.Compose(
        [transforms.ToTensor(),
         transforms.Normalize((0.5, 0.5, 0.5), (0.5, 0.5, 0.5))])
    trainset = torchvision.datasets.CIFAR10(
        root='./data', train=True, download=True,
transform=transform)
    trainloader = torch.utils.data.DataLoader(
        trainset, batch_size=100, shuffle=True, num_workers=2)

    testset = torchvision.datasets.CIFAR10(
        root='./data', train=False, download=True,
transform=transform)
    testloader = torch.utils.data.DataLoader(
        testset, batch_size=100, shuffle=False, num_workers=2)
    return trainloader, testloader
```

The first part of the function does the transformation on the NumPy array from the CIFAR10 dataset. It will be converted to Torch tensors first and then go through the normalization transformation. `ToTensor` does not just convert the NumPy array to the Torch tensor, but it also changes the order of the dimension and range of the value.

All the higher-layer APIs of PyTorch expect the channel (depth of the tensor) to be the first dimension after the batch size. So, the input with shape (height x width x channel (RGB)) in the range [0, 255] will be converted to a `torch.FloatTensor` of shape (channel (RGB) x height x width) in the range [0.0, 1.0]. Then the normalization kicks in with the mean and standard deviation set as 0.5 for each channel (RGB). The normalization operation done by the `torchvision` transformation is the same as the following Python function:

```
def normalize(image, mean, std):
    for channel in range(3):
        image[channel] = (image[channel] - mean[channel]) /
std[channel]
```

`get_data()` returns test and train loaders, which are shuffled iterables. Now that the data is ready, we need to set up the model, loss function, and the optimizer as we did while building the *FizBuz* network.

Model

`SimpleCNNModel` is the model class inherited from `nn.Module` of PyTorch. This is the parent class that uses other custom classes and PyTorch classes to set up the architecture.

```
class SimpleCNNModel(nn.Module):
    """ A basic CNN model implemented with the the basic building
        blocks """

    def __init__(self):
        super().__init__()
        self.conv1 = Conv(3, 6, 5)
        self.pool = MaxPool(2)
        self.conv2 = Conv(6, 16, 5)
        self.fc1 = nn.Linear(16 * 5 * 5, 120)
        self.fc2 = nn.Linear(120, 84)
        self.fc3 = nn.Linear(84, 10)

    def forward(self, x):
        x = self.pool(F.relu(self.conv1(x)))
        x = self.pool(F.relu(self.conv2(x)))
        x = x.view(-1, 16 * 5 * 5)
        x = F.relu(self.fc1(x))
        x = F.relu(self.fc2(x))
        x = self.fc3(x)
        return x
```

The model has two convolutional layers separated by a max-pool layer. The second convolutional layer is wired to three fully connected layers, one after the other, which spit out the score for 10 classes.

We have built the custom convolutional and max-pool layers for the `SimpleCNNModel`. Custom layers are probably the least efficient way of implementing those, but they are highly readable and easily understandable.

```
class Conv(nn.Module):
    """

    Custom conv layer
    Assumes the image is squre
    """

    def __init__(self, in_channels, out_channels, kernel_size,
stride=1, padding=0):
        super().__init__()
        self.kernel_size = kernel_size
```

```
    self.stride = stride
    self.padding = padding
    self.weight = Parameter(torch.Tensor(out_channels,
in_channels, kernel_size, kernel_size))
    self.bias = Parameter(torch.zeros(out_channels))
```

The convolution operation on an image does multiplication and addition on the input image with a filter and creates the single output value. So, now we have one input image and a kernel. For simplicity, let's consider the input image is a single channel (grayscale) image of size 7x7 and assume the kernel is of size 3x3, as shown in the following diagram. We call the middle value of the kernel the anchor, since we keep the anchor on some values in the image to do the convolution.

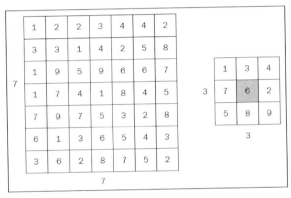

Figure 4.3a

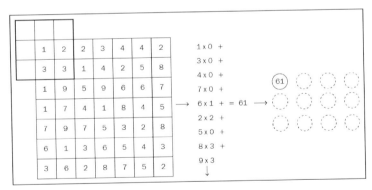

Figure 4.3b

We start the convolution by anchoring the kernel on the top-left pixel of the image, as shown in *Figure 4.3b*. Now we multiply each pixel value from the image with the corresponding value of the kernel and add all of them together to get a single value. But we have a problem to handle. What will the top row and left column of the kernel be multiplied to? For this, we introduce padding.

We add rows and columns to the outer side of the input tensor with the value as zero, so that all the values in the kernel have a corresponding value in the input image to pair with. The single value we got out of multiplication and the addition operation is the output of the convolution operation we did on that instance.

Now we move the kernel one pixel right and do the operation again, like a sliding window, and repeat this until we cover the image. Each output we could get from each convolution operation together creates a feature map or output of that layer. The following code snippet does all these operations in the last three lines.

PyTorch supports normal Python indexing and we use that to find the slot where the sliding window is at for a particular iteration and save that to the variable named `val`. But the indexing creates tensors that might not be a continuous block of memory. Non-continuous memory block tensors cannot be changed by using `view()`, and hence we use the method `contiguous()` to move the tensor to a continuous block. Then we multiply this tensor with the kernel (weight) and add bias to it. The result of the convolution operation is then saved to the `out` tensor, which is initialized with zero as a placeholder. Creating the placeholder beforehand and adding elements to it is an order of magnitude more efficient than doing stacking on a set of single channels at the end.

```
out = torch.zeros(batch_size, new_depth, new_height, new_width)
        padded_input = F.pad(x, (self.padding,) * 4)
        for nf, f in enumerate(self.weight):
            for h in range(new_height):
                for w in range(new_width):
                    val = padded_input[:, :, h:h +
self.kernel_size, w:w + self.kernel_size]
                    out[:, nf, h, w] =
val.contiguous().view(batch_size, -1) @ f.view(-1)
                    out[:, nf, h, w] += self.bias[nf]
```

The `functional` module in PyTorch has methods for helping us with padding. `F.pad` accepts the input tensor and the padding size for each side. In this case, we need constant padding for all four sides of our image, and hence we create a tuple of size four. If you want to know how exactly padding works, the following example shows the size changed to (5, 5) after doing `F.pad` on a tensor of size (1, 1) with padding size (2, 2, 2, 2).

```
>>> F.pad(torch.zeros(1,1), (2,) * 4)
Variable containing:
0 0 0 0 0
0 0 0 0 0
0 0 0 0 0
```

```
0 0 0 0 0
0 0 0 0 0
[torch.FloatTensor of size (5,5)]
```

As you will have realized, we'll get output of the same size as the input by doing convolution over the whole image if we use a kernel of size 1 x 1 x *depth*. In CNNs, if we want to reduce the size of the output regardless of the size of the kernel, we use a nice trick to downsample the size of the output by striding. *Figure 4.4* shows the reduction effect of striding on the output size. The following formula can be used to compute the size of the output with the size of the kernel, padding width, and stride.

$W=(W−F+2P)/S+1$, where W is input size, F is kernel size, S is stride applied, and P is padding.

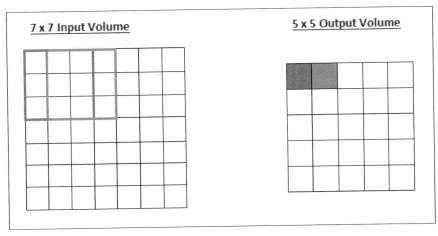

Figure 4.4: Left stride with a value of one

The convolutional layer we have built does not have the capability of doing striding since we did downsampling with max-pooling. But in the advanced examples, we'll use the convolutional layer of PyTorch, which handles striding and padding internally.

The preceding example used a single-channel input and created a single-channel output. We can extend this to use n number of input channels to create n number of output channels and that is the fundamental building block of convolutional networks. By making two changes, the same concept can be extrapolated to handle any number of input channels to create any number of output channels:

- Since the input image has more than one channel, the kernel used to multiply with the corresponding elements needs to be n dimensional. If the input channels are three and the kernel size is five, the kernel shape should be 5 x 5 x 3.

- But how do we create *n* number of output channels? Now we know that regardless of the number of input channels, one convolution always creates a single-valued output and a full sliding window session creates a two-dimensional matrix as output. So, what if we have two kernels that do the exact same thing: sliding through the input and creating the two-dimensional output. Then we'll have two two-dimensional outputs, and stacking them together gives us an output with two channels. We increase the number of kernels as we need more channels in the output.

The custom convolutional layer we have does the same thing to achieve convolution. It accepts the number of input and output channels, kernel size, stride, and padding as arguments. The kernel is being constructed with the shape `[kernel_size, kernel_size, input_channels]`. Instead of creating *n* number of kernels and stacking the output together to get multichannel output, we create a single weight tensor of size (`output_channel, input_channel, kernal_size, kernal_size`), which gives us what we want.

Among all the pooling options, people tend to prefer max-pooling. The pooling operation takes a sub-piece of the tensor and fetches a single value as output. Max-pooling conceptually fetches the prominent feature of that sub-piece, while average-pool takes the average and smoothens the feature. Moreover, historically, max-pooling gives better results than other pooling algorithms, probably because it takes the most prominent feature from the input and passes it to the next level. Hence, we also use max-pooling. The custom max-pool layer has the same structure, but the complex convolution operation is replaced by a simple max operation.

```
out = torch.zeros(batch_size, depth, new_height, new_width)
for h in range(new_height):
    for w in range(new_width):
        for d in range(depth):
            val = x[:, d, h:h + self.kernel_size, w:w +
self.kernel_size]
            out[:, d, h, w] = val.max(2)[0].max(1)[0]
```

The `max()` method of PyTorch accepts the dimension as input and returns a tuple with index/indices to the max value and the actual max value.

```
>>> tensor
1 2

3 4

[torch.FloatTensor of size 2x2]
>>> tensor.max(0)[0]
3

4
```

```
[torch.FloatTensor of size 2]
>>> tensor.max(0)[1]
1
1
[torch.LongTensor of size 2]
```

For instance, `max(0)` in the preceding example returns a tuple. The first element in the tuple is a tensor with values three and four, which are the maximum value in the 0th dimension, and another tensor with values one and one, which are the indices of three and four in that dimension. The last line of the max-pool layer takes the maximum value of the sub-piece by taking the `max()` of the second dimension and `max()` of first dimension.

Convolutional layers and the max-pool layer are followed by three linear layers (fully connected), which reduces the dimensionality to 10, which gives the probability score for each of the classes. What follows is what PyTorch models store as a string representation of the actual network graph.

```
>>> simple = SimpleCNNModel()
>>> simple
SimpleCNNModel(
    (conv1): Conv(
    )
    (pool): MaxPool(
    )
    (conv2): Conv(
    )
    (fc1): Linear(in_features=400, out_features=120, bias=True)
    (fc2): Linear(in_features=120, out_features=84, bias=True)
    (fc3): Linear(in_features=84, out_features=10, bias=True)
)
```

We have wired our neural network in the way we want so that it can give the class score when it sees an image. Now we define the loss function and the optimizers.

```
net = SimpleCNNModel()
loss_fn = nn.CrossEntropyLoss()
optimizer = optim.SGD(net.parameters(), lr=0.001, momentum=0.9)
trainloader, testloader = get_data()
```

We create an instance of our neural network class. Remember how the forward function works? The network class will have the __call__() function defined and that in turn calls the `forward()` function we have defined for forward propagation.

The loss function defined in the next line is also a subclass of `torch.nn.Module`, which also has the `forward()` function, which is being called by `__call__()` and the backward function. That gives us the flexibility of creating a custom loss function.

We will have examples in future chapters. For now, we will use an in-built loss function called `CrossEntropyLoss()`. Like we saw in the previous chapters, we will use the PyTorch optimizer package to get predefined optimizers. We use **stochastic gradient descent (SGD)** for this example, but unlike the last chapter, we will use SGD with momentum, which helps us to accelerate the gradient toward the right direction.

 Momentum is a very popular technique used along with the optimization algorithm nowadays. We add a factor of the current gradient to the current gradient itself to get a bigger value, which is then subtracted from the weights. Momentum accelerates the movement of the loss in the direction of the minima analogous to momentum in the real world.

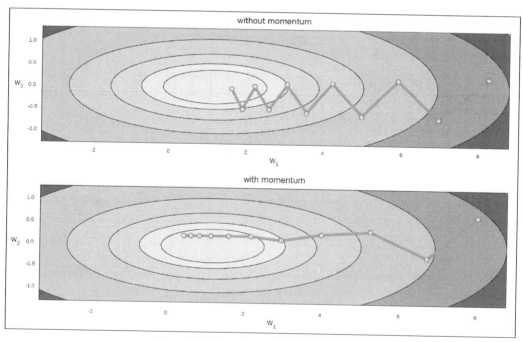

Figure 4.5: SGD without and with momentum

Now we are completely set for training our neural network. From this point, we can use the template code for training:

1. Loop through epoch.
2. Loop through shuffled data for each epoch.
3. Make the existing gradient zero by calling:
    - `optimizer.zero_grad()`
    - `net.zero_grad()`
4. Run the forward pass of the network.
5. Get the loss by calling the loss function with the network output.
6. Run the backward pass.
7. Make the gradient update with the optimizer.
8. Save the running loss if required.

Be careful while saving the running loss because PyTorch saves the whole graph prior to the variable to do the backpropagation. Saving the graph incrementally will be just another operation into your graph, where the graph in each iteration has the previous graph attached to it using the summation operation and you end up running out of memory. Always take the value out of the graph and save it like normal tensors that don't have graph history.

```
inputs, labels = data
optimizer.zero_grad()
outputs = net(inputs)
loss = loss_fn(outputs, labels)
loss.backward()
optimizer.step()
running_loss += loss.item()
```

Semantic segmentation

We have learned the basics of how CNNs work. Now we will take the next step and develop an advanced application of a CNN called semantic segmentation. As the name suggests, this technique marks parts of an image with a category, for example, marking all the trees as green, buildings as red, cars as grey, and so on. Segmentation by itself means identifying the structure, regions, and so on, from an image.

Semantic segmentation is intelligent, and we'll use it when we want to understand what is in the image rather than just identifying the structure or region. Semantic segmentation is recognizing and understanding what's in the image at pixel level.

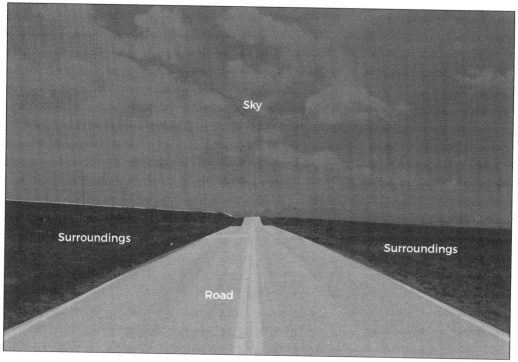

Figure 4.6: An example of semantic segmentation

Semantic segmentation powers several major applications in the real world, from CCTV cameras and self-driving cars, to segmenting different objects. In this chapter, we will implement one of the fastest semantic segmentation architectures called LinkNet [2] [7].

We will use the CamVid dataset for our LinkNet implementation in this chapter. CamVid is a ground truth dataset that consists of high-quality videos converted to frames that are manually segmented and labeled. Manually labeled output images use color as an identification for objects. For example, all the images in the output directory of the dataset use magenta for roads.

LinkNet

LinkNet exploits the idea of autoencoders, which used to be a data compression technique. Autoencoders have two parts in their architecture: an encoder and a decoder. The encoder encodes the input to a low-dimensional space and the decoder decodes/recreates the input from the low-dimensional space. Autoencoders are widely used to reduce dimensionality in compression and so on.

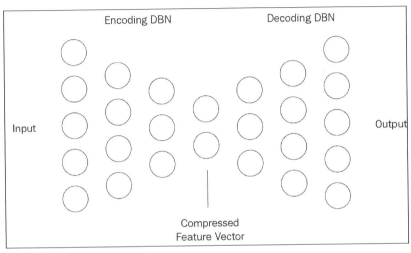

Figure 4.7: An autoencoder

LinkNet consists of an initial block, a final block, an encoder block with four convolutional modules in it, and a decoder with four deconvolution modules. The initial block downsamples the input image twice by using a strided convolution and a max-pooling layer. Then each convolution module in the encoder block downsamples the input once with strided convolution. The encoded output is then passed to the decoder block, which upsamples the input with strided deconvolution once in each deconvolution block; deconvolution is explained in the following section.

The output from the decoder block then passes through the final block, which upsamples twice, just like how the initial block downsamples twice. There is more: LinkNet is capable of reducing the number of parameters in the architecture compared to other semantic segmentation models by using the idea of skip connection.

The encoder block communicates with the decoder block after each convolutional block, which lets the encoder block forget certain information after the forward pass. Since the output of the encoder block does not have to keep that information, the number of parameters can be much less than for other existing architectures. In fact, the authors of the paper used ResNet18 as an encoder and still were able to get state-of-the art results with mind-blowing performance. What follows is the architecture of LinkNet:

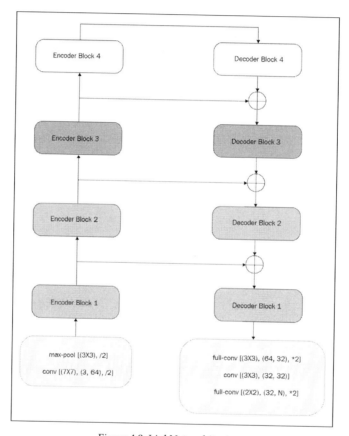

Figure 4.8: LinkNet architecture

So, we have seen certain things that we have not seen before. Let's talk about those.

Deconvolution

Deconvolution can be vaguely described as the reverse of a convolution operation. Matthew Zeiler, the founder and CEO of Clarifai, first used deconvolution in his CNN layer visualization paper [3], though he did not name it then. As it was a success, deconvolution has been used in several papers since.

It makes a lot of sense to name the operation deconvolution, since it is doing the opposite of convolution. It has many names, such as transpose convolution (since the matrix used in between has been transposed) and backward convolution (since the operation is the back pass of convolution while backpropagating). But in reality, we are essentially doing the convolution operation itself, but we change the way the pixels are arranged in the input.

For deconvolution with padding and stride, the input image will have padding around the pixels and will have zero valued pixels in between. The movement of the kernel sliding window will remain the same in all cases.

 More about deconvolution can be found in the paper *A guide to convolution arithmetic for deep learning* [5] or the GitHub repository [6].

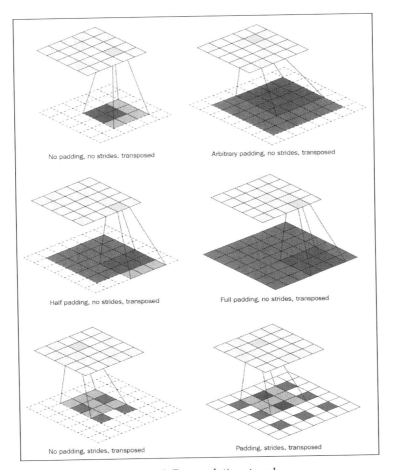

Figure 4.9: Deconvolution at work

Skip connections

The parallel horizontal line between encoder and decoder in the LinkNet architecture is the skip connection representation. Skip connections help the network to forget certain information during encoding and look at it again while decoding. This reduces the number of parameters required for the network, since the amount of information that is needed for the network to decode and generate the image is relatively low. Skip connections can be implemented with the help of different operations. Another advantage of using skip connections is easy gradient flow backward through the same connections. LinkNet adds the hidden encoder output to the corresponding decoder input while Tiramisu [4], another semantic segmentation algorithm, concatenates both and sends this to the next layer.

Model

The encoder of the semantic segmentation model is an extension of the SimpleCNN model we built in the first session but with more convolution modules. Our main class uses five minor components/modules to build up the architecture described earlier:

- ConvBlock is a custom nn.Module class that implements the convolution and the non-linearity.

- DeconvBlock is a custom nn.Module class that implements the deconvolution and non-linearity.

- nn.MaxPool2d is an in-built PyTorch layer that does 2D max-pooling.

- EncoderBlock.

- DecoderBlock.

As we have seen in older sessions, we initialize the classes in __init__() of the major class and link each of them like a chain, while calling it through forward(), but in here, we need to implement a skip connection. We use the output of the encoder layers and pass it to the decoder layer by adding it with the normal input to the decoder.

ConvBlock

```
class ConvBlock(nn.Module):
    """ LinkNet uses initial block with conv -> batchnorm -> relu """

    def __init__(self, inp, out, kernal, stride, pad, bias, act):
        super().__init__()
        if act:
            self.conv_block = nn.Sequential(
```

```
                nn.Conv2d(inp, out, kernal, stride, pad,
        bias=bias),
                nn.BatchNorm2d(num_features=out),
                nn.ReLU())
        else:
            self.conv_block = nn.Sequential(
                nn.Conv2d(inp, out, kernal, stride, pad,
        bias=bias),
                nn.BatchNorm2d(num_features=out))

    def forward(self, x):
        return self.conv_block(x)
```

All the convolutions in LinkNet are followed by a Batch Normalization and ReLU layer almost always, but there are exceptions that don't have a ReLU layer. That's what `ConvBlock` is built for. `ConvBlock`, as mentioned before, is a child class of `torch.nn.Module` that can do backpropagation from whatever happens in the forward pass. `__init__` accepts input and output dimensions, the kernel size, stride value, padding width, a Boolean representing whether bias is required or not, and a Boolean representing whether activation (ReLU) is required or not.

We use `torch.nn.Conv2d`, `torch.nn.BatchNorm2d`, and `torch.nn.ReLu` to configure `ConvBlock`. Conv2D of PyTorch accepts all the arguments to the `__init__` of `ConvBlock`, except the Boolean value representing the analogous activation requirement. Other than that, Conv2D accepts two more optional arguments for dilation and group. The ReLU function from `torch.nn` accepts only one optional argument called `inplace`, which is defaulted to `False`. If `inplace` is `True`, ReLU will be applied on the data in place instead of creating another memory location. This could save memory slightly in many cases but cause issues, since we are destroying the input. The rule of thumb is: unless you are in desperate need of memory optimization, stay away from it.

Batch Normalization is used for normalizing the data inside each batch instead of doing it only once at the beginning. Normalization is essential in the beginning to get an equally scaled input, which in turn gives better accuracy. But as the data flows through the network, non-linearity and augmentation by weight and biases could lead to internal data of a different scale.

Normalizing each layer proved to be a solution for this particular problem, and it increases the accuracy even if we increase the learning rate. Batch Normalization also accelerates the convergence of the network, since it helps the network to learn from a more stable distribution of the input. PyTorch has Batch Normalization implemented for different dimensional inputs just like convolutional layers. Here we use `BatchNorm2d` since we have four-dimensional data where one dimension is the batch size and another dimension is depth.

BatchNorm2d is implemented with two learnable parameters: gamma and beta. PyTorch handles the learning of these features while we backpropagate, unless we set the affine argument to False. Now, BatchNorm2d accepts the number of features, epsilon value, momentum, and affine as arguments.

The epsilon value will be added to the denominator inside the square root to keep numerical stability while the momentum factor decides how much momentum should be gained from the previous layer to speed up the operation.

__init__ checks whether the activation is required or not and creates the layer. This is where torch.nn.Sequential is useful. The obvious approach for defining three different layers (convolution, Batch Normalization, and ReLU) as a single ConvBlock layer is to create Python attributes for all three and pass the output of the first to the second, and then that output to the third in. But with nn.Sequential, we can chain them together and create a single Python attribute. The downside of doing this is that as the network grows, you'll have this extra Sequential wrapper present for all the small modules, which will make interpreting the network graph difficult. The code available in the repository (with the nn.Sequential wrapper) will generate a graph like *Figure 4.10a*, and the layer built without the Sequential wrapper will generate a graph like *Figure 4.10b*.

```
class ConvBlockWithoutSequential(nn.Module):
    """ LinkNet uses initial block with conv -> batchnorm -> relu """

    def __init__(self, inp, out, kernel, stride, pad, bias, act):
        super().__init__()
        if act:
            self.conv = nn.Conv2d(inp, out, kernel, stride, pad,
bias=bias)
            self.bn = nn.BatchNorm2d(num_features=out)
            self.relu = nn.ReLU()
        else:
            self.conv = nn.Conv2d(inp, out, kernel, stride, pad,
bias=bias)
            self.bn = nn.BatchNorm2d(num_features=out)

    def forward(self, x):
        conv_r = self.conv(x)
        self.bn_r = self.bn(conv_r)
        if act:
            return self.relu(self.bn_r)
        return self.bn_r
```

DeconvBlock

The deconvolution block is the building block of the decoder in LinkNet. Just like how we made the convolution block, the deconvolution block consists of three basic modules: a transpose convolution, BatchNorm, and ReLU. In that case, the only difference between the convolution block and deconvolution block is the replacement of torch.nn.Conv2d with torch.nn.ConvTranspose2d. As we have seen before, transpose convolution is doing the same operation as the convolution but giving out the opposite result.

```
class DeconvBlock(nn.Module):
    """ LinkNet uses Deconv block with transposeconv -> batchnorm
        -> relu """

    def __init__(self, inp, out, kernal, stride, pad):
        super().__init__()
        self.conv_transpose = nn.ConvTranspose2d(inp, out, kernal,
stride, pad)
        self.batchnorm = nn.BatchNorm2d(out)
        self.relu = nn.ReLU()

    def forward(self, x, output_size):
        convt_out = self.conv_transpose(x,
output_size=output_size)
        batchnormout = self.batchnorm(convt_out)
        return self.relu(batchnormout)
```

The forward call of DeconvBlock does not use torch.nn.Sequential, and we are doing something extra to what we did with Conv2d in ConvBlock. We pass the expected output_size to the forward call of the transpose convolution for making the dimensions stable. Using torch.nn.Sequential to make the whole deconvolution block into a single variable keeps us from passing a variable into the transpose convolution.

Pooling

PyTorch has several options for pooling operations, from which we choose to use MaxPool. As we have seen in the SimpleCNN example, this is one obvious operation we could use to reduce the dimension of the input by fetching only the prominent feature from a pool. MaxPool2d accepts arguments similar to Conv2d to decide the kernel size, padding, and striding. But apart from those arguments, MaxPool2d accepts two extra arguments, return indices, and ciel. The return indices return the indices of the max value, which can be used while unpooling in some network architecture. ciel is the Boolean argument that decides the output shape by ceiling or flooring the dimension.

EncoderBlock

This encodes part of the network, downsamples the input, and tries to get a compressed version of the input that contains the essence of the input. A basic building block of the encoder is the `ConvBlock` we developed before.

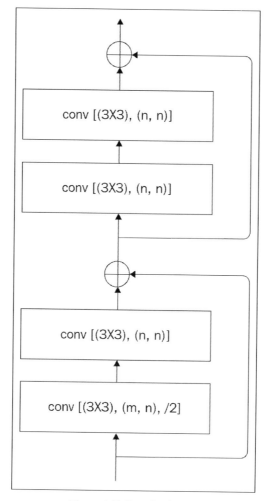

Figure 4.10: Encoder figure

As seen in the preceding diagram, each encoder block in LinkNet consists of four convolution blocks. The first two convolution blocks are grouped together as block one. This is then added with the residue output (an architectural decision motivated by ResNet). The residue output with that addition then goes to block two, which is also similar to block one. The input of block two is then added to the output of block two without passing through a separate residue block.

Block one downsamples the input with the factor of two and block two doesn't do anything with the dimension of the input. That is why we needed a residue net along with block one, while for block two we could add the input and output directly. The code that implements the architecture is as follows. The `init` function is essentially initializing the `conv` blocks and the `residue` blocks. PyTorch helps us to handle the addition of tensors, so that we just have to write the mathematical operations we wanted to do, just like how you do it on a normal Python variable, and PyTorch's `autograd` will take it from there.

```python
class EncoderBlock(nn.Module):
    """ Residucal Block in linknet that does Encoding - layers in
        ResNet18 """

    def __init__(self, inp, out):
        """
        Resnet18 has first layer without downsampling.
        The parameter ''downsampling'' decides that
        # TODO - mention about how n - f/s + 1 is handling output
size in
        # in downsample
        """
        super().__init__()
        self.block1 = nn.Sequential(
            ConvBlock(inp=inp, out=out, kernal=3, stride=2, pad=1,
bias=True, act=True),
            ConvBlock(inp=out, out=out, kernal=3, stride=1, pad=1,
bias=True, act=True))
        self.block2 = nn.Sequential(
            ConvBlock(inp=out, out=out, kernal=3, stride=1, pad=1,
bias=True, act=True),
            ConvBlock(inp=out, out=out, kernal=3, stride=1, pad=1,
bias=True, act=True))
        self.residue = ConvBlock(
            inp=inp, out=out, kernal=3, stride=2, pad=1,
bias=True, act=True)

    def forward(self, x):
        out1 = self.block1(x)
        residue = self.residue(x)
        out2 = self.block2(out1 + residue)
        return out2 + out1
```

DecoderBlock

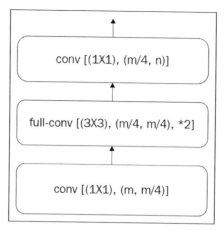

Figure 4.11: Decoder picture from LinkNet

Decoder is the block built on top of `DeconvBlock` and is much simpler than `EncoderBlock`. It doesn't have any residues running along with the network but just a direct chain connection between two convolutional blocks through a deconvolution block. Just like how one encoder block downsamples the input by the factor of two, `DecoderBlock` upsamples the input by a factor of two. So, we have an exact number of encoder and decoder blocks to get the output of the same size back.

```python
class DecoderBlock(nn.Module):
    """ Residucal Block in linknet that does Encoding """

    def __init__(self, inp, out):
        super().__init__()
        self.conv1 = ConvBlock(
            inp=inp, out=inp // 4, kernal=1, stride=1, pad=0,
bias=True, act=True)
        self.deconv = DeconvBlock(
            inp=inp // 4, out=inp // 4, kernal=3, stride=2, pad=1)
        self.conv2 = ConvBlock(
            inp=inp // 4, out=out, kernal=1, stride=1, pad=0,
bias=True, act=True)

    def forward(self, x, output_size):
        conv1 = self.conv1(x)
        deconv = self.deconv(conv1, output_size=output_size)
        conv2 = self.conv2(deconv)
        return conv2
```

With that, our LinkNet model design is complete. We arrange all the building blocks together to make the LinkNet model, and then we use `torchvision` to preprocess the input before starting the training. `__init__` will initialize the whole network architecture. It will create the initial block and max-pool layer, four encoder blocks, four decoder blocks, and two `deconv` blocks that wrap another `conv` block. The four decoder blocks upsample the image to compensate for the downsampling done by the four encoders. The strided convolution and max-pool layer before our encoder blocks (four of them) also downsample the image twice. Compensating for that, we have two `DeconvBlocks` where the `ConvBlock` placed between the `DeconvBlock` doesn't affect the dimension at all.

The forward call just chains all the initialized variables together, but the portion that needs attention is `DecoderBlock`. We will have to pass the expected output to the `DecoderBlock`, which in turn goes to `torch.nn.ConvTranspose2d`. Also, we add the output from the encoder output to the decoder input of the next step. This is the skip connection we have seen before. Since we are passing the encoder output directly to the decoder, we are passing several pieces of information that are needed to recreate the image. This is the fundamental reason why LinkNet works so well even without compromising the speed.

```python
class SegmentationModel(nn.Module):
    """
    LinkNet for Semantic segmentation. Inspired heavily by
    https://github.com/meetshah1995/pytorch-semseg
    # TODO -> pad = kernal // 2
    # TODO -> change the var names
    # find size > a = lambda n, f, p, s: (((n + (2 * p)) - f) / s) + 1
    # Cannot have resnet18 architecture because it doesn't do
    downsampling on first layer
    """

    def __init__(self):
        super().__init__()
        self.init_conv = ConvBlock(
            inp=3, out=64, kernal=7, stride=2, pad=3, bias=True,
            act=True)
        self.init_maxpool = nn.MaxPool2d(kernel_size=3, stride=2,
            padding=1)

        self.encoder1 = EncoderBlock(inp=64, out=64)
        self.encoder2 = EncoderBlock(inp=64, out=128)
        self.encoder3 = EncoderBlock(inp=128, out=256)
        self.encoder4 = EncoderBlock(inp=256, out=512)
```

```
        self.decoder4 = DecoderBlock(inp=512, out=256)
        self.decoder3 = DecoderBlock(inp=256, out=128)
        self.decoder2 = DecoderBlock(inp=128, out=64)
        self.decoder1 = DecoderBlock(inp=64, out=64)

        self.final_deconv1 = DeconvBlock(inp=64, out=32, kernal=3,
stride=2, pad=1)
        self.final_conv = ConvBlock(
            inp=32, out=32, kernal=3, stride=1, pad=1, bias=True,
act=True)
        self.final_deconv2 = DeconvBlock(inp=32, out=2, kernal=2,
stride=2, pad=0)

    def forward(self, x):
        init_conv = self.init_conv(x)
        init_maxpool = self.init_maxpool(init_conv)
        e1 = self.encoder1(init_maxpool)
        e2 = self.encoder2(e1)
        e3 = self.encoder3(e2)
        e4 = self.encoder4(e3)

        d4 = self.decoder4(e4, e3.size()) + e3
        d3 = self.decoder3(d4, e2.size()) + e2
        d2 = self.decoder2(d3, e1.size()) + e1
        d1 = self.decoder1(d2, init_maxpool.size())

        final_deconv1 = self.final_deconv1(d1, init_conv.size())
        final_conv = self.final_conv(final_deconv1)
        final_deconv2 = self.final_deconv2(final_conv, x.size())

        return final_deconv2
```

Summary

The field of computer vision has been dramatically improved in last decade with the help of artificial intelligence. It's now being used not just for traditional use cases, like object detection/recognition, but also for improving the quality of images, rich search from images/videos, text generation from images/videos, 3D modeling, and more.

We have gone through CNNs in this chapter, which are the key to all the success that has happened in computer vision so far. There are multitudes of architectural variants of CNNs that have been used for different purposes, but the core of all those implementations is the fundamental building blocks of CNNs. There have been numerous studies about the technical limitations of CNNs, especially from a human vision simulation point of view. It's been proven that CNNs are not exactly simulating the way the human vision system works. This has led a lot of research groups to believe that there should be an alternative. One most popular approach to replacing CNNs is the use of capsule networks, again from Geoffrey Hinton's lab. But right now, CNNs are acting as the core of thousands of real-time and critical computer vision applications.

In the next chapter, we'll be looking at another of the fundamental network architectures: recurrent neural networks.

References

1. Convolutional network, Udacity, https://www.youtube.com/watch?v=ISHGyvsT0QY

2. LinkNet, https://codeac29.github.io/projects/linknet/

3. Matthew D. Zeiler and Rob Fergus, *Visualizing and Understanding Convolutional Networks*, https://cs.nyu.edu/~fergus/papers/zeilerECCV2014.pdf

4. *The One Hundred Layers Tiramisu: Fully Convolutional DenseNets for Semantic Segmentation*, https://arxiv.org/pdf/1611.09326.pdf

5. *A guide to convolution arithmetic for deep learning*, https://arxiv.org/pdf/1603.07285.pdf

6. GitHub repository for convolution arithmetic, https://github.com/vdumoulin/conv_arithmetic

7. *LinkNet: Exploiting Encoder Representations for Efficient Semantic Segmentation*, Abhishek Chaurasia, and Eugenio Culurciello, 2017, https://arxiv.org/abs/1707.03718

5
Sequential Data Processing

The major challenges that neural networks are trying to solve today are processing, understanding, compressing, and generating sequential data. Sequential data can be described vaguely as anything that has a dependency on the previous data point and the next data point. Handling different types of sequential data requires different techniques, although the basic approach can be generalized. We'll explore what the basic building blocks of sequential data processing units are as well as, the common problems and their widely accepted solutions.

In this chapter, we are going to look at sequential data. The canonical data that people use for sequential data processing is natural language, although time series data, music, sound, and others are also considered to be sequential data. **Natural language processing** (**NLP**) and understanding has been explored extensively and it's an active field of research right now. The human language is insanely complex and the possible combinations of our whole vocabulary are more than the number of atoms in the universe. However, deep networks handle this problem fairly well by using certain techniques like embeddings and attention.

Introduction to recurrent neural networks

Recurrent neural networks (**RNNs**) are the de facto implementation for sequential data processing. As the name indicates, RNNs recur through the data holding the information from the previous run and try to find the meaning of the sequence, just like how humans do.

Although the vanilla RNN, the unrolling of a simple RNN cell for each unit in the input, was a revolutionary idea, it failed to provide production-ready results. The major hindrance was the long-term dependency problem. When the length of the input sequence is increased, the network won't be able to remember information from the initial units (words if it is natural language) when it reaches the last cells. We'll see what an RNN cell contains and how it can be unrolled in the upcoming sections.

Several iterations and years of research yielded a few different approaches to RNN architectural design. The state-of-the-art models now use **long short-term memory (LSTM)** implementations or **gated recurrent units (GRU)**. Both of these implementations use gates inside the RNN cell for different purposes, such as the forget gate, which is responsible for making the network forget unnecessary information. These architectures are built with the long-term dependency problems that the vanilla RNN had and hence use gates not just to forget unnecessary information, but also to remember information that is necessary as it moves to the last cells in a long sequence.

Attention was the next big invention, which helps the network to focus on an important part of the input instead of searching the whole input and trying to find the answer. A team from Google Brain and the University of Toronto had in fact proved that attention could beat LSTM and GRU networks [1]. However, most of the implementations use LSTM/GRU and attention together.

Embedding was another revolutionary idea for finding the conceptual meaning of a word by comparing the distribution of a word in a word cluster. Embeddings keep the relation between words and convert this relation, which it finds from the distribution of words in a word cluster, to a set of floating point numbers. Embeddings reduce the input size drastically and improve performance and accuracy a great deal. We'll use word2vec for our experiments.

Data processing is one of the main challenges when it comes to sequence data, especially natural language. PyTorch provides several utility packages to handle that. We'll be using pre-processed data for our implementation to make things easy, but we'll run through the utility packages to understand how they work. Along with these utility packages, we'll be using `torchtext`, which abstracts away a lot of difficulties we would face when we handle the input data.

Though the chapter is all about sequential data, we'll be focusing on one subset of sequence data, which is natural language. Specific to natural language, some researchers think that the way we handle the input with LSTM or GRU is not how natural language should be processed. Natural language keeps a tree-like hierarchical relation between the words and we should exploit that. **Stack-augmented Parser-Interpreter Neural Network (SPINN)** [2] is one such implementation from the Stanford NLP group. This particular type of network, which handles sequence data with a tree-like structure in mind, is a *recursive neural network* (different from a recurrent neural network). We'll see SPINNs in detail in the last section of this chapter.

The problem

In this chapter, I will first explain a problem to solve and then explain the concepts, while fixing the problem we have. The problem is finding the similarity between two English sentences with three different approaches. To make the comparison fair, we'll use word embeddings in all the implementations. Don't worry, we'll go through word embeddings as well. The problem in hand is commonly called an **entailment problem**, where we have two sentences at each instance and our job is to predict the similarity between these sentences. We could classify the sentences into three categories:

- Entailment: both sentences mean the same thing:
  - A soccer game with multiple males playing.
  - Some men are playing a sport.

- Neutral: both sentences have something in common:
  - An older and younger man smiling.
  - Two men are smiling and laughing at the cats playing on the floor.

- Contradiction: both sentences convey two different meanings:
  - A black race car starts up in front of a crowd of people.
  - A man is driving down a lonely road.

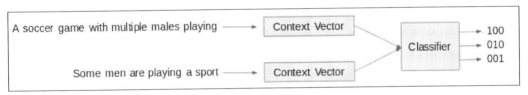

Figure 5.1: Pictorial representation of the problem

Approaches

We'll implement all the three methods: a basic RNN, an advanced RNN like LSTM or GRU, and a recursive network like SPINN, before looping through the SNLI dataset. Each data instance gives us a pair of sentences, a premise, and a hypothesis sentence. The sentences are converted to embeddings first and then passed into each implementation. While the process is the same for simple RNNs and advanced RNNs, SPINNs introduce a completely different flow for training and inference. Let's start with a simple RNN.

Simple RNN

RNNs have been used as the go-to NLP technique for understanding the meaning of data, and we can complete a numerous variety of tasks based on the sequential relations found from it. We will use this simple RNN to show how recurrence works effectively to accumulate the meaning and understand the meaning of words based on the context the words are in.

Before we start building any core modules of our network, we'll have to process the dataset and modify it for our use. We will use the SNLI dataset (a dataset containing sentence pairs labeled for classification between entailment, contradiction, and neutral) from Stanford, which has been pre-processed and saved in torchtext for us.

The loaded dataset contains data instances as pairs of sentences labeled as entailment, contradiction, and neutral. Each sentence is associated with a set of transformations that will be used with recursive networks. The dataset loaded from BucketIterator is shown in the following code block. We can access a pair of sentences by calling batch.premise and .hypothesis (the get_data() function is dummy code kept to avoid showing the long line; the actual code to get the data is available in the GitHub repository):

```
>>> train_iter, dev_iter, test_iter = get_data()
>>> batch = next(iter(train_iter))
>>> batch
[torchtext.data.batch.Batch of size 64 from SNLI]
    [.premise]:[torch.LongTensor of size 32x64]
    [.hypothesis]:[torch.LongTensor of size 22x64]
    [.label]:[torch.LongTensor of size 64]
```

Now that we have everything we need (two sentences for each data instance and a corresponding label), we can start coding the network. But how can we make our neural network process the English language? A normal neural network performs operations on numerical values, but now we have characters. The old approach would be to convert the input to a one-hot encoded sequence. Here is a straightforward example with good old NumPy:

```
>>> vocab = {
        'am': 0,
        'are': 1,
        'fine': 2,
        'hai': 3,
        'how': 4,
```

```
        'i': 5,
        'thanks': 6,
        'you': 7,
        ',': 8,
        '.': 9
    }
>>> # input = hai, how are you -> 3, 8, 4, 1, 7
    seq = [3, 8, 4, 1, 7]
>>> a = np.array(seq)
>>> b = np.zeros((len(seq), len(vocab)))
>>> b[np.arange(len(seq)), seq] = 1
>>> b
array([[0., 0., 0., 1., 0., 0., 0., 0., 0., 0.],
       [0., 0., 0., 0., 0., 0., 0., 0., 1., 0.],
       [0., 0., 0., 0., 1., 0., 0., 0., 0., 0.],
       [0., 1., 0., 0., 0., 0., 0., 0., 0., 0.],
       [0., 0., 0., 0., 0., 0., 0., 1., 0., 0.]])
```

The b variable from this example is what we pass to our neural network. So, our neural network will have a number of input neurons equivalent to the vocabulary size. For each instance, we pass a sparse array with only one element as 1. Do you see what would be the problem with one-hot encoding? You would end up having a huge input layer as your vocabulary size increases. That is when embedding can help you.

Word embedding

The canonical approach to using natural language (or any sequences that consist of discrete individual units) is to convert each word to one-hot encoded vectors and use that for a later stage of the network. The obvious disadvantage with this approach is that as the number of words in the vocabulary increases, the input layer size also increases.

Word embedding is a decades-old idea to reduce the dimensionality of the array or tensors. **Latent Dirichlet allocation (LDA)** and **latent semantic analysis (LSA)** are two such examples that we use for making embeddings. But embedding started being considered as a prerequisite after Tomas Mikolov, a research scientist at Facebook, and his team implemented word2vec in 2013.

Word2vec is an unsupervised learning algorithm where the network makes embeddings without being trained to do so. That means you can train a word2vec model on one English dataset and use it to generate embeddings for another one.

There is one more popular word embedding algorithm called GloVe (we will use this in this chapter), which came from the Stanford NLP group. Although both implementations try to solve the same problem, both use extremely different approaches. Word2vec is using embedding to increase the predictive capability; that is, the algorithm tries to predict the target word by using the context words. As the predictive accuracy goes up, the embedding gets stronger. GloVe is a count-based model where we make a huge table that shows the frequencies of each word corresponding to other words. Obviously, this makes a huge table if the vocabulary is high and if we use large corpora of texts like Wikipedia. So, we do dimensionality reduction on that table to get a reasonably sized embedding matrix.

PyTorch has an embeddings layer created in `torch.nn`, just like other PyTorch layers. It is trainable for our custom dataset, although we could use the pretrained models. The embedding layer requires the size of the vocabulary and size of the embedding dimension we wanted to keep. Normally, we use `300` as the embedding dimension:

```
>>> vocab_size = 100
>>> embedding_dim = 300
>>> embed = nn.Embedding(vocab_size, embedding_dim)
>>> input_tensor = torch.LongTensor([5])
>>> embed(input_tensor).size()
torch.Size([1, 300])
```

The embedding layer nowadays is also used for all types of categorical inputs, not just for embedding natural language. For example, if you are making a winner predictor for the English Premier League, it might be a good idea to embed the team name or the ground name instead of passing them as one-hot encoded vectors to your network.

But for our use case, `torchtext` wrapped the preceding methods into an easy way of converting the input to embeddings. What follows is an example where we transfer learning from GloVe vectors to get the pretrained embeddings trained on six billion tokens from Google News:

```
inputs = data.Field(lower=True)
answers = data.Field(sequential=False)
train, dev, test = datasets.SNLI.splits(inputs, answers)
inputs.build_vocab(train, dev, test)
inputs.vocab.load_vectors('glove.6B.300d')
```

We'll split the SNLI dataset into `training`, `dev`, and `test` sets and pass those as arguments to the `build_vocab` function. The `build_vocab` function loops through the dataset given and finds the number of words, frequencies, and other properties and creates the `vocab` object. This `vocab` object exposes the `load_vectors` API to accept pretrained models to do transfer learning.

RNN cell

Next, we will start building the smallest foundational building block of our network, which is the RNN cell. The way it works is that one RNN cell is capable of processing all the words in the sentence one by one. Initially, we pass the first word from our sentence to the cell, which generates an output and an intermediate state. This state is the running meaning of our sequence, and since this state is not going to output until we finish processing the whole sequence, we call it a hidden state.

After the first word, we have the output and hidden state generated from the RNN cell. Both the output and hidden state have their own purpose. The output can be trained to predict the next character or word in the sentence. This is how most language modeling tasks work.

If you are trying to create a sequential network to predict time series data like stock prices, most probably this is how you will build your network. But in our case, we are worried only about the whole meaning of the sentence, and hence we'll just ignore the output that each cell generates. Instead of the output, we'll focus on the hidden state. The purpose of the hidden state, as I mentioned earlier, is to keep the running meaning of the sentence. Sounds like what we are looking for, right? Each RNN cell takes a hidden state as one of the inputs and spits out another hidden state as given in *Figure 5.2*.

We'll be using the same RNN cell for each word and will pass the hidden state generated from the last word processing as an input to the current word execution. Hence an RNN cell, at each word processing stage, has two inputs: the word itself and the hidden state from the last execution.

What happens when we start the execution? We don't have a hidden state in hand, but we designed the cell to expect the hidden state. Almost always, we create a zero-valued hidden state just to mock the process for the first word, though research has been done to try different values instead of zero.

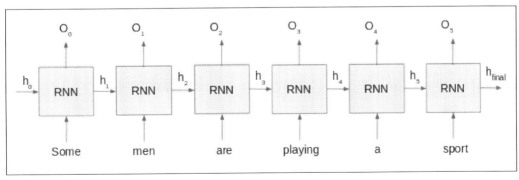

Figure 5.2: A generic RNN cell flow diagram with input, hidden state, and output unrolling our sequence

Figure 5.2 shows the same RNN cell unrolled to visualize how it would be handling each word in the sentence. Since we are using the same RNN cell for each word, we dramatically reduce the number of parameters required for the neural network, and that makes us capable of processing big mini-batches. The way the network parameter learns is to handle the order of the sequence. That is the core principle of RNNs.

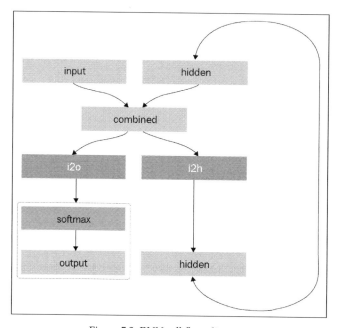

Figure 5.3: RNN cell flow diagram

Different wiring mechanisms have been tried to design the RNN cell to get the most efficient output. In this section, we will use the most basic one, which consists of two fully connected layers and a softmax layer. But in the real world, people use LSTMs or GRUs as an RNN cell, which has proven to provide state-of-the-art results in a huge number of use cases. We'll see them in the next section. In fact, numerous comparisons have been made to find the best architecture for all the sequential tasks, like in *LSTM: A Search Space Odyssey* [3].

We have developed a simple RNN, as shown in the following code. There are no complex gating mechanisms and no architectural patterns; it is just a no-brainer.

```
class RNNCell(nn.Module):
    def __init__(self, embed_dim, hidden_size, vocab_dim):
        super().__init__()

        self.hidden_size = hidden_size
        self.input2hidden = nn.Linear(embed_dim + hidden_size,
```

```
                                    hidden_size)
        self.input2output = nn.Linear(embed_dim + hidden_size,
                                        vocab_dim)
        self.softmax = nn.LogSoftmax(dim=1)

    def forward(self, inputs, hidden):
        combined = torch.cat((inputs, hidden), 2)
        hidden = self.input2hidden(combined)
        # Since it's encoder
        # We are not concerned about output
        # output = self.input2output(combined)
        # output = self.softmax(output)
        return hidden

    def init_hidden(self, batch_size):
        return torch.zeros(1, batch_size, self.hidden_size)
```

As shown in *Figure 5.3*, we have two fully connected layers, each responsible for creating output and a hidden state from the input. The `forward` function of `RNNCell` accepts the current input and hidden state from the previous state, which we then concatenate together.

One `Linear` layer takes the concatenated tensor and generates the hidden state for the next unit, while another `Linear` layer generates output for the current unit. The output is then passed through `softmax` before returning to the training loop. `RNNCell` possesses a class method called `init_hidden`, which is conveniently kept for generating the first hidden state with the hidden state size we passed while initializing the object from `RNNCell`. We'll call `init_hidden` before we start looping through the sequence to get the first hidden state, which will be initialized with zero.

Now we have the smallest component of our network ready. The next task is to create the higher-level component that loops through the sequence and use `RNNCell` to process each word in the sequence to generate the hidden state. We call this `Encoder` node, which initializes `RNNCell` with vocabulary size and hidden size. Remember, `RNNCell` needs the vocabulary dimension for the embedding layer and the hidden size for generating the hidden states. In the `forward` function, we get inputs as arguments, which will be a mini-batch of sequences. In this particular case, we loop through the `BucketIterator` of `torchtext`, which identifies the sequences of the same length and groups them together.

Utilities

What if we are not using `BucketIterator`, or what if we don't have sequences of the same length at all? We have two choices: either we execute sequences one by one, or we pad all the sentences, except the longest sentence, in a batch with zeros, so that all sentences will have same length as the longest sequence.

Though we will not have issues with different sequence lengths if we pass them one by one in PyTorch, we'll end up in trouble if our framework is a static computational graph-based framework. In static computation graphs, even the sequence length has to be static, and that's what makes a static graph-based framework extremely incompatible for NLP-based tasks. But highly sophisticated frameworks like TensorFlow handle this by giving out another API for the user called `dynamic_rnn`.

The first approach seems to work fine since we are processing one word at a time for each sentence separately. But mini-batching the input is much more efficient than processing one data input at a time to get our loss function to converge to the global minima. The obvious and efficient approach to make this happen is padding. Padding the input with zeros (or any predefined value that is not present in the input dataset) helps us to handle this particular problem. But it gets hairy when we try to do it manually and becomes redundant, since we have to do it every time we are working on sequential data. PyTorch has a separate utility package under `torch.nn`, which has utilities we need for RNNs.

Pad sequence

The function `pad_sequence` does what it sounds like it does: it pads the sequence with zeros after identifying the longest sequence in the batch and pads every other sentence to that length:

```
>>> import torch.nn.utils.rnn as rnn_utils
>>> a = torch.Tensor([1, 2, 3])
>>> b = torch.Tensor([4, 5])
>>> c = torch.Tensor([6])
>>> rnn_utils.pad_sequence([a, b, c], True)


1 2 3
4 5 0
6 0 0


[torch.FloatTensor of size (3,3)]
```

In the given example, we have three sequences of three different lengths, where the longest sequence has its length as three. PyTorch pads the other two sequences such that all of them now have length three. The `pad_sequence` function accepts one positional argument, which is the sorted sequence of sequences (that is, the longest sequence (a) first and shortest sequence (c) last) and one keyword argument, which decides whether the user wants it to be `batch_first` or not.

Pack sequence

Do you see the problem with padding the input with zeros and getting it processed with an RNN, especially in our case, where we are so concerned about the last hidden state? A short sentence in a batch that has a really huge sentence will end up having lots of zeros padded to it and while generating hidden state, we'll have to loop through these zeros as well.

The following picture shows an example of batched input with three sentences. The short sentences are padded with zeros to equate the length to the longest sentence. But while processing them, we'll end up processing the zeros as well. For bidirectional RNNs, the problem is more complex since we'll have to process from both ends.

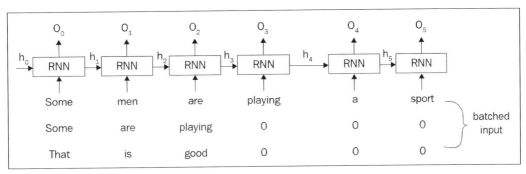

Figure 5.4: A sentence with zeros has the hidden state calculated for the zeros as well

Adding zeros to the input will contaminate the result and that's extremely undesirable. Packing the sequence is done to avoid this effect. PyTorch has the utility function `pack_sequence` exactly for that purpose:

```
>>> import torch.nn.utils.rnn as rnn_utils
>>> import torch
>>> a = torch.Tensor([1, 2, 3])
>>> b = torch.Tensor([1, 2])
>>> c = torch.Tensor([1])
>>> packed = rnn_utils.pack_sequence([a, b, c])
>>> packed
PackedSequence(data=tensor([1., 1., 1., 2., 2., 3.]),
batch_sizes=tensor([3, 2, 1]))
```

The `pack_sequence` function returns an instance of the `PackedSequence` class, which is acceptable by all the RNN modules written in PyTorch. Since `PackedSequence` masks the unwanted part of the input, it improves the efficiency and accuracy of the model. The preceding example shows the content of `PackedSequence`. However, for simplicity, we will refrain from using packed sequences in our models and will always use padded sequence or the output from `BucketIterator`.

Encoder

```
class Encoder(nn.Module):

    def __init__(self, embed_dim, vocab_dim, hidden_size):
        super(Encoder, self).__init__()
        self.rnn = RNNCell(embed_dim, hidden_size, vocab_dim)

    def forward(self, inputs):
        # .size(1) dimension is batch size
        ht = self.rnn.init_hidden(inputs.size(1))
        for word in inputs.split(1, dim=0):
            ht = self.rnn(word, ht)
        return ht
```

In the `forward` function, we first initialize the hidden state for `RNNCell` with zero; this is done by calling `init_hidden`, which we created earlier. Then we loop through the input sequence by splitting it with size one over the dimension one. This is after assuming the input is `batch_first` and hence the first dimension will be the sequence length. For looping through each word, we'll have to loop through the first dimension.

For each word, we call `forward` of `self.rnn` with the current word (the input) and the hidden state from the previous state. `self.rnn` returns the output and the hidden state for the next unit and we continue the loop until the end of the sequence. For our problem case, we are not worried about the output and we are not backpropagating with the loss we could get from the output. Instead, we assume that the last hidden state possesses the meaning of the sentence.

If we could get the meaning of the other sentence in the pair also, we could compare those meanings to predict the class to be contradict, entailment, or neutral and backpropagate the loss. That sounds like an idea. But how will we compare the two meanings? That's up next.

Classifier

The final component of our network is the classifier. So, we have two sentences in hand that we passed through the encoders and we got the final hidden state of both sentences. Now it's time to define the loss function. One approach would be to find the distance between the high-dimensional hidden states from both sentences. The loss can be manipulated as follows:

1. Maximize the loss to a big positive value if it's an entailment.
2. Minimize the loss to a big negative value if it's a contradiction.
3. Keep the loss around zero (within a margin of two or three would work) if it's neutral.

Another approach could be to concatenate the hidden states of both sentences and pass them to another set of layers, and define a final classifier layer that could classify the concatenated value into the three classes we want. This latter approach is used by the actual SPINN implementation but with a more complicated merging mechanism than a simple concatenation.

```
class Merger(nn.Module):

    def __init__(self, size, dropout=0.5):
        super().__init__()
        self.bn = nn.BatchNorm1d(size)
        self.dropout = nn.Dropout(p=dropout)

    def forward(self, data):
        prem = data[0]
        hypo = data[1]
        diff = prem - hypo
        prod = prem * hypo
        cated_data = torch.cat([prem, hypo, diff, prod], 2)
        cated_data = cated_data.squeeze()
        return self.dropout(self.bn(cated_data))
```

Here the `Merger` node is built to simulate the actual implementation of the SPINN. The `forward` function of `Merger` gets two sequences: `prem` and `hypo`. We first identify the difference between the two sentences by normal subtraction and then we find the product between them by element-wise multiplication. We then concatenate the actual sentences with the difference and the product we just found, and pass them through the batch normalization layer and dropout layer.

The `Merger` node is also part of the final classifier layer of our simple RNN, which consists of several other nodes.

The wrapper class `RNNClassifier` wraps all the components we defined so far and creates the final classifier layer as an instance of `torch.nn.Sequential`. The flow of the whole network is shown in the *Figure 5.3* and depicted as code in the following block:

```
class RNNClassifier(nn.Module)

    def __init__(self, config):
        super().__init__()
        self.embed = nn.Embedding(config.vocab_dim, config.embed_dim)
        self.encoder = Encoder(
            config.embed_dim, config.vocab_dim, config.hidden_size)
        self.classifier = nn.Sequential(
```

```
            Merger(4 * config.hidden_size, config.dropout),
            nn.Linear(4 * config.hidden_size, config.fc1_dim),
            nn.ReLU(),
            nn.BatchNorm1d(config.fc1_dim),
            nn.Dropout(p=config.dropout),
            nn.Linear(config.fc1_dim, config.fc2_dim)
        )

    def forward(self, batch):
        prem_embed = self.embed(batch.premise)
        hypo_embed = self.embed(batch.hypothesis)
        premise = self.encoder(prem_embed)
        hypothesis = self.encoder(hypo_embed)
        scores = self.classifier((premise, hypothesis))
        return scores
```

The `RNNClassifier` module has three major layers, which we discussed previously:

- The embedding layer saved into `self.embed`
- The encoder layer that uses `RNNCell`, which is stored into `self.encoder`
- An instance of the `nn.Sequential` layer stored in `self.classifier`

The final sequential layer starts with the `Merger` node. The merged output will have the sequence length dimension augmented by a factor of four because we append both sentences, their difference, and their product to the output of `Merger`. This is then passed through a fully connected layer, which will then be normalized using `batchnorm1d` after a `ReLU` non-linearity. The dropout afterward reduces the chance of overfitting, which is then passed to another fully connected layer, which creates scores for our input data. The input data decides which class among entailment, contradiction, or neutral the data point is part of.

Dropout

Dropout was a revolutionary idea introduced by Nitish Srivastava, a machine learning engineer at Apple. It removes the need for normal regularization techniques that used to be prevalent until dropout was introduced. With dropout, we drop random connections between neurons in the network so that the network has to generalize and cannot be biased toward any type of external factors. To drop a neuron, all you have to do is set its output to zero. Dropping the random neurons prevents the network from co-adapting and hence reduces overfitting to a great extent.

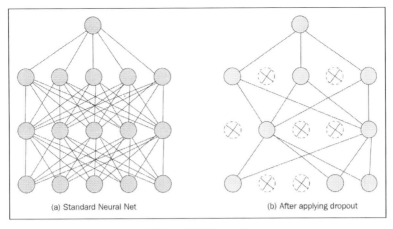

Figure 5.5: Dropout

PyTorch provides a higher-level dropout layer as part of the `torch.nn` package, which accepts the dropout factor while initializing. Its `forward` function just switches off some of the input that goes into it.

Training

We have a single wrapper module for all the small components we have made called `RNNClassifier`. The training process is similar to what we have followed throughout the book. We initialize the `model` class, we define the loss function, and then we define the optimizer. Once we have all of these set and have the hyperparameters initialized, we give the whole control to `ignite`. But in a simple RNN, since we are doing transfer learning from the learned embeddings from the GloVe vectors, we have to transfer those learned weights to the weight matrix of our embed layer. That is done by the second line in the following code snippet.

```
model = RNNClassifier(config)
model.embed.weight.data = inputs.vocab.vectors
criterion = nn.CrossEntropyLoss()
opt = optim.Adam(model.parameters(), lr=lr)
```

Though PyTorch does the backward pass for users and backpropagation is always conceptually the same, backpropagation for the sequential network is not exactly similar to the backpropagation we have seen in the normal network. Here we do **backpropagation through time (BPTT)**. To understand how BPTT works, we have to assume an RNN is long repetitive units of similar RNN cells, rather than considering the same input as being passed through the same RNN cell.

If we have five words in our sentence, then we have five RNN units, but all units have the same weights and when we update the weight of one RNN cell, we update the weight of all RNN cells. Now, if we divide the input into five time steps where each word sits in each time step, we should be able to easily picturize how each word is being passed through each RNN unit. While doing backpropagation, we'll run back through each RNN unit and accumulate the gradient at each time step. Updating the weight of one RNN unit updates the weight of other RNN units as well. Since all five units have got the gradient and each update will update weights of all five, we'll end up updating the weights of each cell five times. Instead of doing updates five times, we accumulate the gradients together and update once; this is BPTT.

Advanced RNNs

Advanced is perhaps a vague term for a network based on LSTMs and GRUs, since these are the network architectures being used in all the sequential data processing networks by default. The GRU network is a relatively new design compared to the LSTM network, which was ideated in the 1990s. Both networks are different forms of gated recurrent networks, where the LSTM network establishes a more complex architecture than the GRU network. These architectures are generalized as gated recurrent networks because they have gates for handling the flow of inputs/gradients through the network. Gates are fundamentally activations, such as sigmoid, to decide the amount of data to flow through. Here we will study more about the architecture of both LSTMs and GRUs and see how PyTorch gives access to the APIs of LSTMs and GRUs.

LSTM

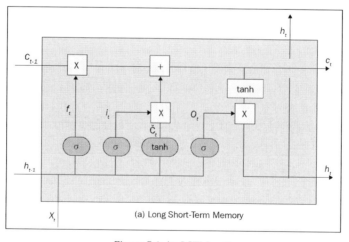

Figure 5.6: An LSTM unit

LSTM networks were introduced in 1991 by Sepp Hochreiter and published in 1997. LSTM networks establish several gates into the recurring unit where the normal `RNNCell` has a `Linear` layer interacting through a `softmax` layer to generate the output and another `Linear` layer that generates the hidden state. A detailed explanation of LSTMs is covered in the original paper or in Christopher Olah's blog titled *Understanding LSTM Networks* [4].

LSTMs are mainly composed of a forget gate, an update gate, and a cell state, which makes LSTMs different from normal RNN cells. The architecture is carefully designed to perform specific tasks. The forget gate uses the input vector and hidden state from the previous state to decide what should be forgotten for instance, and the update gate uses the current input and previous hidden state to decide what should be added to the information repository.

These decisions are based on the output from the sigmoid layer, which always outputs a value in the range of zero to one. Hence, a value of one in the forget gate means to remember everything and a value of zero means to forget everything. The same applies for the update gate as well.

All the operations will be performed on the cell state flowing parallelly through the network, which has only a linear interaction with the information in the network and hence allows data to flow forward and backward seamlessly.

GRUs

GRUs are a relatively new design, which is efficient and less complex than LSTMs. In a nutshell, GRUs merge the forget gate and update gate together and only do one-time updating on the cell state. In fact, GRUs don't have a separate cell state and hidden state, both of which are merged together to create one state. These simplifications reduce the complexity of GRUs to a great extent, without compromising the accuracy of the network. GRUs are being used widely nowadays because of the performance gain GRUs have over LSTMs.

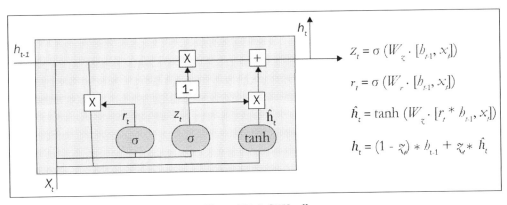

$$z_t = \sigma \left(W_z \cdot [h_{t-1}, x_t] \right)$$

$$r_t = \sigma \left(W_r \cdot [h_{t-1}, x_t] \right)$$

$$\hat{h}_t = \tanh \left(W_z \cdot [r_t * h_{t-1}, x_t] \right)$$

$$h_t = (1 - z_t) * h_{t-1} + z_t * \hat{h}_t$$

Figure 5.7: A GRU cell

Architecture

Our model architecture is similar to that of RNNClassifier, but RNNCell is replaced with LSTM or GRU cells. PyTorch has functional APIs available for using an LSTM cell or GRU cell as the smallest unit of the recurrent network. With the dynamic graph capability, looping through the sequence and calling the cell is completely possible with PyTorch.

The only difference between advanced RNNs and simple RNNs lies in the encoder network. The RNNCell class has been replaced with torch.nn.LSTMCell or torch.nn.GRUCell, and the Encoder class uses these prebuilt cells instead of the custom RNNCell we made last time:

```
class Encoder(nn.Module):

    def __init__(self, config):
        super(Encoder, self).__init__()
        self.config = config
        if config.type == 'LSTM':
            self.rnn = nn.LSTMCell(config.embed_dim,
                    config.hidden_size)
        elif config.type == 'GRU':
            self.rnn = nn.GRUCell(config.embed_dim,
                    config.hidden_size)

    def forward(self, inputs):
        ht = self.rnn.init_hidden()
        for word in inputs.split(1, dim=1):
            ht, ct = self.rnn(word, (ht, ct))
```

LSTMCell and GRUCell

The functional APIs for LSTMCell and GRUCell are absolutely similar, which is exactly how the custom RNNCell was also made. They accept the input size and the hidden size to the initializer. The forward call accepts the mini-batch of input with the input size and creates the cell state and hidden state for that instance, which is then passed to the next execution input. It is extremely difficult to make such an implementation in a static graph framework, since the graph is pre-compiled and static for the whole period of execution; looping statements also should be part of the graph as a graph node. This needs the user to learn those extra op nodes or other functional APIs that handle the loop internally.

LSTMs and GRUs

While PyTorch gives access to granular `LSTMCell` and `GRUCell` APIs, it also takes care of situations where the user doesn't need to be granular. This is especially useful in cases where the user doesn't need to change the internals of how the LSTM works but performance is at its most important, since Python loops are renowned to be slow. The `torch.nn` module has higher-level APIs for LSTM and GRU nets, which wrap `LSTMCell` and `GRUCell` and implement the efficient execution using **cuDNN (CUDA Deep Neural Network)** LSTMs and cuDNN GRUs.

```python
class Encoder(nn.Module):

    def __init__(self, config):
        super(Encoder, self).__init__()
        self.config = config
        if config.type == 'LSTM':
            self.rnn = nn.LSTM(input_size=config.embed_dim, hidden_size=config.hidden_size,
                               num_layers=config.n_layers, dropout=config.dropout,
                               bidirectional=config.birnn)
        elif config.type == 'GRU':
            self.rnn = nn.GRU(input_size=config.embed_dim, hidden_size=config.hidden_size,
                              num_layers=config.n_layers, dropout=config.dropout,
                              bidirectional=config.birnn)

    def forward(self, inputs):
        batch_size = inputs.size()[1]
        state_shape = self.config.cells, batch_size, self.config.hidden_size
        h0 = c0 = inputs.new(*state_shape).zero_()
        outputs, (ht, ct) = self.rnn(inputs, (h0, c0))
        if not self.config.birnn:
            return ht[-1]
        else:
            return ht[-2:].transpose(0, 1).contiguous().view(
                batch_size, -1)
```

Similar to `LSTMCell` and `GRUCell`, LSTMs and GRUs have similar functional APIs to make them compatible with each other. Moreover, LSTMs and GRUs accept more parameters than the cell counterpart, among which `num_layers`, `dropout`, and `bidirectional` are important to look at.

The `dropout` argument, if `True`, adds a dropout layer to the network implementation, which helps with avoiding overfitting and regularizing the network. Using higher-level APIs like LSTM eliminates the need for a Python loop and accepts the complete sequence at a time as input. Though a normal sequence is accepted as input, it is always advisable to pass the packed (masked) input, which increases the performance, since that is how the cuDNN backend expects the input to be.

Increasing the number of layers

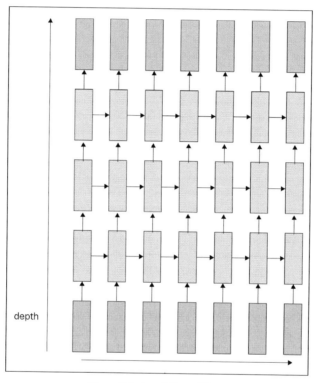

Figure 5.8: A multilayer RNN

The number of layers in RNNs is semantically similar to the increasing number of the layers in any type of neural network. This increases the learning power of the network as it can hold more information about the dataset.

In an LSTM in PyTorch, adding a number of layers is just one parameter to the object initialization: `num_layers`. But that requires the cell state and hidden state to be of the shape [num_layers * num_directions, batch, hidden_size], where `num_layers` is the number of layers and `num_directions` is 1 for single directional and 2 for bidirectional (try to keep the example performance improvements by using a higher number of layers and a bidirectional RNN).

Bidirectional RNN

The RNN implementation would ordinarily be single directional and that is what, we have implemented so far. The difference between a single-directional and bidirectional RNN is that in a bidirectional RNN, the backward pass is equivalent to a forward pass in the opposite direction. So, the input of the backward pass is the same sequence but reversed.

Bidirectional RNNs are proven to be better performants than single directional and it is easy to understand why, especially for NLP. But this cannot be generalized and is not true for all cases. Theoretically, bidirectional RNNs tend to work better if the tasks in hand require past and future information. For example, predicting a word to fill in the gaps requires both the previous sequence and the next sequence.

In our classification task, a bidirectional RNN works better since when the RNN makes the contextual meaning of the sequence, it uses the flow of the sequence on both sides. PyTorch's LSTM or GRU accept a Boolean value for the argument `bidirectional`, which decides whether the network should be bidirectional or not.

Along with the `bidirectional` flag, the hidden state and cell state have to keep the shape [num_layers * num_directions, batch, hidden_size] as described in preceding section, where num_directions need to be 2 if it is bidirectional. Also, I should warn you that bidirectional RNNs are not always the go-to choice, especially for datasets where we don't have future information in hand, such as stock price prediction and others.

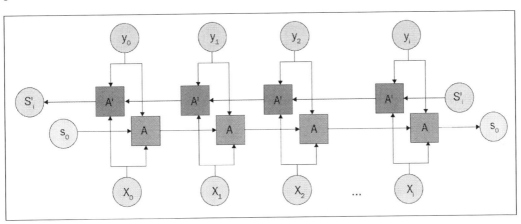

Figure 5.9: A bidirectional RNN

Classifier

The advanced `RNNClassifier` is exactly the same as the simple `RNNClassifier`, with the only exception being that the RNN encoder is being replaced with LSTM or GRU encoders. However, the advanced classifier improves the performance of the network significantly, especially on a GPU, since it is using a highly optimized cuDNN backend.

The model we have developed for advanced RNN is a multilayered bidirectional LSTM/GRU network. Adding attention to the recipe boosts the performance a great deal. But that does not change the classifier, since all these components will be wrapped under the `Encoder` method and the classifier is only worried about the functional API of `Encoder`, which is not changing.

Attention

As mentioned earlier, attention is the process of focusing on the important area along with the normal neural network process. Attention is not part of the existing implementation we make; rather it acts as another module that looks at the input always and is passed as an extra input to the current network.

The idea behind attention is that we focus on the important part of the sentence when we read one. For instance, translating a sentence from one language to another, we'll focus more on the contextual information rather than articles or other words that build the sentence.

Attaining attention in PyTorch is straightforward once the concept is clear. Attention can effectively be used in a number of applications, including voice processing; translation, where autoencoders were the go-to implementation before; and CNN to RNN, which is used for image captioning; and others.

In fact, *Attention Is All You Need* [5] is the paper where authors were able to get SOTA results by just using attention and removing all other complex network architectures like LSTMs.

Recursive neural networks

A portion of linguistic researchers would never approve of the way RNNs work, which is sequentially from left to right, though that is how many human beings read a sentence. Some people strongly believe that language has a hierarchical structure and making use of that structure helps us to solve the NLP problem easily. The recursive neural network is an attempt to solve NLP with that approach, where the sequence is arranged as a tree based on the phrases of the language to be processed. SNLI is the dataset made for this, where each sentence is arranged as a tree.

The specific recursive net we are trying to build is a SPINN, which is made by having the best of both worlds in mind. The SPINN processes data from left to right, just like how human beings read, but still keeps hierarchical flow intact. An approach of reading from left to right has another advantage over parsing it hierarchically: the network can learn eventually to generate the parse tree as it reads from left to right. This is made possible by having a special implementation called shift-reduce parser, along with the use of stack and buffer data structures.

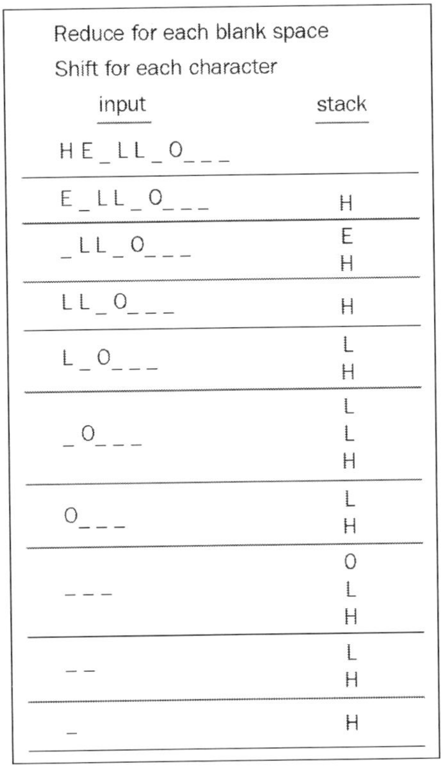

Reduce for each blank space	
Shift for each character	
input	stack
H E _ L L _ O _ _ _	
E _ L L _ O _ _ _	H
_ L L _ O _ _ _	E H
L L _ O _ _ _	H
L _ O _ _ _	L H
_ O _ _ _	L L H
O _ _ _	L H
_ _ _	O L H
_ _	L H
_	H

Figure 5.10: Shift-reduce parser

The SPINN encodes the input sentence into a fixed length vector just like how RNN-based encoders create the "meaning" vector from each sequence. Both sentences from each data points will be passed through the SPINN and create the encoded vector for each, which is then processed with the merger network and classifier network to get the scores for each of those three classes.

If you are wondering what the need is to show SPINN implementation where it is not exposing any other functional APIs of PyTorch, the answer is that a SPINN is the best example to showcase how flexible PyTorch is to fit in with any kind of neural network architecture you develop. PyTorch will never stand in your way, regardless of the architectural requirement you have in mind.

A framework built on top of a static computational graph cannot implement a network architecture like SPINN without messy hacks. This is probably the reason why all the popular frameworks built a dynamic computational graph wrapper around their core implementation, such as TensorFlow's eager, MXNet, CNTK's Gluon API, and others. We'll see how intuitive PyTorch's API is for implementing any kind of conditionals or loops into the computational graph. The SPINN is the perfect example for showcasing those.

Reduce

The reduction network takes the left-most word, right-most word, and sentence context as input and generates the single reduced output in the `forward` call. The sentence context is given by another deep network called `Tracker`. Reduce doesn't care about what is happening in the network; it accepts three inputs always and makes a reduced output out of this. A tree-LSTM, which is a variant of the standard LSTM, is used to batch the heavy operations happening in the `Reduce` network, along with other helper functions, such as `bundle` and `unbundle`.

```
class Reduce(nn.Module):

    def __init__(self, size, tracker_size=None):
        super().__init__()
        self.left = nn.Linear(size, 5 * size)
        self.right = nn.Linear(size, 5 * size, bias=False)
        if tracker_size is not None:
            self.track = nn.Linear(tracker_size, 5 * size,
bias=False)
    def forward(self, left_in, right_in, tracking=None):
        left, right = bundle(left_in), bundle(right_in)
        tracking = bundle(tracking)
        lstm_in = self.left(left[0])
        lstm_in += self.right(right[0])
        if hasattr(self, 'track'):
            lstm_in += self.track(tracking[0])
        out = unbundle(tree_lstm(left[1], right[1], lstm_in))
        return out
```

Reduce is essentially a typical neural network module that does LSTM operations on a three-argument input.

Tracker

The forward method of Tracker is called in each forward call of a SPINN in a loop. Before the reduction operation starts, we need the context vectors to be passed to the Reduce network, and hence we loop through the transition vector and create a buffer, stacks, and a context vector before doing anything in the forward() function of the SPINN. Since PyTorch variables keep track of the historical events, all these loop operations will be tracked and can be backpropagated:

```python
class Tracker(nn.Module):

    def __init__(self, size, tracker_size, predict):
        super().__init__()
        self.rnn = nn.LSTMCell(3 * size, tracker_size)
        if predict:
            self.transition = nn.Linear(tracker_size, 4)
        self.state_size = tracker_size

    def reset_state(self):
        self.state = None

    def forward(self, bufs, stacks):
        buf = bundle(buf[-1] for buf in bufs)[0]
        stack1 = bundle(stack[-1] for stack in stacks)[0]
        stack2 = bundle(stack[-2] for stack in stacks)[0]
        x = torch.cat((buf, stack1, stack2), 1)
        if self.state is None:
            self.state = 2 * [x.data.new(x.size(0),
    self.state_size).zero_()]
        self.state = self.rnn(x, self.state)
        if hasattr(self, 'transition'):
            return unbundle(self.state),
    self.transition(self.state[0])
        return unbundle(self.state), None
```

SPINN

The SPINN module is the wrapper class over all the small components. The initializer for SPINN is as simple as the initialization of the component modules Reduce and Tracker. All the heavy lifting and coordination between internal nodes is managed in the forward call of the SPINN.

```
class SPINN(nn.Module):

    def __init__(self, config):
        super().__init__()
        self.config = config
        assert config.d_hidden == config.d_proj / 2
        self.reduce = Reduce(config.d_hidden, config.d_tracker)
        self.tracker = Tracker(config.d_hidden, config.d_tracker,
                               predict=config.predict)
```

The major part of the forward call is the call on the forward method of Tracker, which will be in a loop. We loop through the input sequence and call the forward method of Tracker for each word in the sequence of transitions and save the output to the context vector list based on the transition instance. If the transition is "shift," the stack is appended with the current word and if the transition is "reduce," then Reduce will be called with trackings already created and the left-most and right-most word, which will be popped from the left and right lists.

```
def forward(self, buffers, transitions):
    buffers = [list(torch.split(b.squeeze(1), 1, 0))
               for b in torch.split(buffers, 1, 1)]
    stacks = [[buf[0], buf[0]] for buf in buffers]
    if hasattr(self, 'tracker'):
        self.tracker.reset_state()
    else:
        assert transitions is not None
    if transitions is not None:
        num_transitions = transitions.size(0)
    else:
        num_transitions = len(buffers[0]) * 2 - 3
    for i in range(num_transitions):
        if transitions is not None:
            trans = transitions[i]
        if hasattr(self, 'tracker'):
            tracker_states, trans_hyp = self.tracker(buffers,
    stacks)
            if trans_hyp is not None:
                trans = trans_hyp.max(1)[1]
        else:
```

```
        tracker_states = itertools.repeat(None)
    lefts, rights, trackings = [], [], []
    batch = zip(trans.data, buffers, stacks, tracker_states)
    for transition, buf, stack, tracking in batch:
        if transition == 3: # shift
            stack.append(buf.pop())
        elif transition == 2: # reduce
            rights.append(stack.pop())
            lefts.append(stack.pop())
            trackings.append(tracking)
    if rights:
        reduced = iter(self.reduce(lefts, rights, trackings))
        for transition, stack in zip(trans.data, stacks):
            if transition == 2:
                stack.append(next(reduced))
return bundle([stack.pop() for stack in stacks])[0]
```

Summary

Sequential data is one of the most active research fields in deep learning, especially because natural language data is sequential. But sequential data processing is not just limited to that. Time series data, which is essentially everything that happens around us, including sound, other waveforms, and more, is all sequential in nature.

The most difficult problem in processing sequence data is long-term dependency, but sequential data comes with a lot more complexities. RNNs were the breakthrough in the sequence data processing field. Thousands of different variations of RNNs have been explored by researchers and it's still an actively growing field.

In this chapter, we have gone through the basic building blocks of sequential data processing. Although we have worked only with the English language, the techniques we have learned here are generally applicable to any type of data. Understanding these building blocks is crucial for beginners because everything that comes afterward is built on top of them.

Even though I have not explained advanced topics in detail, the explanation given in the chapter should be good enough to jump into more advanced explanations and tutorials. There are different combinations of RNNs that exist and even combinations of RNNs with CNNs exist for sequence data processing. Understanding the concepts given in this book will make you start exploring different approaches that people have tried.

In the next chapter, we'll be exploring generative adversarial networks, the most recent huge development in deep learning.

References

1. https://arxiv.org/pdf/1706.03762.pdf

2. https://github.com/stanfordnlp/spinn

3. *LSTM: A Search Space Odyssey*, Greff, Klaus, Rupesh Kumar Srivastava, Jan Koutník, Bas R. Steunebrink, and Jürgen Schmidhuber, IEEE Transactions on Neural Networks and Learning Systems, Vol. 28, 2017, pp. 2222-2232, https://arxiv.org/abs/1503.04069

4. http://colah.github.io/posts/2015-08-Understanding-LSTMs/

5. *Attention Is All You Need*, Vaswani, Ashish, Noam Shazeer, Niki Parmar, Jakob Uszkoreit, Llion Jones, Aidan N. Gomez, Lukasz Kaiser, and Illia Polosukhin, NIPS, 2017

6
Generative Networks

Generative networks are backed by a famous quotation of Richard Feynman, professor of undergraduate physics at Caltech Institute of Technology and a Nobel Prize winner: *"What I cannot create, I cannot understand."* Generative networks are one of the most promising approaches to having a system that can understand the world and store knowledge within it. As their name indicates, generative networks learn the pattern of the true data distribution and try to generate new samples that look like the samples from this true data distribution.

Generative models are a subcategory of unsupervised learning since they learn the underlying pattern by trying to generate samples. They do this by pushing the low-dimensional latent vector and parameter vector to learn the important features it requires to generate the image back. The knowledge that the network acquired while generating images is essentially knowledge about the system and the environment. In a way, we deceive the network by asking it to do something, but the network has to learn what we need without it realizing that it is learning.

Generative networks have shown promising results in different deep learning areas, especially in computer vision. Deblurring or increasing the resolution of the image, image inpainting for filling missing pieces, denoising audio clips, generating speech from text, autoreplying to messages, and generating images/videos from text are some of the active areas of research.

In this chapter, we'll discuss some of the major generative network architectures. More precisely, we'll see one autoregressive model and one **generative adversarial network (GAN)**. First, we'll understand what the fundamental building blocks of both architectures are and how they are different from each other. Along with this explanation, we'll run through some examples and PyTorch code.

Defining the approaches

Generative networks are mostly used in artistic applications nowadays. Style transfer, image optimization, deblurring, resolution improvements, and others are some examples. What follows are two examples of generative models being used in computer vision.

Figure 6.1: Examples of generative model applications such as super resolution and image inpainting
Sources: *Generative Image Inpainting with Contextual Attention,* Jiahui Yu and others and *Photo-Realistic Single Image Super-Resolution Using a Generative Adversarial Network,* Christian Ledig and others

There are several categories of generative networks described by Ian Goodfellow, the creator of GANs:

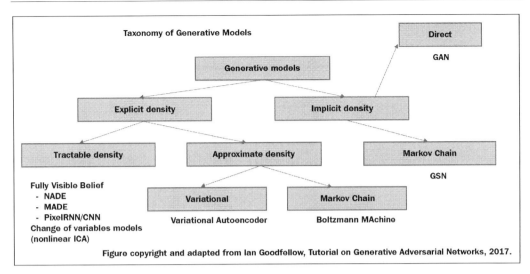

Figure 6.2 Generative network hierarchy

We'll be discussing two major categories that have been discussed a lot in the past and are still active research fields:

- Autoregressive models
- GANs

Autoregressive models are models where the current value is inferred from the previous values, as we discussed in *Chapter 5, Sequential Data Processing*, with RNNs. A **variational autoencoder (VAE)** is a variant of autoencoders that is composed of an encoder and decoder, where the encoder encodes the input into a low-dimensional latent space vector and the decoder decodes the latent vector to generate output similar to the input.

The whole research community agrees that GANs are one of the next big things in the artificial intelligence world. A GAN has a generative network and an adversarial network, and both of them fight each other to generate a high-quality output image. Both GANs and autoregressive models work based on different principles, but each approach has its own advantages and disadvantages. We'll develop one basic example from both approaches in this chapter.

Autoregressive models

Autoregressive models use information from the previous steps and create the next output. RNNs generating text for a language modeling task is a typical example of the autoregressive model.

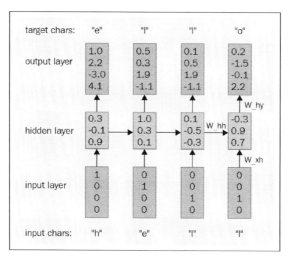

Figure 6.3: Autoregressive model for RNN language modeling

Autoregressive models generate the first input independently, or we give this to the network. For example, in the case of RNNs, we give the first word to the network and the network uses the first word we provided to assume what the second word would be. Then it uses the first and second word to predict the third word and so on.

Although most generation tasks are done on images, our autoregressive generation is on audio. We will build WaveNet, a research result from Google DeepMind, which is the current state-of-the-art implementation of audio generation and especially for text-to-speech processing. Through this, we'll be exploring what the PyTorch APIs for audio processing are. But before looking at WaveNet, we need to implement the foundation block of WaveNet called PixelCNN, which is built on autoregressive **convolutional neural networks (CNNs)**.

Autoregressive models have been used and explored a lot, since each prevalent approach has its own downsides. A major drawback of autoregressive models is their speed, since they generate output sequentially. This becomes worse in PixelRNN, since the forward pass is also sequential.

PixelCNN

Figure 6.4: Images generated from PixelCNN
Source: *Conditional Image Generation with PixelCNN Decoders*, Aäron van den Oord and others

PixelCNN was introduced by DeepMind and it was among the three autoregressive models that DeepMind introduced. There have been several iterations after the first introduction of PixelCNN to improve speed and efficiency, but we'll be going through the basic PixelCNN, which is what we need to build WaveNet.

PixelCNN generates one pixel at a time and uses that to generate the next pixel, and then uses the previous two pixels to generate the next. In PixelCNN, there is a probabilistic density model that can learn the density distribution of all images and generate the images from the distribution. But here, we are trying to condition each pixel generated on all the previously generated pixels by taking the joint probability of all the previous predictions.

Unlike PixelRNN, PixelCNN uses convolutional layers as receptive fields, which improves the reading time of the input. Consider an image partially occluded by something; let's say we only have half of the image. So, we have half of an image and our algorithm needs to generate the second half. While in PixelRNN the network needs to get each pixel one by one, just like a sequence of words, for half of the image and will generate the second half one by one, PixelCNN gets the image in a single shot through the convolutional layer. However, the generation in PixelCNN has to be sequential anyway. You might be wondering how only half of the image goes to convolution; the answer is masked convolution, which we'll be explaining later.

Figure 6.5 shows how the convolution operation is applied on the set of pixels to predict the center pixel. The main advantage of the autoregressive model over other models is that the joint probability learning technique is tractable and can be learned using gradient descent. There is no approximation and there is no workaround; we just try to predict each pixel value given all the previous pixel values and training is completely backed by backpropagation. However, we struggle with scalability using autoregressive models since the generation is always sequential. PixelCNN is a well-architected model to take the product of individual probabilities as joint probabilities of all the previous pixels, while generating new pixels. In an RNN model, this is the default behavior, but the CNN model achieves this by using a cleverly designed mask, as mentioned previously.

PixelCNN captures the distribution of dependencies between pixels in the parameters, which is unlike the other approaches. VAEs learn this distribution by generating the hidden latent vector, which introduces independent assumptions. In PixelCNN, the dependencies learned are not just between the previous pixels but also between the different channels; in a normal color image, it is red, green, and blue (RGB).

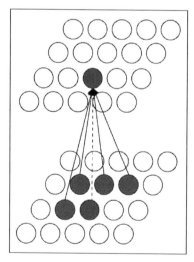

Figure 6.5: Predicting pixel value from surrounding pixels

There is a fundamental problem: what if the CNN tries to use the current pixel or the future pixels to learn the current pixel? This is also managed by the mask, which takes the granularity of **self** to the channel level also. For instance, the current pixel's red channel won't learn from the current pixel but will learn from previous pixels. But the green channel can now use the current red channel and all the previous pixels. Similarly, the blue channel can learn from both the green and red channel of the current pixel, as well as all the previous pixels.

There are two types of masks used in the whole network, but the later layers don't need to have this security, although they still need to emulate the sequential learning while doing the parallel convolution operation. So, the PixelCNN paper [1] introduces two types of masks: type A and type B.

One major architectural difference that makes PixelCNN stand out from other traditional CNN models is the absence of the pooling layers. Since the aim of the PixelCNN is not capturing the essence of the image in a dimensionally reduced form and we cannot afford losing context through pooling, the authors deliberately removed the pooling layer.

```
fm = 64

net = nn.Sequential(
    MaskedConv2d('A', 1, fm, 7, 1, 3, bias=False),
    nn.BatchNorm2d(fm), nn.ReLU(True),
    MaskedConv2d('B', fm, fm, 7, 1, 3, bias=False),
    nn.BatchNorm2d(fm), nn.ReLU(True),
    MaskedConv2d('B', fm, fm, 7, 1, 3, bias=False),
    nn.BatchNorm2d(fm), nn.ReLU(True),
    MaskedConv2d('B', fm, fm, 7, 1, 3, bias=False),
    nn.BatchNorm2d(fm), nn.ReLU(True),
    MaskedConv2d('B', fm, fm, 7, 1, 3, bias=False),
    nn.BatchNorm2d(fm), nn.ReLU(True),
    MaskedConv2d('B', fm, fm, 7, 1, 3, bias=False),
    nn.BatchNorm2d(fm), nn.ReLU(True),
    MaskedConv2d('B', fm, fm, 7, 1, 3, bias=False),
    nn.BatchNorm2d(fm), nn.ReLU(True),
    MaskedConv2d('B', fm, fm, 7, 1, 3, bias=False),
    nn.BatchNorm2d(fm), nn.ReLU(True),
    nn.Conv2d(fm, 256, 1))
```

The preceding code snippet is the complete PixelCNN model, which is wrapped inside a sequential unit. It consists of a bunch of MaskedConv2d instances, which is inherited from torch.nn.Conv2d and uses all the *args and **kwargs of Conv2d from torch.nn. Each convolution unit is followed by a batch norm layer and ReLU layer, which is known to be a successful combination with convolution layers. Instead of using a linear layer at the final layer, the authors decided to use a normal two-dimensional convolution, which is proven to work better than a linear layer.

Masked convolution

Masked convolution is used in PixelCNN to prevent information flow from the future and current pixel to the generation task while training the network. This is essential because while generating the pixels, we don't have access to the future pixels or current pixel. However, there is one exception, which was described previously. The generation of the current green channel value can use the prediction of the red channel and the generation of the current blue channel can use the prediction of both the green and red channels.

Masking is done by zeroing out all the pixels that are not required. A mask tensor of equivalent size to the size of the kernel with values 1 and 0 will be created, which has 0 for all the unnecessary pixels. This mask tensor then multiplies with the weight tensor before doing the convolution operation.

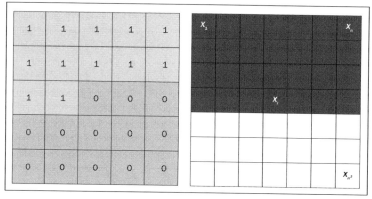

Figure 6.6: On the left is the mask and on the right is the context in PixelCNN

Since PixelCNN doesn't use pooling layers and deconvolution layers, the channel size should remain constant as the flow progresses. While mask A is solely responsible for preventing the network from learning the value from the current pixel, mask B keeps the channel size to three (RGB) and allows more flexibility in the network by allowing the current pixel value depending on its own value as well.

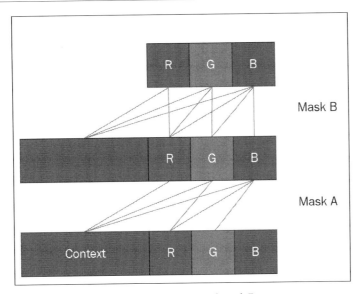

Figure 6.7: Mask A and mask B

```
class MaskedConv2d(nn.Conv2d):
    def __init__(self, mask_type, *args, **kwargs):
        super().__init__(*args, **kwargs)
        assert mask_type in ('A', 'B')
        self.register_buffer('mask', self.weight.data.clone())
        _, _, kH, kW = self.weight.size()
        self.mask.fill_(1)
        self.mask[:, :, kH // 2, kW // 2 + (mask_type == 'B'):] =
        0
        self.mask[:, :, kH // 2 + 1:] = 0

    def forward(self, x):
        self.weight.data *= self.mask
        return super(MaskedConv2d, self).forward(x)
```

The preceding class `MaskedConv2d` is inherited from `torch.nn.Conv2d` instead of being inherited from `torch.nn.Module`. Even though we inherit from `torch.nn.Module` to create a custom model class normally, since we are trying to make `Conv2d` enhance the operation with the mask, we inherit from `torch.nn.Conv2D`, which is in turn being inherited from `torch.nn.Module`. The class method `register_buffer` is one of the convenient APIs that PyTorch provides to add any tensors to the `state_dict` dictionary object, which in turn gets saved to the disk along with the model if you try to save the model to disk.

The obvious way of adding a stateful variable, which can then be reused in the `forward` function, would be to add that as the object attribute:

```
self.mask = self.weight.data.clone()
```

But this would never be part of the `state_dict` and would never be saved to disk. With `register_buffer`, we can make sure that the new tensor we have created will be part of `state_dict`. The mask tensor is then filled with 1s using the in-place `fill_` operation and then has 0 added to it to get a tensor like in *Figure 6.6*, although the figure shows only a two-dimension tensor, where the actual weight tensor is three-dimensional. The `forward` function is just for masking the weight tensor by multiplying with the mask tensor. The multiplication keeps all the values corresponding to the index where the mask had 1, while deleting all the values corresponding to the index where the mask had 0. Then a normal call to the parent `Conv2d` layer uses the weight tensor and does the two-dimensional convolution.

The final layer of the network is a softmax layer, which predicts the value among 256 possible values of a pixel and hence discretizes the output generation of the network, while the previous state-of-the-art autoregressive model used continues value generation at the final layer.

```
optimizer = optim.Adam(net.parameters())
for epoch in range(25):
    net.train(True)
    for input, _ in tr:
        target = (input[:,0] * 255).long()
        out = net(input)
        loss = F.cross_entropy(out, target)
        optimizer.zero_grad()
        loss.backward()
        optimizer.step()
```

Training uses the `Adam` optimizer with default momentum rate. Also, the loss function is created from the `Functional` module of PyTorch. Everything else remains the same as for a normal training operation other than the creation of the `target` variable.

Until now, we had worked with supervised learning, where the labels are given explicitly, but in this case, the target is the same as the input, since we are trying to re-create the same output. The `torchvision` package applies transformation and normalization to the pixels and converts the pixel value ranges from 0 to 255 to -1 to 1. We need to convert back to the 0 to 255 range since we are using softmax at the final layer, and that generates probability distribution over 0 to 255.

Gated PixelCNN

Gated PixelCNN was successfully used by DeepMind in one of the iterative papers of PixelCNN by replacing the ReLU activation function with gates built with sigmoid and tanh. The introductory paper to PixelCNN [1] has three different approaches used for solving the same generation network, where the model with the RNN outperformed the other two. DeepMind still introduced a CNN-based model to show the speed gain compared to PixelRNN. However, with the introduction of gated activation in PixelCNN, the authors were able to match the performance to the RNN variant with greater performance gain. The same paper introduced a mechanism for avoiding the blind spot and adding global and local conditioning on generation, which is out of the scope of this book since that is not necessary for the WaveNet model.

WaveNet

DeepMind introduced WaveNet in another iterative paper [2] for its autoregressive generation networks, which include PixelCNN. In fact, the WaveNet architecture is built on the foundation of PixelCNN, which enables the network to generate output in a relatively faster manner compared to PixelRNN. With WaveNet, we are exploring neural network implementation on audio signals for the first time in the book. We use one-dimensional convolution on audio signals, unlike the two-dimensional convolution of PixelCNN, which is fairly complicated for a beginner to wrap their head around.

WaveNet replaces traditional approaches of using Fourier transformation on audio signals. It does this by making a neural network figure out what transformation to do. So, the transformation becomes backpropagatable and the raw audio data become processable with some techniques like dilated convolution, 8-bit quantization, and others. But people have been doing research on mixing the WaveNet approach with traditional methods, though that converts the loss function to multivariate regression instead of classification, which is what WaveNet uses.

PyTorch exposes the APIs for such traditional methods with a backward pass. What follows is an example of doing fast Fourier transform and inverse Fourier transform on the result of a Fourier transform to get the actual input back. Both operations are on the two-dimensional tensor with the last dimension as two, representing the real and imaginary components of complex numbers.

PyTorch gives an API for fast Fourier transform (`torch.fft`), inverse fast Fourier transform (`torch.ifft`), real-to-complex Fourier transform (`torch.rfft`), inverse of real-to-complex Fourier transform (`torch.irfft`), short-time Fourier transform (`torch.stft`), and several window functions such as Hann window, Hamming window, and Bartlett window.

```
>>> x = torch.ones(3,2)
>>> x


 1 1
 1 1
 1 1
[torch.FloatTensor of size (3,2)]


>>> torch.fft(x, 1)


 3 3
 0 0
 0 0
[torch.FloatTensor of size (3,2)]


>>> fft_x = torch.fft(x, 1)
>>> torch.ifft(fft_x, 1)


 1 1
 1 1
 1 1
[torch.FloatTensor of size (3,2)]
```

WaveNet was not the first architecture that introduced the convolution network of sequence data or dilated convolution network for speeding up an operation. But WaveNet succeeded in using both to hit the sweet spot of generating distinguishable audio. The authors of the first WaveNet had released another iterative paper, which sped up the generation to a great extent, called parallel WaveNet. But we will be focusing on the normal WaveNet in this chapter, which is inspired by golbin's repository.

The fundamental building block of WaveNet is dilated convolution, which replaces the RNN's functionality to get the context information.

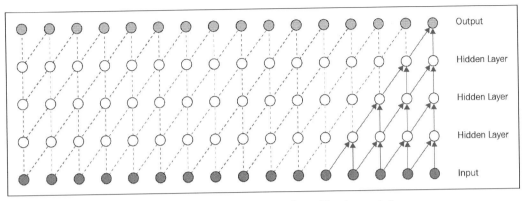

Figure 6.8: WaveNet architecture without dilated convolution
Source: *WaveNet: A Generative Model for Raw Audio*, Aaron van den Oord and others

Figure 6.8 shows how WaveNet pulls the information about the context while working on a new value prediction. The input is given in blue (the bottom layer in the picture), which is raw audio sa mples. For instance, an audio sample of 16 kHz has 16,000 data points for one second of audio, which is humungous if compared to the sequence length of natural language, where each word would be one data point. These long sequences are one good reason why RNNs are not quite effective for raw audio samples.

A practical sequence length for which an LSTM network could remember the context information is 50 to 100. The previous figure has three hidden layers that use information from the previous layer. The first layer input is passed through a one-dimensional convolution layer to generate the data for the second layer. Convolution can be done in parallel, unlike the case with RNNs, where each data point needs the previous input to pass through it sequentially. For collecting more context, we can just increase the number of layers. In *Figure 6.8*, the output, which is in the fourth layer, will get context information from five nodes in the input layer. So, each layer adds one more input node to the context; that is, if we had 10 hidden layers, the final layer would get context information from 12 input nodes.

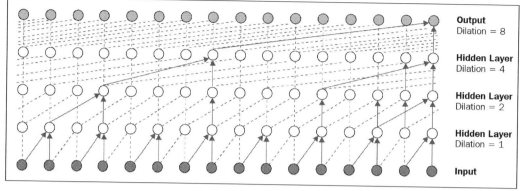

Figure 6.9: Dilated convolution
Source: *WaveNet: A Generative Model for Raw Audio*, Aaron van den Oord and others

By now, it should be obvious that to achieve the practical limit of an LSTM network's context-holding capacity of 50 to 100, the network needs 98 layers, which is computationally expensive. This is where we use dilated convolution. With dilated convolution, we'll have a dilation factor for each layer, and increasing that exponentially will reduce the number of layers needed for any specific context window width logarithmically.

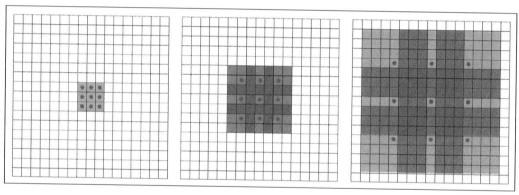

Figure 6.10: Convolutions with dilations 0, 2, and 4
Source: *Multi-scale Context Aggregation By Dilated Convolutions*, Fisher Yu and Vladlen Koltun

Figure 6.9 shows the dilated convolution scheme used in WaveNet (although to understand dilated convolution better, we are using a two-dimensional picture here; WaveNet uses one-dimensional convolution). Although the implementation skips the log of the parameter in between, the final node still gets information from all the nodes in the context with this cleverly designed scheme. With dilated convolution and three hidden layers, the previous implementation covers 16 input nodes, while the previous implementation without dilated convolution covered only five.

```
dilatedcausalconv = torch.nn.Conv1d(
                                    res_channels,
                                    res_channels,
                                    kernel_size=2,
                                    dilation=dilation,
                                    padding=0,
                                    bias=False)
```

The implementation of the dilated convolution can be explained visually with the two-dimensional picture given in *Figure 6.10*. All the three examples use a kernel of size 3x3, where the leftmost block shows the normal convolution or dilated convolution with a dilation factor equal to zero. The middle block is with the same kernel but with a dilation factor of two, and the last block is with a dilation factor of four. The implementation trick of dilated convolution is to add zeros in between the kernel to expand the size of the kernel, as shown in *Figure 6.11*:

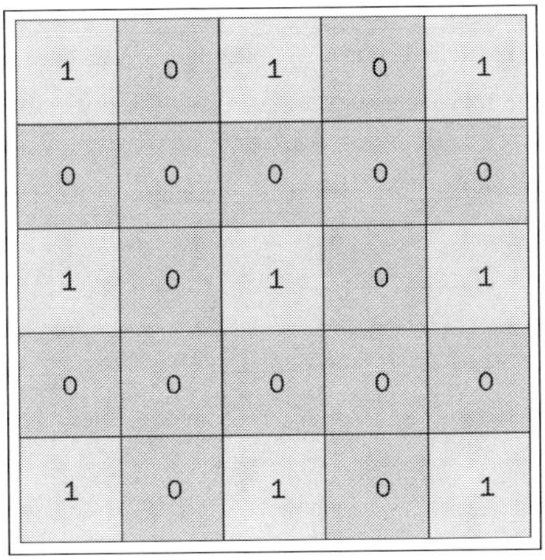

Figure 6.11: Dilated convolution with kernel expansion

PyTorch makes it easy to do dilated convolution by enabling the user to pass dilation as a keyword parameter, as given in the `dilatedcausalconv1d` node in the preceding code block. As described before, each layer has a different dilation factor and that can be passed for the dilated convolution node creation for each layer. Padding is kept as 0 since stride is 1 and the aim is not to upsample or downsample. `init_weights_for_test` is a convenience function made for testing by filling the weight matrix with 1.

The flexibility PyTorch offers enables users to tweak the parameters online, and this is much more useful for debugging the network.

The `forward` pass is just calling the PyTorch `Conv1d` object, which is a callable and saved in the `self.conv` variable:

```
causalconv = torch.nn.Conv1d(
                            in_channels,
                            res_channels,
                            kernel_size=2,
                            padding=1,
                            bias=False)
```

The complete architecture of WaveNet is built on top of the foundation of the dilated convolution network and the gated activation after the convolution. The data flow in WaveNet starts with the causal convolution operation, which is a normal one-dimensional convolution, which is then passed to the dilated convolution node. Each white circle in the WaveNet picture (*Figure 6.9*) is a dilated convolution node. The normally convoluted data point is then passed to the dilated convolution node, which is then passed through the sigmoid gate and tanh activation independently. The output of two operations then goes through a pointwise multiplication operator and a 1x1 convolution. WaveNet uses residual connection and skip connection to smoothen the data flow. The residual thread running parallel to the main flow merges with the output of 1x1 convolution through an addition operation.

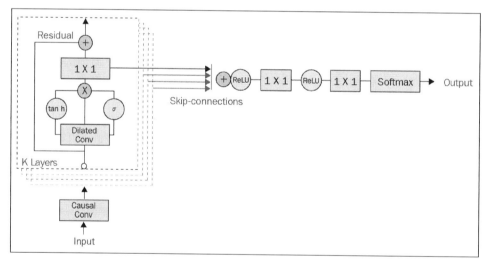

Figure 6.12: WaveNet architecture
Source: *WaveNet: A Generative Model for Raw Audio*, Aaron van den Oord and others

The architectural diagram of WaveNet given in *Figure 6.12* shows all these small components and how they are connected together. The portion after the skip connection is called a dense layer in the program, though it is not the dense layer introduced in the previous chapter.

Normally, the dense layer represents a fully connected layer to introduce non-linearity to the network and get the overview of all the data. But WaveNet's authors found that a normal dense layer can be replaced by a chain of ReLUs and that 1x1 convolution achieves more accuracy with a softmax layer at the end, which fans out to 256 units (8-bit μ-law quantization of a huge fanout of audio frequencies).

```
class WaveNet(torch.nn.Module):
    def __init__(self, layer_size, stack_size, in_channels, res_
channels):
        super().__init__()
        self.rf_size = sum([2 ** i for i in range(layer_size)] *
stack_size)
        self.causalconv = torch.nn.Conv1d(
            in_channels, res_channels, kernel_size=2, padding=1,
bias=False)
        self.res_stack = ResidualStack(
            layer_size, stack_size, res_channels, in_channels)
        self.final_conv = FinalConv(in_channels)


    def forward(self, x):
        x = x.transpose(1, 2)
        sample_size = x.size(2)
        out_size = sample_size - self.rf_size
        if out_size < 1:
            print('Sample size has to be more than receptive field size')
        else:
            x = self.causalconv(x)[:, :, :-1]
            skip_connections = self.res_stack(x, out_size)
            x = torch.sum(skip_connections, dim=0)
            x = self.final_conv(x)
            return x.transpose(1, 2).contiguous()
```

The program given in the preceding code block is the main parent WaveNet module, which uses all the child components to create the graph. init defines the three major components, which are the first normal convolution, then res_stack, which is the residual connection block that consists of all the dilated convolution, and the sigmoid-tanh gates. Then the final_conv is made on top of the 1x1 convolution. forward executes these modules sequentially with the introduction of one summation node. The output created by final_conv is then moved to a single block of the memory with contiguous(). This is required for the rest of the network.

One module that needs more explanation is ResidualStack, which is the core of the WaveNet architecture. ResidualStack is the stack of layers of ResidualBlock. Each small circle in the WaveNet picture is one residual block. After the normal convolution, the data comes to ResidualBlock as it is described previously.

ResidualBlock starts with the dilated convolution and it expects to get the dilation. So, ResidualBlock decides what the dilation factor of each of those small circle nodes in the architecture should be. As described before, the output for the dilated convolution is then passed through the gates similar to the gate we saw in PixelCNN.

After that, it has to go through two separate convolutions for the skip connection and residual connection. Although the authors did not explain this as two separate convolutions, it is much easier to understand with two separate convolutions.

```
class ResidualBlock(torch.nn.Module):
    def __init__(self, res_channels, skip_channels, dilation=1):
        super().__init__()
        self.dilatedcausalconv = torch.nn.Conv1d(
            res_channels, res_channels, kernel_size=2,
dilation=dilation,
            padding=0, bias=False)
        self.conv_res = torch.nn.Conv1d(res_channels, res_channels, 1)
        self.conv_skip = torch.nn.Conv1d(res_channels, skip_channels, 1)
        self.gate_tanh = torch.nn.Tanh()
        self.gate_sigmoid = torch.nn.Sigmoid()

    def forward(self, x, skip_size):
        x = self.dilatedcausalconv(x)

        # PixelCNN Gate
        # --------------------------
        gated_tanh = self.gate_tanh(x)
        gated_sigmoid = self.gate_sigmoid(x)
        gated = gated_tanh * gated_sigmoid
        # --------------------------

        x = self.conv_res(gated)
        x += x[:, :, -x.size(2):]
        skip = self.conv_skip(gated)[:, :, -skip_size:]
        return x, skip
```

ResidualStack uses the count of layers and count of stacks to create the dilation factor. Generally, each layer has 2^l as the dilation factor, where l is the number of the layer. Each stack has the same number of layers and the same pattern of dilation factor list starting from 1 to 2^l.

The method stack_res_block uses ResidualBlock, which we described previously, to create a residual block for each node in each stack and in each layer. We could introduce nn.DataParellel, a new PyTorch API, for parallelism if multiple GPUs are available.

Making the model a data-parallel model lets PyTorch know that the user has more GPU to use and PyTorch takes it from there without giving any more hurdles to the user. PyTorch divides the data into as many numbers of GPUs available and executes the model separately in each GPU in parallel.

It is also responsible for collecting the result back from each GPU and merges this together before proceeding further.

```
class ResidualStack(torch.nn.Module):
    def __init__(self, layer_size, stack_size, res_channels,
    skip_channels):
        super().__init__()
        self.res_blocks = torch.nn.ModuleList()
        for s in range(stack_size):
            for l in range(layer_size):
                dilation = 2 ** l
                block = ResidualBlock(res_channels, skip_channels,
                        dilation)
                self.res_blocks.append(block)

    def forward(self, x, skip_size):
        skip_connections = []
        for res_block in self.res_blocks:
            x, skip = res_block(x, skip_size)
            skip_connections.append(skip)
        return torch.stack(skip_connections)
```

GANs

GANs are one of the major inventions of the last decade in the opinion of lots of deep learning researchers. They are inherently different from other generative networks, especially with the way that they are trained. The first paper about adversarial networks for generating data appeared in 2014, authored by Ian Goodfellow. GANs are considered as an unsupervised learning algorithm where a supervised learning algorithm learns to reason the function $y'=f(x)$ with labeled data, y.

This type of supervised learning algorithm is inherently discriminatory, which means that it learns to model the conditional probability distribution function where it says what the probability of something is given the state of something else.

For instance, what's the probability of the location of a house if the price for buying that house is $100,000? GANs generate output from random distribution and hence the change in the random input lets the output be different.

GANs get the sample from a random distribution, which is then converted to the output by the network. GANs are not supervised in learning the pattern of the input distribution, and unlike other generative networks, GANs won't try to learn a density distribution explicitly. Instead, they use the game theory approach to find the Nash equilibrium between two players. A GAN implementation will always have a generative network and an adversarial network, which are considered as two players trying to beat each other. The core idea of GANs lies in sampling from a data distribution, like uniform or Gaussian, and letting the network convert the sample to a true data distribution-like sample. We will implement a simple GAN to understand the working principle of GANs and then move to an advanced GAN implementation called CycleGAN.

Simple GAN

The intuitive approach to understanding GAN is to understand it from a game theory perspective. A GAN, as briefed, consist of two players, a generator and a discriminator, each trying to beat the other. The generator gets some random noise from a distribution and tries to generate some output distribution from it. The generator always tries to create a distribution that is indistinguishable from true distribution; that is, the fake output should look like it is a real image.

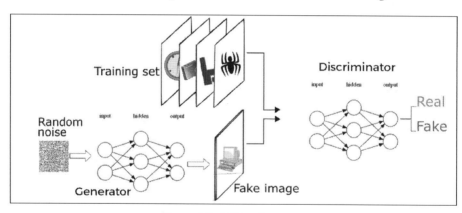

Figure 6.13: GAN architecture

However, without explicit training or labels, the generator has no way to figure out what real images would look like, and the only source it has is a tensor of random floating point numbers. The GAN then introduces the second player to the game, which is a discriminator. The discriminator is only responsible for informing the generator that the generated output doesn't look like a real image, so that the generator changes the way it generates the image to convince the discriminator that it is a real image.

But the discriminator can always tell the generator that an image is not real because the discriminator knows it is generated from the generator. This is where things get interesting. The GAN introduces the actual, real images to the game and isolates the discriminator from the generator. Now the discriminator gets an image from the set of real images and also a fake image from the generator, and the discriminator has to figure out the source of each image. Initially, the discriminator doesn't know anything and predicts random results.

```python
class DiscriminatorNet(torch.nn.Module):
    """
    A three hidden-layer discriminative neural network
    """
    def __init__(self):
        super().__init__()
        n_features = 784
        n_out = 1

        self.hidden0 = nn.Sequential(
            nn.Linear(n_features, 1024),
            nn.LeakyReLU(0.2),
            nn.Dropout(0.3)
        )
        self.hidden1 = nn.Sequential(
            nn.Linear(1024, 512),
            nn.LeakyReLU(0.2),
            nn.Dropout(0.3)
        )
        self.hidden2 = nn.Sequential(
            nn.Linear(512, 256),
            nn.LeakyReLU(0.2),
            nn.Dropout(0.3)
        )
        self.out = nn.Sequential(
            torch.nn.Linear(256, n_out),
            torch.nn.Sigmoid()
        )

    def forward(self, x):
        x = self.hidden0(x)
        x = self.hidden1(x)
        x = self.hidden2(x)
        x = self.out(x)
        return x
```

However, the discriminator's task can be modified to be a classification task. The discriminator could classify the input image as **original** or **generated**, which is binary classification. Also, we train the discriminator network to classify images correctly and eventually, through backpropagation, the discriminator learns to discriminate between the real image and generated image.

The example used in this session will generate MNIST-like output. The preceding code shows the discriminator player on MNIST, which always gets an image either from the real source dataset or from the generator. GANs are notoriously unstable and hence using LeakyReLU is one of the hacks researchers have found works better than normal ReLU. Now, LeakyReLU leaks the negative end through it instead of capping everything under zero to zero. This helps with flowing the gradient through the network better than normal ReLU, which has zero gradient for values less than zero.

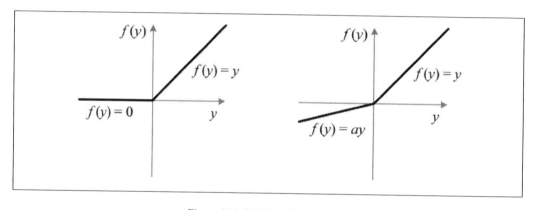

Figure 6.14: ReLU and leaky ReLU

The simple discriminator that we develop has three sequential layers. Each has a linear layer, leaky ReLU, and a dropout layer sandwiched together, which is followed by a linear layer and a sigmoid gate. Normally, the probability prediction network uses a softmax layer as the last layer; a simple GAN like this works best with a sigmoid layer.

```
def train_discriminator(optimizer, real_data, fake_data):
    optimizer.zero_grad()

    # 1.1 Train on Real Data
    prediction_real = discriminator(real_data)
    # Calculate error and backpropagate
    error_real = loss(prediction_real,
                real_data_target(real_data.size(0)))
    error_real.backward()
```

```
# 1.2 Train on Fake Data
prediction_fake = discriminator(fake_data)
# Calculate error and backpropagate
error_fake = loss(prediction_fake,
            fake_data_target(real_data.size(0)))
error_fake.backward()

# 1.3 Update weights with gradients
optimizer.step()

# Return error
return error_real + error_fake, prediction_real,
prediction_fake
```

The function `train_generator` defined in the preceding code block accepts the `optimizer` object, fake data, and real data, which is then passed through the discriminator. The function `fake_data_target` (given in the following code block) creates a zero tensor of the same size as the prediction size, where the prediction is the returned value from the discriminator. The training strategy for the discriminator is to maximize the probability that any real data is classified as belonging to the true distribution and to minimize the probability that any data point is classified as belonging to the true distribution. In practice, a log of the result from the discriminator or the generator is used, since that penalizes the network heavily for incorrect classification. The error is then backpropagated before applying the `optimizer. step` function, which updates the weights with gradients through the learning rate.

Functions for getting the real data target and fake data target are given next, which is essentially aligned with the concept of minimizing or maximizing the probability discussed previously. The real data generator returns a tensor with 1s and of the shape we passed as input. When the generator is being trained, we are trying to maximize the probability of it by generating an image, which should look like it is taken from the true data distribution. This means the discriminator should predict 1 as the confidence score that an image is from the true distribution.

```
def real_data_target(size):
    '''
    Tensor containing ones, with shape = size
    '''
    data = torch.ones(size, 1)
    if torch.cuda.is_available(): return data.cuda()
    return data

def fake_data_target(size):
    '''
```

```
        Tensor containing zeros, with shape = size
        '''
        data = torch.zeros(size, 1)
        if torch.cuda.is_available(): return data.cuda()
        return data
```

So, the discriminator implementation is done with easy flow, since it is essentially just a classification task. The generator network would be a bit complex with all the convolutional upsampling/downsampling involved. But for the current example, since we want it to be as simple as possible, we'll be working on fully connected networks and not convolutional networks.

```
    def noise(size):
        n = torch.randn(size, 100)
        if torch.cuda.is_available(): return n.cuda()
        return n
```

A noise generation function can be defined, which can generate random samples (this sampling is proven to be efficient with a Gaussian rather than random distribution, but we use a random distribution here for simplicity). We transport the random generated noise from CPU memory to GPU memory if CUDA is available and return the tensor with the output size as 100. So, the generative network expects the input noise to have 100 as the number of features and we know the MNIST dataset has 784 data points in it (28x28).

For the generator, we have a similar structure as we had for the discriminator but with a tanh layer at the last layer instead of sigmoid. This change is to synchronize with the normalization we did on the MNIST data to convert it to the range of -1 to 1 so that the discriminator always gets the dataset with data points in the same range. Each of the three layers in the generator upsamples the input noise to an output size of 784, just like how we downsampled it in the discriminator for classification.

```
    class GeneratorNet(torch.nn.Module):
        """
        A three hidden-layer generative neural network
        """
        def __init__(self):
            super().__init__()
            n_features = 100
            n_out = 784

            self.hidden0 = nn.Sequential(
                nn.Linear(n_features, 256),
                nn.LeakyReLU(0.2)
            )
            self.hidden1 = nn.Sequential(
                nn.Linear(256, 512),
```

```
            nn.LeakyReLU(0.2)
        )
        self.hidden2 = nn.Sequential(
            nn.Linear(512, 1024),
            nn.LeakyReLU(0.2)
        )

        self.out = nn.Sequential(
            nn.Linear(1024, n_out),
            nn.Tanh()
        )

    def forward(self, x):
        x = self.hidden0(x)
        x = self.hidden1(x)
        x = self.hidden2(x)
        x = self.out(x)
        return x
```

The generator trainer function is much simpler than the discriminator trainer function, since it doesn't get input from two sources and doesn't have to train for different purposes, whereas the discriminator had to maximize the probability of classifying a real image as a real image and minimize the probability of classifying the noise image as a real image. This function accepts only the fake image data and the optimizer where the fake image is the image generated by the generator. The generator trainer function code can be found in the GitHub repository.

We create the instances of the discriminator and generator networks separately. Until now, all of our network implementation had a single model or single neural network, but for the first time, we have two separate networks working on the same dataset with different goals to optimize. With two separate networks, we need to create two separate optimizers also. Historically, the Adam optimizer has worked best for GANs with a very slow learning rate.

Both the networks are trained with the output from the discriminator. The only difference is that while training the discriminator, we try to minimize the probability of the fake image being classified as a real image, and while training the generator, we try to maximize the probability of the fake image being classified as a real image. Since it is always a binary classifier trying to predict 0 and 1, we use BCELoss from torch.nn, which tries to predict 0 or 1:

```
discriminator = DiscriminatorNet()
generator = GeneratorNet()
d_optimizer = optim.Adam(discriminator.parameters(), lr=0.0002)
g_optimizer = optim.Adam(generator.parameters(), lr=0.0002)
loss = nn.BCELoss()
```

What follows is the output generated by the simple GAN in different epochs, which shows how the network learned to map the input random distribution to the output true distribution.

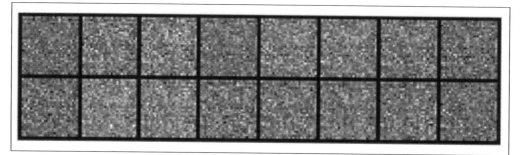

Figure 6.15: Output after 100 epochs

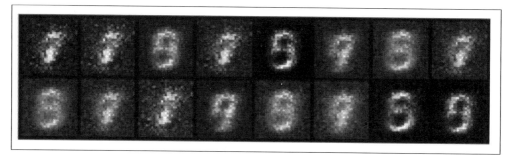

Figure 6.16: Output after 200 epochs

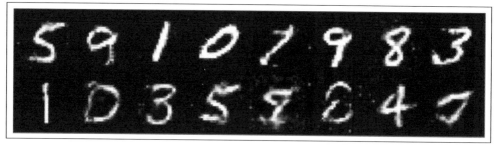

Figure 6.17: Output after 300 epochs

CycleGAN

Figure 6.18: CycleGAN in practice

Source: *Unpaired Image-to-Image Translationusing Cycle-Consistent Adversarial Networks*, Jun-Yan Zhu and others

CycleGAN is one of the smart variants of the GAN genre. A cleverly designed cyclical flow between two GANs in the same architecture teaches the mapping between two different distributions. Previous approaches required pairs of images from different distributions for the network to learn the mapping. For example, if the aim is to build a network that can convert black-and-white images to color, the dataset needs a black-and-white and color version of the same image as a pair in the training set. This is possible to an extent, although difficult. However, if the aim is to make an image that is taken in winter look like it's taken in summer, the pair of images in the training set needs to be the exact same image with the same objects and same frame taken in winter and summer. This is quite impossible, and that's where CycleGAN could help.

CycleGAN learns the pattern of each distribution and tries to map an image from one distribution to another distribution. A simple architectural diagram of CycleGAN is given in *Figure 6.19*. The diagram on top shows how to train one GAN and the diagram on the bottom shows how to train another with the canonical example of CycleGAN at work: horse and zebra.

In CycleGAN, instead of starting with randomly sampled data from a distribution, we use a real image from set A, which is in this case a set of horses. Generator A to B (we call it A2B) is delegated to convert the same horse to a zebra, but without a paired image of a horse converted into a zebra. When the training starts, A2B generates a meaningless image.

Discriminator B gets either the image generated by A2B or a real image from set B, which is the set of zebras. Just like any other discriminator, it is responsible for predicting whether the image is generated or real. This process is the normal GAN and it never guarantees the conversion of the same horse to a zebra; rather, it converts an image of a horse to any image of a zebra, since the loss is just to make sure that the image looks like the set B distribution; it doesn't need any correlation with set A. To impose that correlation, CycleGAN introduces the cycle.

The generated image from A2B is then passed through another generator, B2A, to get Cyclic_A. The loss being applied to Cyclic_A is the crucial part of the CycleGAN. Here we try to reduce the distance between Cyclic_A and Input_A. The idea behind this second loss is that the second generator must be able to generate the horse back, since the distribution we started with was a horse. If A2B knows how to map a horse to zebra without changing anything else in the picture, and if the B2A knows how to map a zebra to a horse without changing anything else in the picture, this assumption we made about the loss should be correct.

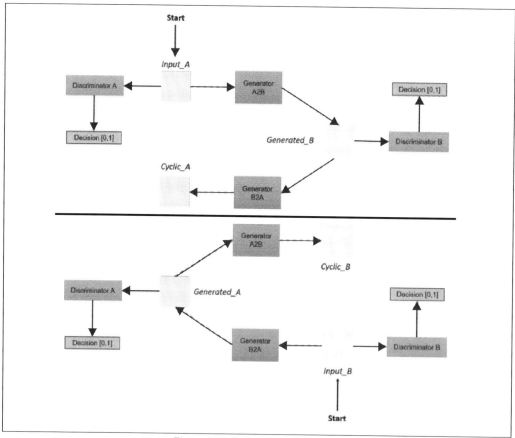

Figure 6.19: CycleGAN architecture

When Discriminator A gets the real image of a horse, Discriminator B gets the generated image of a zebra from A2B, and when Discriminator B gets the real image of a zebra, Discriminator A gets the generated image of a horse from B2A. The point to be noted is that Discriminator A always gets to predict whether the image is from the horse set or not, and Discriminator B gets to predict whether the image is from the zebra set or not. Also, A2B is always responsible for mapping the horse set to the zebra distribution and B2A is always responsible for mapping the zebra set to the horse distribution.

This cyclic training of both generators and both discriminators makes sure the networks learn to map the image with the pattern change but every other feature of the image intact.

```
Generator(
  (model): Sequential(
    (0): ReflectionPad2d((3, 3, 3, 3))
    (1): Conv2d(3, 64, kernel_size=(7, 7), stride=(1, 1))
    (2): InstanceNorm2d(64, eps=1e-05, momentum=0.1, affine=False,
        track_running_stats=False)
    (3): ReLU(inplace)
    (4): Conv2d(64, 128, kernel_size=(3, 3), stride=(2, 2),
        padding=(1, 1))
    (5): InstanceNorm2d(128, eps=1e-05, momentum=0.1,
        affine=False, track_running_stats=False)
    (6): ReLU(inplace)
    (7): Conv2d(128, 256, kernel_size=(3, 3), stride=(2, 2),
        padding=(1, 1))
    (8): InstanceNorm2d(256, eps=1e-05, momentum=0.1,
        affine=False, track_running_stats=False)
    (9): ReLU(inplace)
    (10): ResidualBlock()
    (11): ResidualBlock()
    (12): ResidualBlock()
    (13): ResidualBlock()
    (14): ResidualBlock()
    (15): ResidualBlock()
    (16): ResidualBlock()
    (17): ResidualBlock()
    (18): ResidualBlock()
    (19): ConvTranspose2d(256, 128, kernel_size=(3, 3), stride=(2,
        2), padding=(1, 1), output_padding=(1, 1))
    (20): InstanceNorm2d(128, eps=1e-05, momentum=0.1,
        affine=False, track_running_stats=False)
    (21): ReLU(inplace)
    (22): ConvTranspose2d(128, 64, kernel_size=(3, 3), stride=(2,
```

```
            2), padding=(1, 1), output_padding=(1, 1))
    (23): InstanceNorm2d(64, eps=1e-05, momentum=0.1,
          affine=False, track_running_stats=False)
    (24): ReLU(inplace)
    (25): ReflectionPad2d((3, 3, 3, 3))
    (26): Conv2d(64, 3, kernel_size=(7, 7), stride=(1, 1))
    (27): Tanh()
  )
)
```

PyTorch gives the user complete flexibility for getting inside the network and manipulating it. Part of this is printing the model to the terminal to show the topographically ordered graph with all the modules in it.

Earlier we saw the graph of our generator in CycleGAN. Both A2B and B2A have the same internal architecture with convolutions inside it, unlike the first simple GAN we explored. The whole generator is wrapped inside a single sequence module starting with `ReflectionPad2D`.

Reflection padding involves padding the boundary of the input, skipping the batch dimension and channel dimension. Padding is followed by a typical convolution module arrangement, which is two-dimensional convolution.

Instance normalization normalizes every output batch separately rather than normalizing the whole set together like in Batch Normalization. Two-dimensional instance normalization does instance normalization over 4D input with the batch dimension and channel dimension as the first and second dimension. PyTorch allows the instance normalization layer to be trainable by passing `affine=True`. The parameter `track_running_stats` decides whether to store the running mean and variance from the training loop for use in the evaluation mode for instance normalization. By default, it is set to `False`; that is, it uses the statistics collected from the input in both training and evaluation mode.

A visual comparison of batch normalization and instance normalization is given in the following figure. In the image, the data is represented as a three-dimensional tensor where C is the channel, N is the batch, and D is the other dimensions represented in one dimension for simplicity. As given in the image, batch normalization normalizes data across the batch while instance normalization normalizes one instance of data in both dimensions, thereby keeping the variance between batches intact.

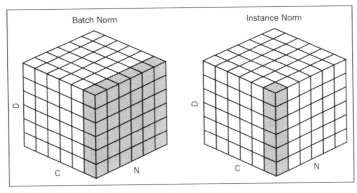

Figure 6.20
Source: *Group Normalization*, Yuxin Wu and Kaiming He

The generator of the original CycleGAN uses nine residual blocks after three convolution blocks, where each convolution block consists of convolution, normalization, and activation layers. The residual blocks are followed by several transpose convolutions, which are then followed by one convolution layer with a tanh function at the last layer. As described in a simple GAN, the tanh output ranges from -1 to 1, which is the normalized value range of all the images.

The internals of the residual block are another set of padding, convolution, normalization, and activation units arranged in a sequence. But the `forward` method makes a residual connection, like in `residueNet`, with the summation operation. The sequential wrapper of all the internal blocks is saved to the variable `conv_block` in the following example. Data passed through this block is then fed through a summation operator along with the input to the network, `x`. This residue connection helps the network to become stable by allowing information to flow in both directions much more easily:

```python
class ResidualBlock(nn.Module):
    def __init__(self, in_features):
        super().__init__()

        self.conv_block = nn.Sequential(
                            nn.ReflectionPad2d(1),
                            nn.Conv2d(in_features,
                                    in_features, 3),
                            nn.InstanceNorm2d(in_features),
                            nn.ReLU(inplace=True),
                            nn.ReflectionPad2d(1),
                            nn.Conv2d(in_features,
                                    in_features, 3),
                            nn.InstanceNorm2d(in_features))
    def forward(self, x):
        return x + self.conv_block(x)
```

Summary

In this chapter, we learned about a whole new array of neural networks that have turned the artificial intelligence world upside down. Generative networks were always important to us, but we could not reach human-comparable accuracy with them until recently. Although there are a few successful generative network architectures, we have discussed only the two most popular networks in this chapter.

Generative networks use basic architectures like CNNs or RNNs as the building blocks of the overall network, but use some nice techniques to make sure the network is learning to generate some output. So far, generative networks have been widely used in art, and we could easily predict that generative networks will become the foundation of many sophisticated networks, since the model has to learn data distribution to generate output. Perhaps the most promising use of generative networks won't be generation but learning data distribution through generation and using that information for other purposes.

In the next chapter, we'll be looking at the networks that got the most attention from the masses: reinforcement learning algorithms.

References

1. *Conditional Image Generation with PixelCNN Decoders*, Oord, Aäron van den, Nal Kalchbrenner, Oriol Vinyals, Lasse Espeholt, Alex Graves and Koray Kavukcuoglu, NIPS, 2016, `https://arxiv.org/pdf/1606.05328.pdf`

2. *Parallel WaveNet: Fast High-Fidelity Speech Synthesis*, Oord, Aäron van den, Yazhe Li, Igor Babuschkin, Karen Simonyan, Oriol Vinyals, Koray Kavukcuoglu, George van den Driessche, Edward Lockhart, Luis C. Cobo, Florian Stimberg, Norman Casagrande, Dominik Grewe, Seb Noury, Sander Dieleman, Erich Elsen, Nal Kalchbrenner, Heiga Zen, Alex Graves, Helen King, Tom Walters, Dan Belov and Demis Hassabis, ICML, 2018, `https://DeepMind.com/documents/131/Distilling_WaveNet.pdf`

3. golbin's WaveNet repository, `https://github.com/golbin/WaveNet`

7
Reinforcement Learning

Let's talk about the nature of learning. We aren't born into this world knowing anything. By interacting with the world, we learn about the effects of our actions. Once we have an understanding of how the world works, we can use that knowledge to make decisions that can lead us to specific goals.

In this chapter, we will formulate this approach to learning computationally using a method called reinforcement learning. It's very different to the other types of deep learning algorithms covered in this book and is a vast field on its own.

Applications of reinforcement learning range from playing games in a digital environment to governing the actions of robots in a real-life environment. It also happens to be the technique you use to train dogs and other animals. These days, reinforcement learning is being used to drive self-driving cars and is a hugely popular field.

One of the major recent breakthroughs happened when a computer (AlphaGo) was able to beat the world Go champion, Lee Sedol [1]. It was a breakthrough because Go has been considered as the holy grail of games for a computer to master for a very long time. This is because it's said that the number of configurations in the game of Go is greater than the number of atoms in our universe.

After the world champion lost to AlphaGo, he was even said to have learned some things from the computer. This sounds crazy, but it is true. What sounds even more crazy is that the input to the algorithm is nothing but the image of the current state of the board game and AlphaGo trained itself by playing against itself over and over again. But before doing that, it learned from watching videos of world champions for hours.

These days, reinforcement learning is being used to enable robots to learn how to walk. The inputs in this case would be the forces a robot can apply to its joints and the state of the ground it is about to walk on. Reinforcement learning is also being used to predict stock prices and is gaining much attention in that area.

These real-world problems might seem very complex. We would need to formulate all these things mathematically so that a computer could solve them. To do that, we would need to simplify the environment and the decision-making process to reach a specific goal.

In the whole paradigm of reinforcement learning, we are only concerned with learning from interactions, and the learner or decision-maker is considered an agent. In the case of the self-driving car, the agent would be the car, whereas in the case of ping-pong, the agent would be the bat. When the agent is initially brought into the world, it will not know anything about the world. The agent will have to observe its environment and make decisions or take actions based on it. The response that it gets back from its environment is called the reward, which can be either positive or negative. Initially, the agent will be taking actions randomly until it gets a positive reward, and that tells it that these decisions might benefit it.

This seems pretty simple, as all the agent has to do is make decisions considering the current state of the environment, but we would like more. In general, an agent's goal is to maximize its cumulative reward over its lifetime, with emphasis on the word cumulative. The agent is not only concerned with the reward it gets in the next step, but also with future rewards it might get. This requires foresight and will make the agent learn better.

This element makes the problem a little more complicated, as we have to balance two factors: exploration and exploitation. Exploration would mean making random decisions and testing them out, while exploitation would mean making the decisions that the agent already knows will give it positive results, so the agent now needs to find out a way to get the maximum cumulative result by balancing these two factors. This is a very important concept in reinforcement learning. The concept has spawned various algorithms for balancing these two factors and is an extensive field of research.

In this chapter, we will be using a library called Gym by OpenAI. It's an open source library that set a standard in training and benchmarking reinforcement learning algorithms. Gym provides a lot of environments that researchers have been using to train reinforcement learning algorithms. It includes a lot of Atari games, robot simulations for picking stuff up, various robot simulations for walking and running, and driving simulations. The library provides the parameters for an agent and the environment that are necessary for them to interact with each other.

The problem

Now we are ready to formulate the reinforcement learning problem mathematically, so let's get right into it.

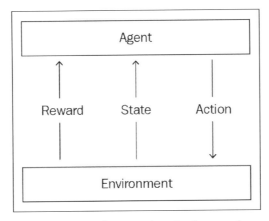

Figure 7.1: Reinforcement learning framework

In the preceding diagram, you can see the setup of any reinforcement learning problem. In general, a reinforcement learning problem is characterized by an agent trying to learn things about its environment, as stated earlier.

Assuming that time evolves in discrete time steps, at time step 0, the agent looks at the environment. You can think of this observation as the situation the environment presents to the agent. It is also known as observing the state of the environment. Then the agent must select an appropriate action for that particular state. Next, the environment presents a new situation to the agent in response to the action taken by it. In the same time step, the environment gives the agent a reward, which gives some indication of whether the agent has responded appropriately or not. Then the process continues. The environment gives the agent a state and reward and in turn, the agent takes an action.

$$S_t \quad A_t \quad R_t \quad \bigg| \quad S_{t+1} \quad A_{t+1} \quad R_{t+1} \quad \bigg| \quad S_{t+2} \quad A_{t+2} \quad R_{t+2}$$

Figure 7.2: Each time step has a state, action, and reward

So, now the sequence of states, actions, and rewards flows through time, and in this process, the most important thing for the agent is its award. That being said, the goal of the agent is to maximize the cumulative reward. In other words, the agent needs to formulate a strategy that can help it to take actions that maximize the accumulated reward. This can only be done by interacting with the environment.

This is because it is the environment that decides how much reward is given to the agent for each action. To formulate this mathematically, we would need to specify the states, actions, and rewards, and also the rules of the environment.

Episodic versus continuous tasks

A lot of the tasks that we specify in the real world have a well-defined ending point. For example, if an agent is playing a game, then the episode or the task ends when the agent wins or loses, or dies.

In the situation of a self-driving car, the task ends when the car reaches the destination or it crashes. These tasks with well-defined ending points are called episodic tasks. The reward that the agent gets is given to it at the end of each episode and this is when the agent decides how well it has done in the environment. Then the agent goes on to the next episode, when it starts from scratch but has the prior information of the last episode with it and can perform better.

As time passes, over a period of episodes, the agent will learn to play the game or drive the car to a particular destination, and thus it will be trained. As you will remember, the agent's goal is to maximize the cumulative reward at the end of the episode.

However, there can be some tasks that go on forever; for example, a bot that trades stocks on a stock market does not have a well-defined ending point and has to learn and improve itself at every time step. These tasks are called continuing tasks. So, in that scenario, the reward is presented to the agent at specific time intervals but the task has no end, so the agent has to learn from the environment and predict at the same time.

In this chapter, we will be focusing only on episodic tasks, but formulating the problem statement for a continuous task would not be very different.

Cumulative discounted rewards

For an agent to maximize the cumulative reward, one method to think about is to maximize the reward at each time step. Doing this may have a negative effect because maximizing the reward in an initial time step might lead to the agent failing in the future quite quickly. Let's take an example of a walking robot. Assuming the speed of the robot is a factor in the reward, if the robot maximizes its speed at every time step, it might destabilize it and make it fall sooner.

We are training the robot to walk; thus, we can conclude that the agent cannot just focus on the current time step to maximize the reward; it needs to take all time steps into consideration. This would be the case with all reinforcement learning problems. Actions may have short- or long-term effects and the agent needs to understand the complexity of the action, and the effects that come from it from the environment.

In the preceding case, if the agent will learn that it cannot move faster than a certain limit that could destabilize it and have a long-term effect of it falling, it will learn the threshold velocity on its own. Hence the agent will get a lower reward at each time step but will avoid falling in the future, and this maximizes the cumulative reward.

Let's say that the rewards at all future timesteps are represented by R_t, R_{t+1}, R_{t+2}, and so on:

$$\text{Goal} = \text{maximize} \ \underbrace{(R_{t+1} + R_{t+2} + R_{t+3} \cdots)}_{\text{return}}$$

Because these time steps are in the future, the agent does not know with great certainty what the future rewards will be. It can only estimate or predict them. The sum of the future rewards is also called the return. We can more clearly specify that the goal of the agent is to maximize the expected return.

Let's also consider that all the rewards in the future return are not as important as each other. To illustrate that, let's say you want to train a dog. You give it commands and if it follows them correctly, you give it a treat as a reward. Can you expect the dog to weigh the rewards that it might get tomorrow in the same way it weighs the rewards it might get years from now? This does not seem feasible.

For the dog to decide what actions it needs to take now, it needs to give a lot more importance to the rewards it might be getting sooner and give less importance to the rewards that it might be getting years from now. This would also be considered logical because the dog is not sure of what the future holds, especially when the dog is still learning about the environment and is changing its strategies for getting the greatest reward out of the environment. Because the rewards that lie a couple of time steps in the future are more predictable than the rewards that lie thousands of time steps in the future, the concept of discounted returns comes into the picture.

$$\text{Goal} = \text{maximize} \ (R_{t+1} + \gamma R_{t+2} + \gamma^2 R_{t+3} + \gamma^3 R_{t+4} \cdots)$$

$$\text{where } \gamma \in (0,1)$$

You can see that we have introduced a variable gamma to our *Goal* equation. A Gamma close to 1 would signify that you value each reward in the future equally. A Gamma close to 0 would signify that only the most recent rewards are very highly weighted.

A good practice is to keep Gamma = 0.9, as you want the agent to look far enough into the future but not infinitely far. You would set Gamma at the training time and it would stay fixed until your experiment ends. It's important to note that discounting can be very useful in continuing tasks, as there is no end to them. But continuing tasks are out of the scope of this chapter.

Markov decision processes

Let's complete the definition of the reinforcement learning problem by learning about a mathematical framework called the **Markov decision process (MDP)**.

An MDP definition has five things:

- A finite set of states
- A finite set of actions
- A finite set of rewards
- A discount rate
- The one-step dynamics of the environment

We have learned about how to specify the states, actions, rewards, and discount rates. Let's find out how to specify the one-step dynamics of the environment.

The image that follows describes an MDP for a trash-collecting robot. The goal of the robot is to collect trash cans. The robot will go in search of the trash cans and keep collecting them until the battery runs out and then come back to the docking station to recharge the battery. The states of the robot can be defined as high and low, representing its battery level. The set of actions the robot can take are searching for the trash cans, waiting at its own position, and going back to the docking station to recharge the battery.

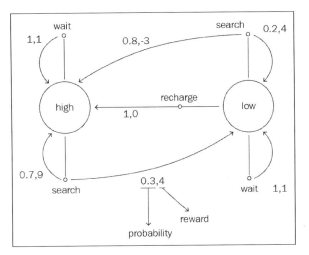

Figure 7.3: MDP for a trash-collecting robot

For example, let's say that the robot is in a state of high battery. If it decides to search for trash cans, there is a 70% probability that the state remains high and a 30% probability that the state becomes low, and the reward it would get for each is 4.

Similarly, if being in a high-battery state it decides to wait at its current location, the probability of it being in the high battery state is 100%, but the reward that it gets is also low.

Take a moment to go through all the actions and states to understand them better. This is how you can specify the environment by detailing all the states the agent can be in, as well as all the actions that it can take in all its states, and deciding the probabilities for each action. Once all these are specified, you would have specified the one-step dynamic of the environment.

In any MDP, the agent would know the states, actions, and the discount rate, whereas it would not know the reward and the one-step dynamic of the environment.

Now you know everything about formulating any real-world problem to be solved with reinforcement learning.

The solution

Now that we have learned how to specify the problem using an MDP, the agent needs to formulate a strategy to solve it. This strategy can also be called a policy.

Policies and value functions

A policy defines the learning agent's way of behaving at a given time. A policy is denoted by the Greek letter Pi. The policy cannot be defined by a formula; it's more of an intuition-based concept.

Let's take an example. For a robot that needs to find a way out of a room, it may have the following policies:

- Go randomly
- Go along the walls
- Find the shortest path to the door

For us to mathematically predict which action to take in a particular state, we need a function. Let's define a function that takes in the current state and outputs a number that signifies how valuable that state is to be in. For example, if you want to cross the river, a position near the bridge would be more valuable than the state far from it. This function is called the value function, also denoted by V.

There's another function we can use that can help us to measure things: a function that gives us values of all the future states led by all the actions we can take.

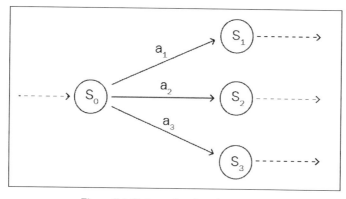

Figure 7.4: States and actions in an MDP

Let's take an example. Let's consider a generic state, S_0. Now we need to predict what actions to be taken between a_1, a_2, and a_3 to get the maximum return (cumulative discounted reward). Let's name this function Q. Our function, Q, would predict the expected return (value (V)) for each of the actions. This Q function is also called the action value function, as it takes into consideration the states and actions, and predicts the expected return for the combination for each of them.

We would choose the maximums most of the time. Thus, these maximums would guide the agent to the end and this would be our policy. Notice that I said most of the time. We generally keep a small random chance where we choose non-maximum action-value pairs. We do this to improve the explorability of the model. This percentage of random chance for exploration is termed as epsilon, and this policy is called the epsilon-greedy policy. It is the most common policy used by people to solve reinforcement learning problems. If we choose only the maximum all the time without any exploration, that policy is simply called a greedy policy. We will use both policies in our implementation.

But initially, we might not know the optimal action-value function. Thus, the policy resulting from it will also not be the optimal one. We would need to iterate over the action value function and find the one that gives the best reward. Once we find it, we would have our optimal Q. Optimal Q is also termed as Q^*. Thus, we would be able to find the optimal Pi, which is also termed as Pi*.

This Q function is the one the agent will have to learn. We will be using a neural network to learn this function, as neural networks are also universal function approximators. Once we have the action-value function, the agent can learn the optimal policy for the problem and we will have completed the goal.

Bellman equation

If we redefine the goal equation with the recently defined Q function, we can write:

$$Q^{\pi}_{(s,a)} = r_{t+1} + \gamma r_{t+2} + \gamma^2 r_{t+3} \cdots$$

Now let's define the same equation recursively. We would come up with what is called the Bellman equation:

$$Q^{\pi}_{(s,a)} = r + \gamma Q^{\pi}_{(s',\pi(s'))}$$

Simply put, the Bellman equation states that the return at each point is equal to the estimated reward for the next time step plus the discounted reward for the states that follow. It is safe to say that any value function for some policy obeys the Bellman equation.

Finding the optimal Q-function

We know now that if we have the optimal Q-function, we can find out the optimal policy by choosing the action that gives the highest return.

Deep Q-learning

The deep Q-learning algorithm uses neural networks to solve the Q-learning problem. It works really well with reinforcement learning problems with continuous spaces; that is, tasks that don't end.

Earlier we talked about value functions (V) and action-value functions (Q). As neural networks are universal function approximators, we can assume any of them are neural networks with some weights that can be trained.

Thus, the value function will now take in the states and the weights of the network and output a value for the current state. We would need to calculate some kind of error and backpropagate to the network, and train it using gradient descent. We need to compare the output of the network (value function) to a value we can consider optimal.

According to the Bellman equation:

$$Q^{\pi}_{(s,a)} = r + \gamma Q^{\pi}_{(s',\pi(s'))}$$

We can calculate the expected Q by taking the value of the next state into account. We can calculate the current Q by taking the cumulative reward until now into account. Using a **mean squared error** (MSE) over the difference between these Q functions can be our loss. One improvement that researchers have suggested is using mean absolute error instead of the MSE when the error is large. This makes it more robust to outliers when the estimates of the Q function are very noisy. This type of loss is called Huber loss.

$$\underset{\text{(Loss)}}{\text{Error}} = \underbrace{R + \gamma \max(Q)}_{\substack{\text{target} \\ \text{using greedy policy}}} - \underbrace{\text{actual } Q}_{\substack{\text{current } Q \\ \text{using } \in \text{greedy} \\ \text{policy}}}$$

The training loop of our code will look like this:

- Initialize w randomly
- $\pi \leftarrow \in$ - greedy
- For all no of episodes:
  - Observe S
  - While S is not terminal for each time step:
  - Choose A from S using π, Q
  - Observe R and S'
  - Update Q
  - $S \leftarrow S'$

One thing to notice here is we would use the same epsilon-greedy policy for choosing an action in *step 6* and we update the same policy in *step 8*. Such an algorithm is called an on-policy algorithm. This is good in the sense that the policy will be learned faster as we are observing and updating the same policy. It converges very quickly. It has some drawbacks too, namely that the policy being learned and the policy for making decisions are intimately tied to each other. What if we wanted a more exploratory policy for selecting observations in *step 6* and updating a more optimal policy in *step 8*? Such an algorithm is called an off-policy algorithm.

Q-learning is an off-policy algorithm, so, in Q-learning, we'll have two policies. The policy we use to infer the actions would be an epsilon-greedy policy and a network we would call policy network. The network we would update using our update step would be our target net. That would be governed by just a greedy policy, which means we would always choose the maximum value with epsilon equals zero. We will not take random actions for this policy. We do that so that we progress faster toward the higher value. We would update the target net's weights by copying the policy net's weights once in a while, such as once every other episode.

The idea behind this is to not chase a moving target. Let's take an example: imagine you want to train a donkey to walk. If you sit on a donkey and dangle a carrot in front of its mouth, the donkey might step forward, the carrot still remaining the same distance away from the donkey. Contrary to popular belief, though, this doesn't work that well. The carrot is likely to bounce around more randomly and might throw the donkey away from its path. Instead, decoupling the donkey and the carrot by getting down from the donkey and standing in a place where you want the donkey to come, seems like a better option. It makes for a more stable learning environment.

Experience replay

One more improvement that we can make to our algorithm is to add a limited memory bank of our experiences and saved transactions. Each transaction consists of all the relevant information needed to learn something. It is a tuple of a state, the taken action, the next state that follows, and the reward given for that action.

```
Transition = namedtuple('Transition',
                        ('state', 'action', 'next_state', 'reward'))
```

We will randomly sample some experiences or transactions and learn from them when we optimize the model.

```python
class ReplayMemory(object):
    def __init__(self, capacity):
        self.capacity = capacity
        self.memory = []
        self.position = 0

    def push(self, *args):
        if len(self.memory) < self.capacity:
            self.memory.append(None)
        self.memory[self.position] = Transition(*args)
        self.position = (self.position + 1) % self.capacity

    def sample(self, batch_size):
        return random.sample(self.memory, batch_size)

    def __len__(self):
        return len(self.memory)

memory = ReplayMemory(10000)
```

Here we've defined a memory bank for the transactions. There is a function called push that pushes the transactions into memory. There's another function to randomly sample from the memory.

Gym

We will be using OpenAI's Gym to get the parameters from the environment, env. There are a lot of environment variables, like the speed of the agent and the location. We'll be training a cartpole to balance itself.

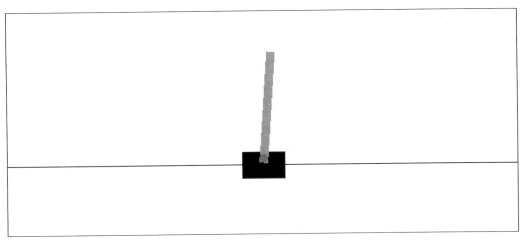

Figure 7.5: Cartpole balancing environment

```
class CartPoleEnv(gym.Env):
    """

    Description:
        A pole is attached by an un-actuated joint to a cart, which moves along a frictionless track. The pendulum star

    Source:
        This environment corresponds to the version of the cart-pole problem described by Barto, Sutton, and Anderson

    Observation:
        Type: Box(4)
        Num     Observation             Min         Max
        0       Cart Position           -4.8        4.8
        1       Cart Velocity           -Inf        Inf
        2       Pole Angle              -24°        24°
        3       Pole Velocity At Tip    -Inf        Inf

    Actions:
        Type: Discrete(2)
        Num     Action
        0       Push cart to the left
        1       Push cart to the right
```

Figure 7.6: Environment variables exposed by Gym

Every observation or state in the environment has four values in the cartpole environment (env). The preceding screenshot is from the Gym code of the cartpole environment. Every observation has the position, velocity, pole angle, and pole velocity at the tip. The actions you can take are to move left or right.

```
env = gym.make('CartPole-v0').unwrapped
device = torch.device("cuda" if torch.cuda.is_available() else
"cpu")
```

```
screen_width = 600


def get_screen():
    screen = env.render(mode='rgb_array').transpose((2, 0, 1))
# transpose into torch order (CHW)
    screen = screen[:, 160:320]
# Strip off the top and bottom of the screen

    # Get cart location
    world_width = env.x_threshold * 2
    scale = screen_width / world_width
    cart_location = int(env.state[0] * scale + screen_width / 2.0)
    # MIDDLE OF CART

    # Decide how much to strip
    view_width = 320
    if cart_location < view_width // 2:
        slice_range = slice(view_width)
    elif cart_location > (screen_width - view_width // 2):
        slice_range = slice(-view_width, None)
    else:
        slice_range = slice(cart_location - view_width // 2,
                            cart_location + view_width // 2)

    # Strip off the edges, so that we have a square image centered
on a cart
    screen = screen[:, :, slice_range]

    screen = np.ascontiguousarray(screen, dtype=np.float32) / 255
    screen = torch.from_numpy(screen)
    resize = T.Compose([T.ToPILImage(),
                        T.Resize(40, interpolation=Image.CUBIC),
                        T.ToTensor()])

    return resize(screen).unsqueeze(0).to(device)
# Resize, and add a batch dimension (BCHW)
```

Here we have defined a `get_screen` function. The cartpole environment renders and returns a screen (3D array of pixels). We would want to cut out a square image with the cartpole in the center. We get the cartpole location from `env.state[0]`. As per the documentation, the first parameter is the cart location. Then we strip the top, bottom, left, and right to get the cartpole in the center. Next, we convert it into a tensor, do some transformations, add another dimension, and return the image.

```
class DQN(nn.Module):
    def __init__(self):
        super(DQN, self).__init__()
        self.conv1 = nn.Conv2d(3, 16, kernel_size=5, stride=2)
        self.bn1 = nn.BatchNorm2d(16)
        self.conv2 = nn.Conv2d(16, 32, kernel_size=5, stride=2)
        self.bn2 = nn.BatchNorm2d(32)
        self.conv3 = nn.Conv2d(32, 32, kernel_size=5, stride=2)
        self.bn3 = nn.BatchNorm2d(32)
        self.head = nn.Linear(448, 2)

    def forward(self, x):
        x = F.relu(self.bn1(self.conv1(x)))
        x = F.relu(self.bn2(self.conv2(x)))
        x = F.relu(self.bn3(self.conv3(x)))
        return self.head(x.view(x.size(0), -1))


policy_net = DQN().to(device)
target_net = DQN().to(device)
target_net.load_state_dict(policy_net.state_dict())
target_net.eval()
```

Next, we define our network. The network takes in the current state, applies some convolutions on it and in the end, converges to a linear layer, and gives an output of the value of the current state and a value signifying how much of an advantage it is being in that state.

We've defined two networks, `policy_net` and `target_net`. We copy the weights of `policy_net` to `target_net` so that they represent the same network. We keep `target_net` on evaluation mode so that we don't update the weights of the network while backpropagating. We'll be inferring `policy_net` at every step but will be updating `target_net` once in a while.

```
EPS_START = 0.9
EPS_END = 0.05
EPS_DECAY = 200
steps_done = 0


def select_action(state):
    global steps_done
    eps_threshold = EPS_END + (EPS_START - EPS_END) * \
        math.exp(-1. * steps_done / EPS_DECAY)
    steps_done += 1
```

```
sample = random.random()
if sample > eps_threshold:

    # freeze the network and get predictions
    with torch.no_grad():
        return policy_net(state).max(1)[1].view(1, 1)

else:

    # select random action
    return torch.tensor([[random.randrange(2)]],
device=device, dtype=torch.long)
```

Next, we define a method to take the actions for us using an epsilon-greedy policy. We can infer from the policy net for a certain percentage of time, but there is also a chance of `eps_threshold`, which means that we would choose the action randomly.

```
num_episodes = 20
TARGET_UPDATE = 5


for i_episode in range(num_episodes):
    env.reset()
    last_screen = get_screen()
    current_screen = get_screen()
    state = current_screen - last_screen

    for t in count():  # for each timestep in an episode
        # Select action for the given state and get rewards
        action = select_action(state)
        _, reward, done, _ = env.step(action.item())
        reward = torch.tensor([reward], device=device)

        # Observe new state
        last_screen = current_screen
        current_screen = get_screen()
        if not done:
            next_state = current_screen - last_screen
        else:
            next_state = None

        # Store the transition in memory
        memory.push(state, action, next_state, reward)

        # Move to the next state
```

```
        state = next_state

        # Perform one step of the optimization (on the target
network)
        optimize_model()
        if done:
            break

    # Update the target network every TARGET_UPDATE episodes
    if i_episode % TARGET_UPDATE == 0:
        target_net.load_state_dict(policy_net.state_dict())

env.close()
```

Let's look at our training loop. For each episode, we reset the environment. We get two screens from the environment, defining the current state as the difference between the two screens. Then, for each timestep in the episode, we use the `select_action` function to select an action. We ask the environment to take that action and give back the reward and the `done` flag (it tells us whether the episode ended, whether that is, the cartpole fell). We observe the new state that has been presented. Then we push the transaction we just experienced into the memory bank and move to the next state. The next step is to optimize the model. We'll come to that function shortly.

We also update `target_net` with a copy of the weights of `policy_net` every five episodes.

```
BATCH_SIZE = 64
GAMMA = 0.999
optimizer = optim.RMSprop(policy_net.parameters())


def optimize_model():

    # Dont optimize till atleast BATCH_SIZE memories are filled
    if len(memory) < BATCH_SIZE:
        return

    transitions = memory.sample(BATCH_SIZE)
    batch = Transition(*zip(*transitions))

    # Get the actual Q
    state_batch = torch.cat(batch.state)
    action_batch = torch.cat(batch.action)
    state_values = policy_net(state_batch)
    # Values of States for all actions
```

```
# Values of states for the selected action
state_action_values = state_values.gather(1, action_batch)

# Get the expected Q
# # Mask to identify if next state is final
non_final_mask = torch.tensor(tuple(map
                                 (lambda s: s is not None,
                                  batch.next_state)),
                                 device=device,
                                 dtype=torch.uint8)
non_final_next_states = torch.cat([s for s in batch.next_state
if s is not None])
next_state_values = torch.zeros(BATCH_SIZE, device=device)
# init to zeros
# predict next non final state values from target_net using
next states
next_state_values[non_final_mask] =
target_net(non_final_next_states).max(1)[0].detach()
reward_batch = torch.cat(batch.reward)
# calculate the predicted values of states for actions
expected_state_action_values = (next_state_values * GAMMA) +
reward_batch

# Compute Huber loss
loss = F.smooth_l1_loss(state_action_values,
expected_state_action_values.unsqueeze(1))

# Optimize the model
optimizer.zero_grad()
loss.backward()
for param in policy_net.parameters():
    param.grad.data.clamp_(-1, 1)
optimizer.step()
```

Then here is the main part: the optimizer step. This is where we find out loss and backpropagate using RMSProp. We sample some experiences from the memory bank. Then we convert all the states, actions, and rewards into batches. We pass the states through policy_net and get the corresponding values.

```
tensor([[2.0429, 1.4886],
        [1.2952, 1.2798],
        [1.1960, 1.1665],
        [1.3114, 1.1780],
        [1.2970, 1.2814],
        [1.4016, 1.4096],
        [1.5460, 1.2322],
        [2.1189, 1.5717],
        [1.4563, 1.1823],
        [1.2912, 1.2759],
        [2.0797, 1.6504],
        [1.2814, 1.2050],
        [1.3184, 1.3216],
        [1.3782, 1.3824],
        [1.4194, 1.4275],
        [1.4445, 1.1700].
```

We then gather the values corresponding to the actions batch.

```
tensor([[0.9818],
        [0.8832],
        [1.2682],
        [0.9230],
        [0.9572],
        [0.8275],
        [1.0659],
        [1.1392],
        [1.2381],
        [1.1048],
        [0.9397],
        [0.8558],
        [1.0015],
        [1.0669],
        [1.0863],
        [1.1538],
        [1.0786],
        [0.9248],
        [0.9540],
        [0.9916]
```

Now we have the state-action pairs, and the values associated with them. This corresponds to the actual Q-function.

Next, we need to find the expected Q-function. We create a mask consisting of 0s and 1s that maps non-0 states as 1, and 0 states (terminal states) as 0. We know by the design of the algorithm that the terminal state will always have a value of 0. Every other state has a positive value, but the terminal state has 0. A mask would look like this:

```
tensor([1, 1, 1, 1, 1, 1, 1, 1, 1, 0, 1, 1, 1, 1, 1, 1, 1, 1, 1, 1, 1, 1, 1,
        1, 1, 1, 1, 1, 1, 1, 1, 0, 1, 1, 1, 1, 1, 1, 1, 1, 1, 1, 1, 1, 1, 1,
        1, 1, 1, 1, 1, 1, 1, 1, 1, 1, 1, 1, 1, 1, 1], dtype=torch.uint8)
```

In that batch of states, the 1s placed at 0 are terminal states. All others are non-final states. We concatenate all non-final next states into `non_final_next_states`. After that, we initialize `next_state_values` as all 0s. Then we pass `non_final_next_states` through `target_network`, get the value for the action that would give the maximum value from it, and apply it in `next_state_values[non_final_mask]`. We put all the values predicted from the non-final states into the non-final `next_state_values` array. This is how `next_state_values` would look:

```
tensor([-0.0286, -0.0289, -0.0286, -0.0287, -0.0287, -0.0287, -0.0281, -0.0285,
        -0.0285, -0.0285, -0.0285, -0.0284, -0.0285, -0.0281, -0.0288, -0.0280,
        -0.0281, -0.0286, -0.0283, -0.0285, -0.0281, -0.0289, -0.0282, -0.0285,
        -0.0286, -0.0281, -0.0288, -0.0284, -0.0284, -0.0281, -0.0288, -0.0280,
        -0.0282, -0.0291, -0.0285, -0.0282, -0.0287, -0.0288, -0.0287, -0.0286,
         0.0000, -0.0284, -0.0285, -0.0283, -0.0289, -0.0282, -0.0286, -0.0285,
        -0.0283, -0.0286, -0.0285, -0.0284, -0.0288, -0.0287, -0.0283, -0.0280,
```

Finally, we calculate the expected Q-function. As per our prior discussion, it will be R + gamma (next state values). Then we calculate the loss from the actual Q-functions and the expected Q-function, and we backpropagate the error to the policy network (remember that `target_net` is in `eval` mode). We are also using gradient clamping to ensure that the gradients are small and don't divert out far.

Training the neural network would take some time, as the process renders each frame and calculates the errors on that. We could have used a far simpler approach by taking the velocities and positions directly to formulate a loss function, and that would take less time to train as it won't be rendering each frame; it would just directly take inputs from `env.state`.

There are many improvements to this algorithm, like adding imagination to the agent so that it can explore better and imagine the actions in its head, and make better predictions.

Summary

In this chapter, we learned about a whole new field of unsupervised learning: reinforcement learning. It is a whole different field and we have just touched on this topic in this chapter. We learned how to phrase a problem for reinforcement learning, and then we trained a model that sees a few measurements provided by the environment and can learn how to balance a cartpole. You can apply the same knowledge to teach robots to walk, to drive cars, and also to play games. This is one of the more physical applications of deep learning.

In the next and closing chapter, we'll be looking at productionizing our PyTorch models so that you can run them on any framework or language, and scale your deep learning applications.

References

1. Google DeepMind Challenge Match: Lee Sedol versus AlphaGo, `https://www.youtube.com/watch?v=vFr3K2DORc8`

This chapter was contributed by Sudhanshu Passi.

8
PyTorch to Production

In 2017, when PyTorch released its usable version, the promise was for it to be a Python-first framework for researchers. The PyTorch community was strict about this for a year, but then it saw the abundance of production requirements and decided to merge production capability with PyTorch's first stable release, 1.0, but without compromising the usability and flexibility it was created for.

PyTorch is known for being a clean framework, and hence it was a challenging task to achieve the production capability and flexibility needed for research. I think that the major hurdle for pushing production support to the core was going out of Python's realm and moving the PyTorch model to a faster, thread-safe language that has multithreading capability. But then, that violated the Python-first principle that PyTorch had up to that point.

The first step toward solving this problem was to make the **Open Neural Network Exchange** (**ONNX**) format stable and compatible with all popular frameworks (at least with those that have good serving modules). ONNX defines the fundamental operator and standard data types that a deep learning graph requires. That led the way for ONNX coming into the core of PyTorch and it, along with the ONNX converters, has been built for the popular deep learning frameworks such as CNTK, MXNet, TensorFlow, and others.

ONNX was great and everybody loved it, but one of the major disadvantages of ONNX is its scripting mode; that is, ONNX runs the graph once to fetch the information about the graph, which is then converted to an ONNX format. Hence, ONNX can't migrate control flow in a model (using a `for` loop for different sequence lengths of recurrent neural network (RNN) models).

The second approach to productionizing PyTorch was to build a high-performance backend in PyTorch itself. Instead of building one from scratch, Caffe2's core was merged with the PyTorch core, but the Python APIs were kept the same. However, that did not solve the problem that the Python language had.

Next was the introduction of TorchScript, which converts the native Python model to a serialized form that can be loaded in a high-performance universe, like in a C++ thread. TorchScript is readable by LibTorch, the backend of PyTorch, which makes PyTorch efficient. With this, a developer can prototype the model and perhaps train it in Python itself. After the training, the model can be converted to an **intermediate representation (IR)**. Right now, only the C++ backend is developed, and hence the IR can be loaded as a C++ object, which then can be read from PyTorch's C++ APIs. TorchScript can even convert the control flow in the Python program, which makes it superior to the ONNX approach in the case of production support. TorchScript itself is a subset of operations possible in the Python language, and hence no Python operations are allowed to write in TorchScript. A very detailed explanation is available in the official documentation itself, discussing what is possible and what is not, along with numerous examples [1].

In this chapter, we will start with serving a normal Python PyTorch model using Flask (a popular Python web framework). A setup such as this is good enough, mostly, especially if you are setting up a sample web app or something for your personal needs, or for similar use cases. Then we'll explore ONNX and convert the PyTorch model to MXNet, which can then be served using the MXNet model server. From there, we'll go to TorchScript, the new kid on PyTorch's block. Using TorchScript, we'll make C++ executables, which can then be executed from C++ with the help of LibTorch. The highly efficient C++ executable can then be served from a stable, performant C++ server or even from a Go server using cgo. For all the servings, we will use the fizbuz network we built in *Chapter 2, A Simple Neural Network*.

Serving with Flask

Serving the PyTorch model in Python itself is the easiest way of serving your model in production. But before going into explaining how it can be done, let's have a quick look at what Flask is. Explaining Flask completely is out of the scope of this chapter, but we'll still go through the most fundamental concepts of Flask.

Introduction to Flask

Flask is a microframework that's been used in production by several big companies in the Python world. Even though Flask comes up with a template engine that can be used to push the UI to the client, we are not using that; instead, we will make a RESTful backend that serves APIs.

Flask can be installed using `pip`, just like any other Python package:

```
pip install Flask
```

This will install the additional dependencies Werkzeug (the Python interface between the application and the server), Jinga (as the template engine), itsdangerous (for securely signing the data), and Click (as the CLI builder).

Once installed, the user will have access to the CLI and invoking our script with `flask run` will bring up the server:

```
from flask import Flask
app = Flask(__name__)

@app.route("/")
def hello():
    return "Hello World!"
```

The example has four components in it:

- The first line is where we import the Flask package.
- We make a Flask object, which is our big web application object that will be used by the Flask server to run our server.
- Once we have the application object, we need to store the information about what URL the object should do actions on. For this purpose, the application object comes with a `route` method, which accepts the desired URL and returns a decorator. This is the URL we want the application to serve now.
- The decorator returned by the application object decorates a function, and this function will be triggered when the URL gets a hit. We will name this function `hello`. The name of the function doesn't have much importance here. In the preceding example, it just checks for the input and responds accordingly. But for our model server, we make this function slightly complex so that it can accept the input and feed that input to the model we have built. The return value of our model will then be pushed back to the user as an HTTP response.

We start our implementation by making a `flask_trial` directory and save this file as `app.py` in that directory:

```
mkdir flask_trial
cd flask_trial
```

Then we execute the CLI command that comes with Flask to bring the server up. After the execution, you'll see the server being served from `http://127.0.0.1:5000` if you haven't given custom parameters.

```
flask run
```

We can test the simple Flask application by making an HTTP request to the server location. If everything worked fine, we should get a "Hello, World!" message from the server.

```
-> curl "http://127.0.0.1:5000"

-> Hello World!
```

We have set up our simple Flask application. Now let's bring the fizbuz model into our application. The following snippet shows the same model from *Chapter 2, A Simple Neural Network*, for your reference. This model will be called from the router function. We have trained the model in *Chapter 2, A Simple Neural Network*, and hence we'll be loading the trained model here instead of training it again:

```python
import torch.nn as nn
import torch


class FizBuzNet(nn.Module):
    """
    2 layer network for predicting fiz or buz
    param: input_size -> int
    param: output_size -> int
    """

    def __init__(self, input_size, hidden_size, output_size):
        super(FizBuzNet, self).__init__()
        self.hidden = nn.Linear(input_size, hidden_size)
        self.out = nn.Linear(hidden_size, output_size)

    def forward(self, batch):
        hidden = self.hidden(batch)
        activated = torch.sigmoid(hidden)
        out = self.out(activated)
        return out
```

Model serving with Flask

The directory structure of our application is given in the following screenshot. The assets folder has the trained model, which will be used by the controller.py file while loading the model. app.py in the root location is the entry point for our Flask application. Flask prefers app.py as the default name of the entry point file.

When you execute flask run, Flask looks for the app.py file in the current directory and executes that. The controller.py file is where we are loading the model from the model.py file. The loaded model will then wait for the input from the user through the HTTP endpoint. app.py redirects the user input to controller, which is then converted to Torch tensors.

The tensor object will be passed through the neural network and `controller` returns the result from the neural network after passing it through the post-processing operations.

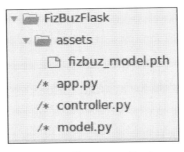

Figure 8.1: The current directory

We have four components in our directory for making the Flask app. The `assets` folder is where we kept our model. The other three files are where the code resides. Let's look into each of those. We'll start with our entry file, `app.py`. It is an extended version of the simple Flask application given earlier. The file taught us how to define the URL endpoint and how to map a URL endpoint to a Python function. Our extended `app.py` file is shown in the following code block:

```python
import json

from flask import Flask
from flask import request

import controller

app = Flask('FizBuzAPI')


@app.route('/predictions/fizbuz_package', methods=['POST'])
def predict():
    which = request.get_json().get('input.1')
    if not which:
        return "InvalidData"
    try:
        number = int(which) + 1
        prediction = controller.run(number)
        out = json.dumps({'NextNumber': prediction})
    except ValueError:
        out = json.dumps({'NextNumber': 'WooHooo!!!'})
    return out
```

Flask gives us the `request` utility, which is a global variable but local to the current thread that stores information about the current request. We use the `get_json` function of the `request` object to get the body POST parameters from the `request` object. String data that came through HTTP is then converted to an integer. This integer is the number we are passing from the frontend. Our application's task is to predict what the state will be of the next number. Will that be the next number itself or fizz, or buzz, or fizz buzz? But, if you remember, we train our network to predict the status of the number we pass. However, we need the status of next number. So, we'll add one to the current number we have and then pass the result to our model.

The next import we have is `controller`, where we have loaded our model file. We are calling the `run` method and passing the number to the model. The predicted value from `controller` is then passed back to the user as a dictionary. Flask will convert that to a response body and send it back to the user.

Before moving forward, there are two more main differences we could see in the extended version from the previous simple Flask app. One is the URL routing: / `predictions/fizbuz_package`. As we have seen before, Flask allows you to map any URL endpoint to a function of your choice.

Secondly, we used another keyword argument in the decorator: `methods`. With that, we are telling Flask that this function needed to be called not only by the URL rule, but also only on the POST method call on that URL. So, we run the application with `flask run`, like we did before, and we test it with our `curl` command.

```
-> curl -X POST http://127.0.0.1:5000/predictions/fizbuz_package \
      -H "Content-Type: application/json" \
      -d '{"input.1": 14}'


-> {"NextNumber": "FizBuz"}
```

In the HTTP POST request, we are passing the JSON object with the input number as 14 and our server returns the next number as `FizBuz`. All of that magic happens in the `controller.run()` method that our `app.py` is calling. Now let's see what that function is doing.

Next is the `controller` file with the `run()` method. Here we convert the input number to a 10-digit binary (remember, this is what we passed as input to our fizbuz network in *Chapter 2, A Simple Neural Network*) and make it a Torch tensor. The binary tensor is then passed to our model's forward function to get the 1 x 4 tensor that has the prediction.

Our model is made by calling the `FizBuz` class from the model file loaded with the saved `.pth` file. We use Torch's `load_state_dict` method to load the parameters to the initialized model. After that, we convert our model to `eval()` mode, which sets the model to evaluation mode (it switches off batchnorm dropout layers in the evaluation mode). The model's output is the probability distribution on which we run `max` and figure out which index has the maximum value, and then convert that to readable output.

A production-ready server

This is a very basic walkthrough of how we can deploy a PyTorch model to a server using Flask. But Flask's in-built server is not production-ready and should only be used for development purposes. Once the development is done, we should use some other server package to serve our Flask application in production.

Gunicorn is one of the most popular server packages used by Python developers and it is so easy to bind it with the Flask application. You can install Gunicorn using `pip`, like how we installed Flask:

```
pip install gunicorn
```

Gunicorn needs us to pass the module name for it to pick up the module and run the server. But Gunicorn expects the application object to have the name `application`, which is not the case with our project. Hence, we need to explicitly pass the application object name along with the module name. Gunicorn's command-line tool has numerous options, but we are trying to make it as simple as possible:

```
gunicorn app:app
```

```python
import torch
from model import FizBuzNet

input_size = 10
output_size = 4
hidden_size = 100


def binary_encoder():
    def wrapper(num):
        ret = [int(i) for i in '{0:b}'.format(num)]
        return [0] * (input_size - len(ret)) + ret
    return wrapper
```

```
net = FizBuzNet(input_size, hidden_size, output_size)
net.load_state_dict(torch.load('assets/fizbuz_model.pth'))
net.eval()
encoder = binary_encoder()


def run(number):
    with torch.no_grad():
        binary = torch.Tensor([encoder(number)])
        out = net(binary)[0].max(0)[1].item()
    return get_readable_output(number, out)
```

ONNX

The ONNX protocol was built to create interoperability between different frameworks. This helps AI developers and organizations to choose the right framework to develop AI models where they spend most of their time. Once the development and training phases are over, they can migrate the model to any framework of their choice to serve it in production.

Different frameworks could be optimized for different purposes, such as mobile deployment, readability and flexibility, production deployment, and others. Converting the model to different frameworks is sometimes inevitable and manual conversion is time-consuming. This is another use case that ONNX is trying to solve with interoperability.

Let's take any framework example to see where ONNX is going to fit in. The framework will have a language API, which is used by developers, then a graph representation of the model developed by them. This IR then goes to the highly optimized runtime for execution. ONNX provides a unified standard for this IR and makes all the frameworks understand ONNX's IR. With ONNX, developers can use the API to make the model, which is then converted to the framework's IR. ONNX converters could convert that IR to ONNX's standard IR, which is then convertible to the other framework's IR.

This is the readable representation of PyTorch's IR of the fizbuz net:

```
graph(%input.1 : Float(1, 10)
      %weight.1 : Float(100, 10)
      %bias.1 : Float(100)
      %weight : Float(4, 100)
      %bias : Float(4)) {
  %5 : Float(10!, 100!) = aten::t(%weight.1),
       scope: FizBuzNet/Linear[hidden]
```

```
%6 : int = prim::Constant[value=1](),
      scope: FizBuzNet/Linear[hidden]
%7 : int = prim::Constant[value=1](),
      scope: FizBuzNet/Linear[hidden]
%hidden : Float(1, 100) = aten::addmm(%bias.1, %input.1, %5, %6,
          %7), scope: FizBuzNet/Linear [hidden]
%input : Float(1, 100) = aten::sigmoid(%hidden),
          scope: FizBuzNet
%10 : Float(100!, 4!) = aten::t(%weight),
      scope: FizBuzNet/Linear[out]
%11 : int = prim::Constant[value=1](),
      scope: FizBuzNet/Linear[out]
%12 : int = prim::Constant[value=1](),
      scope: FizBuzNet/Linear[out]
%13 : Float(1, 4) = aten::addmm(%bias, %input, %10, %11, %12),
      scope: FizBuzNet/Linear[out]
  return (%13);
}
```

The representation clearly says what the structure of the whole network is. The first five lines show the parameters and the input tensors, and mark a name for each. For example, the whole network addresses our input tensor as input.i, which is a float tensor with the shape 1 x 10. Then it shows the weight and bias tensors of our first and second layers.

From the sixth line onward, the structure of the graph is shown. The first part of each line (the characters before the full colon that start with the % sign) is the identifier for each line, which is what is used in other lines to refer to these lines. For example, a line with %5 as an identifier does a transpose of the weight of the first layer represented by aten::t(%weight.i), which gives a float tensor of shape 10 x 100 as output.

Figure 8.2: The other IR converted to ONNX's IR, which is then converted to the other IR

PyTorch has a built-in ONNX exporter, which helps us to create the ONNX IR without leaving the comfort of PyTorch. In the example given here, we are exporting our fizbuz net to ONNX, which is then served by the MXNet model server. In the following snippet, we use PyTorch's in-built export module to convert the fizbuz net to ONNX's IR:

```
>>> import torch
>>> dummy_input = torch.Tensor([[0, 0, 0, 0, 0, 0, 0, 0, 1, 0]])
```

```
>>> dummy_input
    tensor([[O., 0., 0., 0., 0., 0., 0., O., 1., 0.]])
>>> net = FizBuzNet(input_size, hidden_size, output_size)
>>> net.load_state_dict(torch.load('assets/fizbuz_model.pth'))
>>> dummy_input = torch.Tensor([[0, 0, 0, 0, 0, 0, 0, 0, 1, 0]])
>>> torch.onnx.export(net, dummy_input, "fizbuz.onnx", verbose=True)
```

In the last line, we call the export module and pass PyTorch's net, a dummy input, and the output file name. ONNX does the conversion by tracing the graph; that is, it executes the graph once with the dummy input we give.

While executing the graph, it keeps track of PyTorch operations we execute and then converts each of those operations to ONNX format. The key-value parameter verbose=True writes the output to the terminal screen while exporting. It gives us the IR representation of the same graph in ONNX:

```
graph(%input.1 : Float(1, 10)
      %1 : Float(100, 10)
      %2 : Float(100)
      %3 : Float(4, 100)
      %4 : Float(4)) {
  %5 : Float(1, 100) = onnx::Gemm[alpha=1, beta=1,
      transB=1](%input.1, %1, %2),
      scope: FizBuzNet/Linear[hidden]
  %6 : Float(1, 100) = onnx::Sigmoid(%5), scope: FizBuzNet
  %7 : Float(1, 4) = onnx::Gemm[alpha=1, beta=1,
      transB=1](%6, %3, %4),
      scope: FizBuzNet/Linear[out]
  return (%7);
}
```

It also shows all the operations that are needed for the graph execution but on a smaller scale than PyTorch's graph representation. While PyTorch shows us each operation (including the transpose operation), ONNX abstracts that granular information under high-level functions such as `onnx:Gemm`, assuming the `import` modules of other frameworks can read through these abstractions.

The `export` module of PyTorch saves the ONNX model in the `fizbuz.onnx` file. This can be loaded from ONNX itself or the ONNX importers built into other frameworks. Here we are loading the ONNX model into ONNX itself and doing a model check. ONNX also has a highly performant runtime managed by Microsoft, which is out of this book's scope to explain but is available on `https://github.com/Microsoft/onnxruntime`.

Since ONNX has become the norm of interoperability between frameworks, other tools have been built around it. The most used/useful one would probably be Netron, the visualizer for ONNX models. Even though it's not as interactive as TensorBoard, Netron is good enough for basic visualization.

Once you have the `.onnx` file, you can pass the file location as an argument to the Netron command-line tool, which builds the server and shows the graph in the browser:

```
pip install netron

netron -b fizbuz.onnx
```

The preceding command brings up the Netron server with the graph visualization of our fizbuz net, which is shown in the following diagram. Apart from the zoomable graph, Netron can visualize other basic information as well, such as the version, producer, how the graph is produced, and more. Plus, each of the nodes is clickable, which will show information about that particular node. Of course, this is not complex enough to cover all the requirements we need from a visualizer, but it is good enough to give some idea about the whole network.

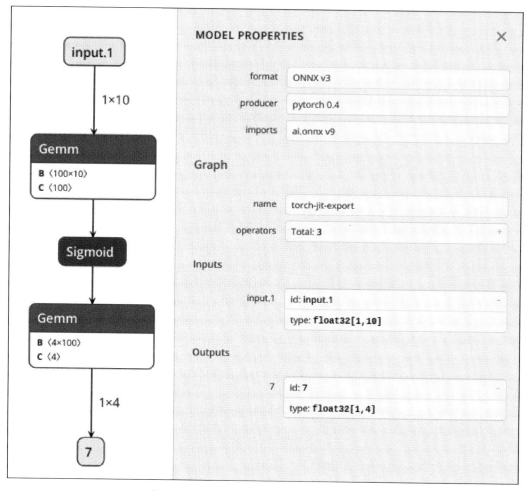

Figure 8.3: Netron visualization of the fizbuz net

From just being an ONNX visualizer, Netron grew to accept exported models of all the popular frameworks. Right now, as per the official documentation, Netron accepts models of ONNX, Keras, CoreML, Caffe2, MXNet, TensorFlow Lite, TensorFlow.js, TensorFlow, Caffe, PyTorch, Torch, CNTK, PaddlePaddle, Darknet, and scikit-learn.

MXNet model server

Now we have left the PyTorch world. We have different model servers available now but we chose the MXNet model server. The MXNet model server is maintained by the community and led by the Amazon team and is also referred to as MMS. From here onward, I'll be using both MMS and MXNet model server interchangeably.

MXNet works better than other serving modules. At the time of writing, TensorFlow is not compatible with Python 3.7 and MXNet's serving module has integration with the built-in ONNX model, which makes it easy for a developer to serve the model with very few lines of commands, without learning the complexities of distributed or highly scalable deployments.

Other model servers, such as TensorRT and Clipper, are not as easy as the MXNet server for setup and management. Also, MXNet comes with another utility called MXNet archiver, which makes a single bundled package with all the required files that can be independently deployed without having to worry about other dependencies. Apart from all of these cool features that the MXNet model server comes up with, the top benefit is being able to customize the pre-processing and post-processing steps. We'll see how all of this can be done in the upcoming sections.

The flow of the whole process starts from where we try to create a single archive file with the `.mar` format using the model archiver. The single bundle file needs the ONNX model file, `signature.json`, which provides information about the input size, name, and more. Consider that to be a configuration file that can be changed at any time. It doesn't even have to be part of your archive if you decide to hardcode all the values into your code instead of reading from the configuration. Then you need the service file, which is where you define the pre-process, inference function, post-process function, and other utility functions.

Once the model archive is made, we can call the model server and pass the location to our model archive as input. That's it; you have your model being served from a super-performant model server now.

MXNet model archiver

We'll start our journey by installing the MXNet model archiver. The default model archiver that comes along with the MXNet model server doesn't have ONNX support, and hence we need to install it separately. The model archiver for ONNX has a dependency on the protocol buffer and the MXNet package itself. The guide for installing the protobuf compiler for each operating system is available in the official documentation. The MXNet package can be installed via `pip`, just as we have installed other packages (for GPUs, MXNet has another package, but here we are installing the base version of MXNet):

```
pip install mxnet
pip install model-archiver[onnx]
```

Now we can install the MXNet model server. It's built on the **Java virtual machine (JVM)**, and hence multiple threads running with instances of our model are being called from the JVM. With the JVM supporting the complexities, the MXNet server can be scaled up to multiple processes handling thousands of requests.

The MXNet server comes with a management API, which is served over HTTP. This helps the production team to increase/decrease the resources as required. Apart from handling the scale of workers, the management API has other options as well. But we are not going into depth on those here. Since the model server is running on the JVM, we need to install Java 8. Also, the MXNet model server is still in experimental mode on Windows, but it is stable in Linux flavors and Mac.

```
pip install mxnet-model-server
```

Now, with all the prerequisites installed, we can start coding up our production-ready PyTorch model with the MXNet model server. First, we make a new directory for saving all the required files for our model archiver to make the bundle file. Then we move the `.onnx` file we made in the last step.

The one mandatory requirement MMS has is the service file with a service class in it. MMS executes the `initialize()` and `handle()` functions of the only class that's available in the service file. We'll go through each of those in the next section, but here is the skeleton that we can use to make our service file.

Figure 8.4: Directory structure of fizbuz_package

```
class MXNetModelService(object):

    def __init__(self):
        ...
    def initialize(self, context):
        ...
    def preprocess(self, batch):
        ...
    def inference(self, model_input):
        ...
    def postprocess(self, inference_output):
        ...
    def handle(self, data, context):
        ...
```

Then we need a signature file. As we have seen before, the signature file is just the configuration file. We can avoid having this by hardcoding values to the script itself, but this is recommended by MMS folks as well. We made our minimal signature file for the fizbuz net, which looks like this:

```
{
  "inputs": [
    {
      "data_name": "input.1",
      "data_shape": [
        1,
        10
      ]
    }
  ],
  "input_type": "application/json"
}
```

In the signature file, we are describing the data name, input shape, and input type. While reading the data stream from over the HTTP, this is what our server assumes the data information will be. In general, we can make our API accept any type of data by configuring it in the signature file. But then our script should be able to handle those types as well. Let's finish up the service file and then we can bundle the files together with MMS.

As you have seen before, MMS calls the `initialize()` method of the only single class available in the service file. If you have more classes present in the service file, that's a whole other story, but let's make it simple enough for us to comprehend. As the name indicates, the `initialize()` file initializes the required attributes and methods:

```python
def initialize(self, context):
    properties = context.system_properties
    model_dir = properties.get("model_dir")
    gpu_id = properties.get("gpu_id")
    self._batch_size = properties.get('batch_size')
    signature_file_path = os.path.join(
        model_dir, "signature.json")
    if not os.path.isfile(signature_file_path):
        raise RuntimeError("Missing signature.json file.")
    with open(signature_file_path) as f:
        self.signature = json.load(f)
    data_names = []
    data_shapes = []
    input_data = self.signature["inputs"][0]
    data_name = input_data["data_name"]
    data_shape = input_data["data_shape"]
    data_shape[0] = self._batch_size
    data_names.append(data_name)
    data_shapes.append((data_name, tuple(data_shape)))
```

```
self.mxnet_ctx = mx.cpu() if gpu_id is None else
    mx.gpu(gpu_id)
sym, arg_params, aux_params = mx.model.load_checkpoint(
    checkpoint_prefix, self.epoch)
self.mx_model = mx.mod.Module(
    symbol=sym, context=self.mxnet_ctx,
    data_names=data_names, label_names=None)
self.mx_model.bind(
    for_training=False, data_shapes=data_shapes)
self.mx_model.set_params(
    arg_params, aux_params,
    allow_missing=True, allow_extra=True)
self.has_initialized = True
```

MMS passes context parameters while calling `initialize()`, which has information it acquired while unpacking the archive file. When calling MMS first with the archive file path as an argument, before calling the service file, MMS unpacks the archive file and installs the model, and collects information about where the model is stored, how many cores MMS could use, whether it has GPU, and more. All this information is passed to `initialize()` as a context argument.

The first part of `initialize()` is to collect this information and the information from the signature JSON file. The second part of the function fetches input-related data from the information collected in the first part. Then the third part of the function is to create the MXNet model and load the trained parameters into the model. And at the end, we set the `self.has_initialized` variable to `True`, which is then used to check the status of initialization from other parts of the service file:

```
def handle(self, data, context):
    try:
        if not self.has_initialized:
            self.initialize()
        preprocess_start = time.time()
        data = self.preprocess(data)
        inference_start = time.time()
        data = self.inference(data)
        postprocess_start = time.time()
        data = self.postprocess(data)
        end_time = time.time()

        metrics = context.metrics
        metrics.add_time(self.add_first())
        metrics.add_time(self.add_second())
        metrics.add_time(self.add_third())
        return data
```

```
        except Exception as e:
            request_processor = context.request_processor
            request_processor.report_status(
                500, "Unknown inference error")
            return [str(e)] * self._batch_size
```

MMS is programmed to call the `handle()` method of the same class on each request, which is where we take the control of the flow. The `initialize()` function will only be called once while initiating the thread; the `handle()` function will be called for each user request. Since the `handle()` function gets called for each user request, along with the context information, it gets the current data as well in the argument. But for making the program modular, we are not doing any operations in `handle()`; instead, we are calling other functions, which are designated to do only one thing: what the function is supposed to do.

We have divided the whole flow into four: the pre-processing, inference, post-processing, and matrix logging. In the first line of `handle()`, we verify whether the thread is being initialized with the context and data information. Once that's done, we'll get into the flow. We'll run through our flow step by step now.

We first call the `self.preprocess()` function with `data` as the parameter, where `data` will be the POST body content of the HTTP request. The `preprocess` function fetches the data we passed with the same name we have configured in the `signature.json` file. Once we have the data, this is the integer for which we need the system to predict the next number. Since we have trained our model to predict the fizz buzz status of the current number, we'll add one to the number from the data and then create an MXNet array on the binary of the new number:

```
def preprocess(self, batch):
    param_name = self.signature['inputs'][0]['data_name']
    data = batch[0].get('body').get(param_name)
    if data:
        self.input = data + 1
        tensor = mx.nd.array(
            [self.binary_encoder(self.input, input_size=10)])
        return tensor
    self.error = 'InvalidData'
```

The `handle()` function gets the processed data and passes that to the `inference()` function, which calls the MXNet model saved on the `initialize()` function with the processed data. The `inference()` function returns the output tensor of size 1 x 4, which is then returned to the `handle()` function.

```
def inference(self, model_input):
    if self.error is not None:
        return None
```

```
self.mx_model.forward(DataBatch([model_input]))
model_output = self.mx_model.get_outputs()
return model_output
```

The tensor is then passed to the `postprocess()` function to convert it to human-readable output. We have the `self.get_readable_output()` function, which converts the output of the model to fizz, buzz, fizz buzz, or the next number as needed.

The post-processed data then goes back to the `handle()` function, where it does the matrices creation. After that, the data is returned to the callee of the `handle()` function, which is part of MMS. MMS converts that data to the HTTP response and returns it to the user. MMS also logs the matrices' output so that operations can look into the matrices in real time and take decisions based on that:

```
def postprocess(self, inference_output):
    if self.error is not None:
        return [self.error] * self._batch_size
    prediction = self.get_readable_output(
        self.input,
        int(inference_output[0].argmax(1).asscalar()))
    out = [{'next_number': prediction}]
    return out
```

Once we have all the files in the directory as given previously, we can create the `.mar` archive file:

```
model-archiver \
        --model-name fizbuz_package \
        --model-path fizbuz_package \
        --handler fizbuz_service -f
```

This will create a `fizbuz_package.mar` file in the current directory. That then can be passed to MMS as a CLI argument:

```
mxnet-model-server \
        --start \
        --model-store FizBuz_with_ONNX \
        --models fizbuz_package.mar
```

Now our model server is up and running on port 8080 (if you haven't changed the port). We can try executing the same `curl` command we used for the Flask application (obviously, we have to change the port number) and check the model. We should have exactly the same result as the Flask application, but now we have the ability to scale up or down the number of workers dynamically on the fly, as required. MMS gives the management API for this purpose. The management API comes with a couple of configurable options, but here we are focusing only on scaling up or down the number of workers.

Along with the server running on port 8080, there will be a management API service running on 8081 to which we can make calls and control the configurations. Hitting that endpoint with a simple GET request will give you the status of the server. But before probing that, we'll make the number of workers one (by default, it is four). The API endpoint is a proper REST endpoint; we specify the model name in the path and pass the argument max_worker=1 to make the number of workers one. We can increase the number of workers by passing min_worker=<number> as well. A thorough explanation of possible configurations over the management API is given in the official doc [2].

```
-> curl -v -X PUT
"http://localhost:8081/models/fizbuz_package?max_worker=1"

...

{

    "status": "Processing worker updates..."

}

...
```

Once the number of workers has been brought down, we can hit the endpoint to figure out the status of our server. A sample output (right after we brought down the number of workers) is as follows:

```
-> curl "http://localhost:8081/models/fizbuz_package"
{
  "modelName": "fizbuz_package",
  "modelUrl": "fizbuz_package.mar",
  "runtime": "python",
  "minWorkers": 1,
  "maxWorkers": 1,
  "batchSize": 1,
  "maxBatchDelay": 100,
  "workers": [
    {
      "id": "9000",
      "startTime": "2019-02-11T19:03:41.763Z",
      "status": "READY",
      "gpu": false,
      "memoryUsage": 0
    }
  ]
}
```

We have set up the model server and we now know how to configure the server as per the scale. Let's use Locust to load test our server and check how our server is holding up, and how easy it is to increase/decrease the resources as per our needs. Deploying AI models to production can't be this easy.

Load testing

A sample Locust script follows, which should be saved as `locust.py` in the current directory. If Locust is installed (you can install it using `pip`), then calling `locust` will bring up the Locust server and open up the UI, where we can input the scale we want to test. We can bring up the scale gradually and check at what point our server starts breaking, and then hit the management API to increase the workers and make sure our server can hold the scale:

```python
import random
from locust import HttpLocust, TaskSet, task


class UserBehavior(TaskSet):
    def on_start(self):
        self.url = "/predictions/fizbuz_package"
        self.headers = {"Content-Type": "application/json"}

    @task(1)
    def success(self):
        data = {'input.1': random.randint(0, 1000)}
        self.client.post(self.url, headers=self.headers,
                         json=data)


class WebsiteUser(HttpLocust):
    task_set = UserBehavior
    host = "http://localhost: 8080"
```

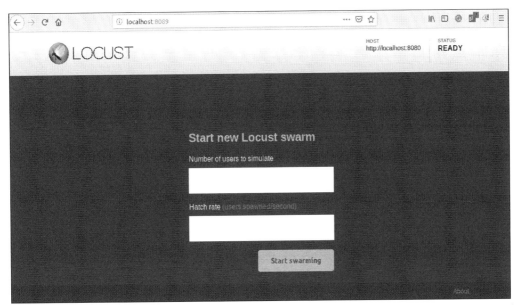

Figure 8.5: Locust UI, where we can configure the number of users to simulate production load

Efficiency with TorchScript

We have set up the simple Flask application server to serve our model and we have implemented the same model using the MXNet model server, but if we need to go away from the Python world and make a highly efficient server in C++ or Go, or in other efficient languages, PyTorch came up with TorchScript, which can generate the most efficient form your model, which is readable in C++.

Now the question is: isn't this what we did with ONNX; that is, creating another IR from the PyTorch model? Yes, the processes are similar, but the difference here is that ONNX creates the optimized IR using tracing; that is, it passes a dummy input through the model and while the model is being executed, it records the PyTorch operation and then converts those operations to intermediate IR.

There is a problem with this approach: if the model is data-dependent, like loops in RNNs, or if the if/else condition is based on the input, then tracing can't really get that right. Tracing will discover only what happened in that particular execution cycle and ignore the other cases. For example, if our dummy input is a 10-word sentence and our model is a loop-based RNN, then the traced graph will hardcode the 10-times execution of the RNN cell and it will break if we have a longer sentence than 10 words or a short sentence with fewer words. TorchScript has been introduced with this in mind.

There is a subset of such Python control flows supported by TorchScript, and the only thing you have to do is to convert your existing program to a stage where all the control flows are TorchScript-supported control flows. The intermediate stage created by TorchScript can be read by LibTorch. In this session, we will create the TorchScript output and write a C++ module to load it using LibTorch.

A usable and stable version of TorchScript was introduced in PyTorch 1.0 even though TorchScript was part of the early releases of PyTorch as a JIT package. TorchScript can serialize and optimize models that are written in PyTorch.

Just like ONNX, TorchScripts can be saved into the disk as an IR, but unlike ONNX, this IR is optimized to run in production. Saved TorchScript models can be loaded in environments without Python dependency. Python was always a bottleneck for production deployments because of performance and multithreading reasons, even though the scale Python can take you to is good enough for most use cases in the real world.

Avoiding this fundamental bottleneck was the primary task for all the production-ready frameworks, and that's why static computational graphs ruled the framework world. PyTorch solved this problem by introducing a C++-based runtime with a high level of APIs, which are accessible for developers if they wish to code in C++.

PyTorch was made production-ready by pushing TorchScript to the core. TorchScript can convert models written in Python to highly optimized IR, which then can be read by LibTorch. A model loaded by LibTorch then can be saved as a C++ object and can be run in a C++ program or other highly efficient programing languages such as Go.

PyTorch allows you to make a TorchScript IR through two methods. The easiest is by tracing, just like ONNX. You can pass the model (even a function) to torch.jit.trace with a dummy input. PyTorch runs the dummy input through the model/function and traces the operations while it runs the input.

The traced functions (PyTorch operations) then can be converted to the optimized IR, which is also called a static single assignment IR. Like an ONNX graph, instructions in this graph also have primitive operators that A TENsor library (ATen, the backend of PyTorch) would understand.

This is really easy but comes with a cost. Tracing-based inference has the basic problem ONNX had: it can't handle the model structure changes that are dependent on the data, that is, an `if/else` condition check or a loop (sequence data). For handling such cases, PyTorch introduced scripting mode.

Scripting mode can be enabled by using the `torch.jit.script` decorator for normal functions and `torch.jit.script_method` for methods on the PyTorch model. By this decorator, the content inside a function/method will be directly converted to TorchScript. Another important thing to remember while using `torch.jit.script_method` for model classes is about the parent class. Normally, we inherit from `torch.nn.Module`, but for making TorchScript, we inherit from `torch.jit.ScriptModule`. This helps PyTorch to avoid using pure Python methods, which can't be converted to TorchScript. Right now, TorchScript doesn't support all Python features, but it has all the necessary features to support data-dependent tensor operations.

We'll start the C++ implementation of our fizbuz model by first exporting our model to the `ScriptModule` IR, exactly like we did for the ONNX export:

```
net = FizBuzNet(input_size, hidden_size, output_size)
traced = torch.jit.trace(net, dummy_input)
traced.save('fizbuz.pt')
```

The saved model can be loaded back into Python by the `torch.load()` method, but we'll be using the similar API LibTorch introduced into C++ for loading the model into C++. Before we go into the logic, let's import the required headers to the current scope:

```
#include <torch/script.h>
#include <iostream>
#include <memory>
#include <string>
```

The most important header is the `torch/script.h`, which brings all the required methods and functions from LibTorch. We decided to pass the model name and the sample input as a command-line argument. So, the first part of our main program is to read command-line arguments and parse them for the rest of the program:

```
std::string arg = argv[2];
int x = std::stoi(arg);
float array[10];
```

```
int i;
int j = 9;
for (i = 0; i < 10; ++i) {
    array[j] = (x >> i) & 1;
    j--;
}
```

The program reads the second command-line argument, which is the number the user gave to get the prediction. The number, when read from the command line, is of the `string` type. We'll convert it to `int`. For the loop after the `string`-to-`int` conversion, we need to convert it to a binary array. This is where the LibTorch execution starts:

```
std::shared_ptr<torch::jit::script::Module> module =
torch::jit::load(argv[1]);
auto options = torch::TensorOptions().dtype(torch::kFloat32);
torch::Tensor tensor_in = torch::from_blob(array, {1, 10},
                             options);
std::vector<torch::jit::IValue> inputs;
inputs.push_back(tensor_in);
at::Tensor output = module->forward(inputs).toTensor();
```

In the first line, we load the model from the path, which is passed as a first command-line argument (we declare the variable as `ScriptModule`). On the third line, we convert our binary array to a two-dimensional LibTorch tensor using the method `from_blob`. On the last line, we execute the `forward` method of our model with the tensor we made and return the output to the user. This is probably the most basic example we could implement to show TorchScript in action. There are numerous examples in the official doc that show the power of scripting mode (unlike tracing mode) to comprehend the Python control flows and push the model to C++ world.

Exploring RedisAI

We have seen the optimization we can get through TorchScript, but what will we do with the optimized binary? Yes, we can load it in the C++ world and make a Go server, and load it there, but that's still painful.

Redis Labs and Orobix brought us another solution called RedisAI. It is a highly optimized runtime built on top of LibTorch and can accept compiled TorchScript binaries for serving through the Redis protocol. For people who don't have prior experience with Redis, http://redis.io has good documentation and the introduction doc given there [3] should be a good start.

RedisAI comes with three options to configure three backends: PyTorch, TensorFlow, and ONNX Runtime. It doesn't stop there: RedisAI uses DLPack in the backend to enable tensors to pass through different frameworks without much conversion cost.

What does that even mean? Let's say you have a TensorFlow model that converts the human face to a 128-dimensional embedding (this is what FaceNet does). And now you can make a PyTorch model use this 128-dimensional embedding to do classification. In the normal world, passing the tensors from TensorFlow to PyTorch requires deep knowledge of how things work under the hood, but with RedisAI, you could do it with a couple of commands.

RedisAI is built as a module to the Redis server (`loadmodule` switch). The benefit of serving models through RedisAI is not just the option of having more than one runtime and the interoperability between them. In fact, that's the least important thing when it comes to production deployment. The most important feature that comes with RedisAI is the failover and distributed deployment options baked into the Redis server already.

With Redis Sentinel and Redis Cluster, we could deploy RedisAI in a multicluster, highly available setup without much knowledge of DevOps or infrastructure building. Also, since Redis has clients in all the popular languages, once you deploy the TorchScript model through RedisAI, you can essentially use any language client of Redis to communicate to the server for running models, passing input to models, getting output from models, and more.

The next highlight of using RedisAI is the availability of the whole big ecosystem of Redis, such as RedisGears (to run any Python function as part of a pipeline), RedisTimeSeries, Redis Streams, and others.

Let's start with loading the fizbuz network model that we compiled using TorchScript to RedisAI. First of all, we need to set up the environment with the Redis server and RedisAI installed. The `installation.sh` file has three parts that do this:

```
sudo apt update
sudo apt install -y build-essential tcl libjemalloc-dev
sudo apt install -y git cmake unzip


curl -O http://download.redis.io/redis-stable.tar.gz
tar xzvf redis-stable.tar.gz
cd redis-stable
make
sudo make install
cd ~
rm redis-stable.tar.gz


git clone https://github.com/RedisAI/RedisAI.git
```

```
cd RedisAI
bash get_deps.sh cpu
mkdir build
cd build
cmake -DDEPS_PATH=../deps/install ..
make
cd ~
```

The first part is where we install the dependencies required. The second part is where we download the Redis server binary and install it. The third part is for cloning the RedisAI server and building it using `make`. Once the installation is done, we could run the `run_server.sh` file to make the Redis server up with RedisAI as the loaded module.

```
cd redis-stable
redis-server redis.conf --loadmodule ../RedisAI/build/redisai.so
```

Now we are all set with our Redis server. Setting up the RedisAI server is as easy as that. Now scaling it with Sentinel or Cluster is also not that scary. Official documentation has enough information for you to get started.

Here we start with our minimal Python script to run the fizbuz example with RedisAI. We are using the Python package `Redis` to communicate with the Redis server. RedisAI has an official client being built, but it's not at a stage where we can use it at the time of writing.

```
r = redis.Redis()
MODEL_PATH = 'fizbuz_model.pt'
with open(MODEL_PATH,'rb') as f:
    model_pt = f.read()
r.execute_command('AI.MODELSET', 'model', 'TORCH', 'CPU',
                  model_pt)
```

The preceding script opens the Redis connection with localhost first. It reads the binary model we have saved previously using TorchScript and uses the command `AI.MODELSET` to set the Torch model in RedisAI. The command needs us to pass the name we need for the model in the server, which backend we want to use, whether we want to use CPU or GPU, and lastly, the binary model file itself. The model set command returns with an okay message, and then we loop through and wait for user input. The user input is passed through the encoder, as we have seen before, to convert it to binary-encoded format.

```
while True:
    number = int(input('Enter number, press CTRL+c to exit: ')) +
            1
```

```
inputs = encoder(number)

r.execute_command(
    'AI.TENSORSET', 'a', 'FLOAT', *inputs.shape, 'BLOB',
    inputs.tobytes())
r.execute_command('AI.MODELRUN', 'model', 'INPUTS', 'a',
    'OUTPUTS', 'out')
typ, shape, buf = r.execute_command('AI.TENSORGET', 'out',
    'BLOB')
prediction = np.frombuffer(buf, dtype=np.float32).argmax()
print(get_readable_output(number, prediction))
```

Then we use `AI.TENSORSET` to set the tensor and map it to a key. You might have seen the way we are passing the input NumPy array to the backend. NumPy has a convenient function, `tobytes()`, that gives the string format of how data is being stored in memory. We explicitly tell the command that we need to save the model as `BLOB`. The other option to save the model is `VALUES`, which is not very useful when you have a bigger array to save.

We also have to pass the data type and the shape of the input tensor. One thing we should consider while doing a tensor set is the data type and the shape. Since we are passing input as a buffer, RedisAI tries to convert the buffer to the DLPack tensor using the shape and data type information that we have passed. And if that doesn't match with the length of the byte string we have passed, RedisAI will throw an error.

Once the tensor is set, we have our model saved in a key called `model` and our tensor is saved in a key called a. We can now run the `AI.MODELRUN` command by passing the model key name and tensor key name.

If we have more than one input to pass, we use the tensor set more than once and pass all the keys as `INPUTS` to the `MODELRUN` command. The `MODELRUN` command saves the output to the key mentioned under `OUTPUTS`, which is then readable by `AI.TENSORGET`.

Here we read the tensor as `BLOB` like we have saved it. The tensor command gets us the type, shape, and buffer itself to us. The buffer is then passed to NumPy's `frombuffer()` function, which gives us the NumPy array of the result.

Once we have the data out of RedisAI, then things are the same as in other chapters. RedisAI seems to be the most promising production deployment system available for AI developers in the current market. It's still in the early stages even now and was released at RedisConf 2019 in April. We could see a lot of amazing features coming out of RedisAI in the near future, which makes it the de facto deployment mechanism for a large portion of the AI community.

Summary

In this chapter, we have gone through three different approaches to take PyTorch to production, starting from the easiest but least performant way: using Flask. Then we moved to the MXNet model server, which is a pre-built, optimized server implementation that can be managed using management APIs. The MXNet model server is useful for people who don't need a lot of complexity but need an efficient server implementation that can be scaled as required.

Lastly, we tried with TorchScript to create the most efficient version of our model and imported that in C++. For those who are ready to take up the complexity of building and maintaining a low-level language server like C++, Go, or Rust, you can take this approach and build a custom server until we have better runtime available that can read the script module and serve that like MXNet does on ONNX models.

The year 2018 was the year of model servers; there were numerous model servers from different organizations with different views in mind. But the future is bright and we could see a lot more model servers coming out day by day, which will probably make all of the previously mentioned approaches obsolete.

References

1. `https://pytorch.org/docs/stable/jit.html`
2. `https://github.com/awslabs/mxnet-model-server/blob/master/docs/management_api.md`
3. `https://redis.io/topics/introduction`

Another Book You May Enjoy

If you enjoyed this book, you may be interested in another book by Packt:

Deep Reinforcement Learning Hands-On

Maxim Lapan

ISBN: 978-1-78883-424-7

- Understand the DL context of RL and implement complex DL models
- Learn the foundation of RL: Markov decision processes
- Evaluate RL methods including Cross-entropy, DQN, Actor-Critic, TRPO, PPO, DDPG, D4PG and others
- Discover how to deal with discrete and continuous action spaces in various environments

- Defeat Atari arcade games using the value iteration method
- Create your own OpenAI Gym environment to train a stock trading agent
- Teach your agent to play Connect4 using AlphaGo Zero
- Explore the very latest deep RL research on topics including AI-driven chatbots

Leave a review - let other readers know what you think

Please share your thoughts on this book with others by leaving a review on the site that you bought it from. If you purchased the book from Amazon, please leave us an honest review on this book's Amazon page. This is vital so that other potential readers can see and use your unbiased opinion to make purchasing decisions, we can understand what our customers think about our products, and our authors can see your feedback on the title that they have worked with Packt to create. It will only take a few minutes of your time, but is valuable to other potential customers, our authors, and Packt. Thank you!

Index

41846012R00140

Made in the USA
San Bernardino, CA
06 July 2019